THE PRESS
AND ABORTION,
1838–1988

COMMUNICATION

A series of volumes edited by:
Dolf Zillmann and **Jennings Bryant**

Zillmann/Bryant • Selective Exposure to Communication

Beville • Audience Ratings: Radio, Television, Cable, Revised Edition

Bryant/Zillmann • Perspectives on Media Effects

Goldstein • Reporting Science: The Case of Aggression

Ellis/Donohue • Contemporary Issues in Language and Discourse Processes

Winett • Information and Behavior: Systems of Influence

Huesmann/Eron • Television and the Aggressive Child: A Cross-National Comparison

Gunter • Poor Reception: Misunderstanding and Forgetting Broadcast News

Olasky • Corporate Public Relations: A New Historical Perspective

Donohew/Sypher/Higgins • Communication, Social Cognition, and Affect

Van Dijk • News Analysis: Case Studies of International and National News in the Press

Van Dijk • News as Discourse

Wober • The Use and Abuse of Television: A Social Psychological Analysis of the Changing Screen

Kraus • Televised Presidential Debates and Public Policy

Masel-Walters/Wilkins/Walters • Bad Tidings: Communication and Catastrophe

Salvaggio/Bryant • Media Use in the Information Age: Emerging Patterns and Consumer Use

Salvaggio • The Information Society: Economic, Social, and Structural Issues

Olasky • The Press and Abortion, 1838–1988

THE PRESS
AND ABORTION,
1838–1988

Marvin N. Olasky
The University of Texas at Austin

LEA LAWRENCE ERLBAUM ASSOCIATES, PUBLISHERS
1988 Hillsdale, New Jersey   Hove and London

Lawrence Erlbaum Associates, Inc., Publishers
365 Broadway
Hillsdale, New Jersey 07642

Production, interior, and cover
design: Robin Marks Weisberg

Library of Congress Cataloging-in-Publication Data
Olasky, Marvin N.
  The press and abortion, 1838–1988 / by Marvin Olasky.
  p.   cm.
  Includes bibliographical references and index.
  ISBN 0-8058-0199-5
  ISBN 0-8058-0485-4 (Pbk.)

  1. Abortion in the press—United States.   I. Title.
  PN4888.A2044   1988
  070.4′4936346—dc19
                                                    88-12112
                                                    CIP
Printed in the United States of America
10 9 8 7 6 5 4 3 2

For *Eli* and *Ida Olasky*

OTHER BOOKS BY MARVIN N. OLASKY

Turning Point (with Herbert Schlossberg)

Corporate Public Relations: A New Historical Perspective

Patterns of Corporate Philanthropy

Prodigal Press

Freedom, Justice and Hope (with Herbert Schlossberg, Clark Pinnock, and Pierre Berthoud)

Contents

Acknowledgments   ix
Introduction   xi

_____ PART I

ABORTION WAR ONE, 1838–1910

Chapter 1   Madame Restell Builds a Business   3
Chapter 2   Abortion Advances, 1840–1870   14
Chapter 3   The New York *Times* Versus Abortion   24
Chapter 4   Danger and Dollars, 1878–1898   34
Chapter 5   Driving Abortion Underground   44

_____ PART II

SPIKING THE UNBORN CHILD, 1910–1965

Chapter 6   Sounds of Silence   57
Chapter 7   Greed and Corruption, 1930–1939   67
Chapter 8   Building the Abortion Rationale   76
Chapter 9   Heading Toward the Moon, 1950–1959   83
Chapter 10 From Murder to Liberation   92

_____ PART III

ABORTION WAR TWO, 1965–

Chapter 11 The Triumph of Public Relations   103

Chapter 12   Pulpits for Abortion, 1970–1974   113
Chapter 13   "That No Fetus Will Be Born Alive"   123
Chapter 14   Ideology Versus Investigation, 1978–1985   133
Chapter 15   A Lap Dog for the Abortion Lobby   142

Notes   152
Index   195

Acknowledgments

Research for this book could not have been completed without the aid of many organizations and individuals. I am grateful to librarians at the San Diego *Union* and the Chicago *Sun-Times* for allowing me into their clipping files; to the Christian Action Council, the Pro-Life Action League, the Pearson Institute, Planned Parenthood of New York City, the National Abortion Federation, and the Religious Coalition for Abortion Rights, for providing clippings; to librarians at the University of Texas and the Chicago Historical Society; and to Ken Craven, archivist of the old New York *Journal-American* morgue (now housed at the University of Texas) for promptly locating many yellowed articles.

I also thank Tim Walters, Lori Burton, Rick Rutledge, and other students at the University of Texas who became interested in this subject and who located some hard-to-find articles and 19th century ads. Leslie Wilson, Evan Olson, Don Wagner, and several other students at CBN University looked at New York *Times* coverage. Colleagues and administrators at the University of Texas, and my children Peter, David, and Daniel, continued to make both school and home pleasant places to teach, research, and write.

My wife Susan made this book possible in many ways. She helped to open my eyes originally to the abortion problem, wrote with me two magazine articles that began the research for chapter 9, and co-authored with me also a *Journalism Quarterly* article that was an earlier version of chapter 10. She also provided emotional support and intellectual stimulation during long walks through Austin. I have dedicated a previous book to Susan and do not want to embarrass her further by dwelling on many wonderful traits, but, as E.B. White noted in *Charlotte's Web*, it is hard to find a good friend and a good writer.

Earlier versions of parts of chapters 1, 2, 3, 9, and 15 appeared in *Journalism History*, *Media History Digest*, *Journalism Quarterly*, *Eternity*, *Human Life Review*, and *Public Relations Review*.

Introduction

In January, 1988, forces favoring and opposing abortion demonstrated in Washington and around the country on the 15th anniversary of the Supreme Court's *Roe v. Wade* legalization of widespread abortion. Fifteen years seems like an eternity in a land where the trend is toward 15-second commercials for presidential candidates; by 1988 both sides were hoping that their opponents would weary of the struggle and diminish their efforts. But if history is any guide, it appears that America's abortion wars have a long way to go, for they have gone a long way already. As this book shows, the year 1988 brought with it not the 15th but the 150th anniversary of the struggle.

The history of abortion and the press is an exciting tale of "trunk murders" and buried bodies, doctors' crusades and behind-the-scenes manipulation, courage, and timidity. And yet, despite all the billions of words written about the current abortion debate, the vibrant history of America's abortion wars remains a largely untold story. One book on 19th century practice, brief overviews in a few chapters of some other books, a handful of articles, and a few stories about particularly colorful characters, are all we have.[1]

Many people, even those active in the abortion debate, believe that the conflict originated in the 1960s. Others are vaguely aware of some skirmishing in the 19th century, but incorrectly call the first half of the 20th century "the silent years." An examination of abortion history over the past 150 years, as strained through the press, may help us to understand more deeply the nature of the continuing warfare.

A parallel gap exists in the literature concerning media handling of issues in which world views and basic philosophical views come strongly into play. Countless articles decry "media bias" or defend the press, but few scholars have devoted the time necessary to chronicle coverage of a sensitive question over a long period of time.[2] I recently dealt with some questions of bias in another book, *Prodigal Press*,[3] and I will not repeat its arguments here; yet, the debate about the relationship of views to news will not be advanced without some detailed historical perspective on the problem.

This book, then, has two subjects — abortion and the press — and its goal is to provide information that will deepen the level of discussion concerning both. For example, 19th century press coverage showed clear concern for the life of the unborn child as well as the health of the mother; Justice Blackmun's *Roe v. Wade* decision, relying for its historical evidence on one faulty article, got the story wrong.[4] The cozy financial relationships of editors and abortionists, and the impact of political power and advertising money on abortion coverage, also are explored.

The Press and Abortion, 1838-1988 reports the sensationalism of 19th century abortion stories filled with specific detail concerning the depravity of abortionists, the misery of young women who sought them out, and the tragedy of unborn children victimized. It shows the triumphs of the anti-abortion campaigns — legislation tightened, abortion advertising turned down, abortionists arrested or publicly disgraced — but also points out press tendencies to back away from hard-hitting exposes that could alienate some readers and advertisers. The history shows that when investigative journalism lagged, public interest decreased and laws against abortion were not enforced rigorously.

The early 20th century brought both victory and defeat for anti-abortion forces. Doctors in Chicago and other cities pushed hard against newspapers that continued to accept abortion advertising. Although anti-abortionists were winning the advertising wars, they were losing the news pages. News stories emphasized the greed of abortionists but not the evil of abortion, and coverage shifted from concern for the unborn child to issues of corruption that supposedly could be dealt with through legalization of abortion. As pro-abortion public relations slowly emerged, reporting of abortion became neutral and a new set of cozy relationships developed. Newspapers from mid-century on both set a pro-abortion agenda and were used by those setting agendas.

With such a broad expanse to cover, research for this volume necessarily was eclectic. From 1838 to 1962 press information concerning abortion is a trickle, and I simply tried to drink in every drop of evidence from city newspapers, news magazines, and other journalistic writing — including news articles, editorials, ads, and a few popular books — that I could find. In 1962 the trickle became a torrent, and I had to be more selective to avoid being drowned; each of those later chapters emphasizes major aspects of coverage and does not pretend to be comprehensive. Throughout, the emphasis is on coverage by broad-based, general interest print media, and not by explicitly religious, political, or interest group magazines and newsletters.

Two other limitations of this book need noting here. First, this is a history of abortion and print media; an overall examination of broadcast coverage of abortion since 1962 still needs doing, and would be very valuable. Second, due in part to the availability of sources, this history of press coverage of abortion in America is dominated by the history of press coverage by New York-based newspapers. Readers should keep that tilt in mind, but should also realize that New York newspapers from the 1830s on have been the leaders in advertising for, crusading against, gradually legitimizing, and eventually legalizing abortion.

I have tried to be fair to both sides in terminology, and that means I may anger both sides. Language helps to define what is moral and honorable, and for that reason both sides in the abortion battle have tried to grab the high ground: "pro-choice" and "pro-life." The subject of this book, however, is abortion, and the debate is between those who favor abortion in several or all circumstances and those who oppose it[5]; I teach my children and students that it is better to be specific rather than vague, and for that reason, with the likelihood of angering both sides, I use the terms *pro-abortion* and *anti-abortion* rather than *pro-life* and *pro-choice.*[6]

Another basic question in terminology concerns the name of that being in the womb. George Orwell noted that political language often seeks to defend the indefensible by softening the force of some images[7] that is certainly what happened in the abortion war when, just as abortion was gaining wide acceptance, the press began using the dehumanizing word "fetus" rather than the traditional "unborn child." Whether a person is for or against abortion, the honest position is that taken by an American Medical Association panel in 1871: "We had to deal with human life. In a matter of less importance we could entertain no compromise. An honest judge on the bench would call things by their proper names. We could do no less."[8] This book uses the term *unborn child.*[9]

This book, I hope, honors my parents who did not leave me unborn. It is dedicated to them.

PART I

ABORTION WAR ONE, 1838–1910

The New York *Times* on abortion: "It is useless to talk of such matters with bated breath, or to seek to cover such terrible realities with the veil of a false delicacy. . . . From a lethargy like this it is time to rouse ourselves. The evil that is tolerated is aggressive."

Chapter 1

Madame Restell Builds a Business

Abortion first emerged as a social issue in America not in 1973, nor even in 1900, but in 1712, 20 years before the birth of George Washington. In that year, Benjamin Wadsworth, later to be president of Harvard College, declared that "If any purposely indeavor [sic] to destroy the Fruit of their Womb (whether they actually do it or not) they're guilty of Murder in God's account."[1] In 1716 New York City midwives were required to swear that they would abide by "A law Regulating Mid Wives within the City of New York"; one part of the law stated "You Shall not Give any Counsel or Administer any Herb Medicine or Potion, or any other thing to any Woman being with Child whereby She Should Destroy or Miscarry of that she goeth withall before her time."[2] In 1719 Wadsworth once again attacked abortion.[3]

Wadsworth's statements were part of a long theological tradition familiar to colonial ministers and the church-going populace. In an age of frequent Scripture-reading it would be difficult to avoid noticing that the Bible states, over 40 times, that human life begins with conception.[4] The Anglican and Lutheran Churches strongly opposed abortion;[5] Presbyterian and Congregationalist churches were founded on the doctrines of John Calvin, who wrote that an unborn child, "though enclosed in the womb of its mother, is already a human being" and should not be "rob[bed] of the life which it has not yet begun to enjoy."[6]

The existence of statements such as those of Wadsworth and New York officialdom suggests that abortion was not entirely unknown in colonial days. Yet, with abortion considered both grossly unethical and traditionally illegal (according to British common law),[7] it seems likely that abortion in

colonial days was rare. Evidence to the contrary is slight: Newspapers that
reported rumor of scandal did not discuss abortion, and Puritan preachers
who dwelled on sinful activities generally did not list abortion as one of
the activities indicating a decline in piety.

During the first half century of American independence some abortion
activity is recorded.[8] Doctors' comments and several court cases suggest
that abortion was on the rise — but only slightly. Until the 1830s abortion
remained an aberration in the early American tendency to be fruitful and
multiply.[9] Again, that is unsurprising, for as late as 1835 the French observer Alexis de Tocqueville was able to write that "there is no country in
the world where the Christian religion retains a greater influence over the
souls of men than in America."[10]

The great change began in 1838 through a combination of theological,
demographic, and cultural changes — and the entrepreneurial initiative of
Anna Lohman, a 26-year-old midwife married to a printer employed by
New York's leading newspaper, the *Herald*. Most newspapers at that time
accepted advertisements only for those products that the editor saw as ethical, but the *Herald* would admit sellers of any variety as long as they paid
cash. "Business is business, money is money," *Herald* owner James Gordon
Bennett said, "and we permit no blockhead to interfere with our business."[11] Most newspapers at that time cost 6¢ and had circulations in the
hundreds, but the *Herald* sold for a penny and was read by thousands and
then tens of thousands.

The *Herald* prospered greatly through lively writing, aggressive news
coverage (except when stories might injure major advertisers), and the willingness to turn its pages over to the highest bidder. *Herald* managing editor Frederick Hudson called each advertiser a promoter of "the hopes, the
thoughts, the joys, the plans, the shames . . . the religion of the people.
Each advertiser is therefore a reporter, a sort of penny-a-liner, he paying
the penny."[12] Anna and Charles Lohman saw the opportunity to build a
new business, an abortion business, not just by whispering to a few, but
by becoming ad-buying reporters for the *Herald* and proclaiming to many
the idea that abortion was a legitimate and appropriate way to get out of
trouble.

SELLING THE IDEA OF ABORTION

Using Anna's midwifery as a base, the Lohmans adopted the trade names
Madame Restell and Dr. Mauriceau (for the French were considered most
up-to-date in such matters) and began advertising in 1838. Madame Restell
was not the first to advertise abortion — small and scattered abortion ads
may be found in the *Herald* and its main competitor, the New York *Sun*,

as early as 1836 — but she was the first to advertise consistently and to attempt to sell the *idea* of abortion, rather than just announcing its availability. She sold the idea in five ways: Her ads made abortion seem loving to husbands, kind to children already born, easy to accomplish, fair to women, and maybe not even abortion at all.

First, Madame Restell suggested that a woman might decide to abort out of love for her husband: "In how many instances does the hard working father" of a large family become a slave, "tugging at the oar of incessant labor, toiling but to live and living but to toil?" Having another baby might leave the other children fatherless: "If care and toil have weighed down the spirit, and at last broken the health of the father, how often is the widow left unable, with the most virtuous intentions, to save her fatherless offspring from becoming degraded objects of charity or profligate votaries of vice?"[13]

Second, Madame Restell's ads expressed concern about the wife dying from pregnancy or overwork and leaving "young and helpless children" without "those endearing attentions and watchful solicitudes, which a mother alone can bestow."[14] She then asked, "Is it desirable, then — is it moral — for parents to increase their families, regardless of consequences to themselves, or the well being of their offspring, when a simple, easy, healthy and certain remedy is within our control?"[15] The answer, for Restell, definitely supported abortion: "Every dispassionate, virtuous and enlightened mind, will unhesitating answer in the affirmative."[16]

Third, the ads made abortion seem easy to accomplish. Abortion operations were extremely hazardous to women, and few would want to contemplate such surgery initially. Pills, containing substances such as ergot, calomel, aloe, black hellebore, or ergot mixed with oil of tansy, were an easier sell. Such abortifacients were to be ingested, on the theory that a horrible shock in the lower digestive tract might so disrupt the uterus that a miscarriage would result. Sometimes the procedure worked; at other times, after a few attempts by medication, women would be psychologically reconciled to abortion and determined to have one.[17] An operation resisted previously might now be accepted.

Fourth, Madame Restell's ads made abortion seem an attempt to alleviate strains that no person should have to bear. Pregnancy, she suggested in her ads, was a miserable bringer of "violent and convulsive headaches, derangement of the stomach, gnawing in the side, burning in the chest, disturbed and feverish sleep, frightful dream, languor, debility, weakness, a most distressing lethargy."[18] Some women who become pregnant, the ad continued, fall into "that melancholy of mind and depression of Spirits that make existence itself but a prolongation of suffering and wretchedness, and which alas! not infrequently dooms the unhappy victim to the perpetration of suicide."[19] For women who were suffering through the physical problems that sometimes do occur during the first trimester of pregnancy, the Restell ad would strike home.[20]

Fifth, Madame Restell gave women the opportunity to pretend that abortion was actually something else. In those days before pregnancy tests there was no sure proof of pregnancy until "quickening" (when the mother can feel fetal movement, generally in the fifth month of pregnancy). Madame Restell termed abortion before quickening "an attempt to remove female blockages" or "a cure for stoppage of the menses." Those expressions were accurate in one sense, because pregnancy *is* the leading cause of menstrual stoppage among women of childbearing age. She called her abortifacients "female monthly regulating pills," with the pretense that the only goal was regulation of the monthly cycle.

In connection with that pretense, and to reduce criticism from those opposed to publicizing abortion, Madame Restell's ads, like those of similar advertisers, did not use the word "abortion." Madame Restell's ads were ostensibly designed to "inform the ladies that her pills are an infallible regulator of ******. They must not be taken when ********."[21] Anyone could see, even in those days before *Wheel of Fortune*, that the asterisks stood for "menses" and "pregnant."[22] Madame Restell also publicized her "FEMALE MONTHLY REGULATING PILLS" that would cure "all cases of suppression, irregularity, or stoppage of the menses, however obdurate, or from whatever causes produced."[23] A New York *Sun* ad in 1839 came close to mentioning abortion, but merely spoke of pills so strong that they should not be taken during pregnancy, because they would "produce a******n."[24] The "warnings" not to use abortifacients were a clear tip-off as to when they were supposed to be used, because they were good for nothing else except their illegal purpose.

The very thin language veil disguised little. One observer said the abortion advertisements' code words were known to "every schoolgirl" in New York.[25] A physician complained that the ads were "intelligible not only to fathers and mothers, but also to boys and girls."[26] But all of the abortionists followed the code; language such as "suppression," "irregularity," or "stoppage of the menses" was customary, with "obdurate," "obstinate," or "persistent" cases being those pregnancies that continued after use of abortifacients and might lead to a visit to the abortionist.[27] And, like other abortionists, Madame Restell always emphasized that she could "be consulted with the strictest confidence on complaints incident to the female frame."[28]

Madame Restell, in short, was a thoroughly modern anticipator of the arguments that would be used for abortion over a century later. Freedom for parents, love for "wanted" children by avoiding the "unwanted," and a tendency to use euphemisms (today, removing "tissue" or "products of conception"), all figured prominently in her advertising strategy. Her copy took what was viewed as immoral, abortion, and made it the moral choice. Madame Restell also took what was seen as moral—"be fruitful and multiply"—and turned it into immorality.

She could not do this just by herself, of course. The times were right for a Madame Restell because of three great changes the United States began going through in the 1830s.

The first of these was theological. As long as ministers were telling their flocks to work for God's kingdom on earth as in Heaven by following the teachings of the Bible, abortion would have a hard time winning general acceptance. Yet, even as de Tocqueville wrote of Christian consensus, American popular theology was changing, with orthodox Christianity soon to be hard-pressed by emerging doctrines such as Transcendentalism and pantheism, "higher criticism" and "free thinking." Some began saying the Bible was not God's Word—and if it were not so, its anti-abortion stance could be disregarded.

The second revolution was the urban revolution. From 1830 on city populations surged; New York City grew from 203,000 in 1830 to 1 million in 1860. Some of the new inhabitants came from abroad, with an entirely different set of theological understandings and practical applications. Many came from upstate New York or rural Vermont and grew up with the Bible, but saw the big city as a place to throw off restraints. "City air makes man free," the saying goes, and freedom allowed for more experimentation—economic, social, and sexual.

The third revolution was in newspaper production. When entrepreneurs such as Bennett of the *Herald* sold their newspapers for a penny, they also made themselves captive to advertisers. Because the lowered sales price did not meet production costs, publishers became very dependent on revenue brought in through the sale of higher priced ads to those who wanted to appeal to a vastly increased readership.[29] The press revolution would thus allow advertisers such as Madame Restell access to a vastly increased audience while providing them with so much clout that only a brave editor would be willing to criticize on news pages the hands that fed him.

The three revolutions, then, gave Madame Restell a clear path to building a major business. Theological objections were decreasing as her potential market and means of reaching that market enormously expanded. Newspapers in which she advertised would probably not criticize her or abortion, so she and fellow abortionists could publish pro-abortion messages without having anti-abortion messages on news pages cutting into their advertising potency.

That is exactly what happened. None of the newspapers in which Madame Restell advertised was found to have run any editorial comments on Madame Restell's views, or to have covered her illegal activity during the early 1840s. The New York *Sun* once noted some complaints against it from Christians for "its constant advertisements of Madame Restell," but called the complaints "spiteful attacks from fanatics, hypocrites, and corrupt partizans [sic]. . . . When we are attacked from such quarters, it gives us strong assurance that we are doing our duty to the public."[30] The New York *Tribune* did not accept Madame Restell's ads during 1841, and criticized the *Herald* and the *Sun* for taking them,[31] but by the 1850s the *Tribune* also was accepting abortion ads.

The economic impact of abortion on the press at that time is evident. At the price of $2.50 for running a six-line unit for 2 weeks, with about a 60-line average in 1839, Restell's annual bill for reaching the New York *Sun*'s 32,000 readers would have been $650 — at a time when decent New York apartments cost $5 or $6 per month.[32] A similar computation for the *Herald*, which charged $2.50 for an eight-line unit in 1840, would put her annual advertising costs in that newspaper alone at about $430 — an appreciable sum, in that Bennett had founded the *Herald* with just $500 in 1835.[33] With other abortionists also advertising, abortion-related advertising revenue for newspapers such as the *Sun* and the *Herald* would run into the thousands of dollars — and perhaps make the difference between press profit and subsistence.

The effect of advertising on Madame Restell's business also appears to have been large. During the early 1840s she was doing so well that she opened branch offices in Boston and Philadelphia. She also had abortifacient-selling franchises in Newark, Providence, and five New York locations. By 1845, she was keeping her main office open from 9 a.m. to 9 p.m.[34] She even gave herself a pedigree: Madame Restell had absolutely no formal medical training or hospital experience, but her ads stated that she had worked "in the two principal Female Hospitals in Europe — those of Vienna and Paris — where favored by her great experience and opportunities, she attained that celebrity in those great discoveries in medical science so specially adapted to the female frame."[35]

There is much we do not know about the economics of abortion in the 1840s. Given the illegality of her business, the informality of all medical practice at that time, and the absence of income taxes, it is not surprising that no financial records apparently exist of Madame Restell's business or customer load. (Even today, with a massive tax enforcement structure and much more required paperwork, much of the income of certain escort services and massage parlors remains hidden.)[36] Similarly, we just do not know whether most of her customers came because of print advertising or word-of-mouth. We do know that Madame Restell and her fellow New York abortionists must have seen continual advertising as a good investment, because they kept running ads.

By the early 1840s many abortionists advertised in New York newspapers.

Dr. Bell promised to cure "irregularity of females."[37] Dr. Ward treated suppression, irregularity, and female obstructions.[38] Dr. Vandenburgh contended that his "Female Regeneracy Pills" were "an effectual remedy for suppression, irregularity, and all cases where nature has stopped from any cause whatsoever."[39] Madame Vincent offered her own pills, and ads for "Portuguese Female Pills" and "FRENCH LUNAR PILLS" appeared in 1841.[40] The latter were called "lunar pills on account of their efficacy in producing the monthly turns of females. . . . The effects are truly astonishing. They are never attended with any distressing operation, are always certain, and therefore pregnant women should not take them."[41] Mrs. Mott, Mrs. Bird, Madame Costello, and many others jumped into the market.[42]

With abortionists running ads and no one running counter ads or investigative stories, the newspaper view of abortion was clearly one-sided. The precise impact of the ads cannot be measured now, but by the mid-1840s doctors such as Amos Dean of the Albany Medical College, *Medical Jurisprudence* editor R. E. Griffith, and many others were writing of a great upsurge in abortion.[43] In 1844 the *Boston Medical and Surgical Journal* noted an increase in the number of abortionists and the number of their customers, including married women, and attacked the practice of abortion that was "still more deplorable" than the practice of infanticide believed to be common in China.[44] In the 1850s and 1860s Professor Jesse Boring of the Atlanta Medical College, Professor Walter Channing of Harvard, and physicians in Buffalo, Detroit, Vermont, Ohio, and many other cities and states bemoaned the increase in abortion.[45]

Evidence and historical parallel suggest that advertising had a role in that increase. Although laws banning abortion rarely were enforced, occasional arrests led to trials in which some women testified that they had seen abortion advertisements and had begun thinking about what appeared to be an easy way out of trouble.[46] One physician believed that "a large proportion of the increase of abortion" could "be traced to the dissemination of immoral and criminal advertisements in daily journals."[47] Theoretically, this was unsurprising, because we have learned that advertising of new products and services can actually create some demand; for example, advertising expenditures underlay the auto industry boom early in the 20th century.[48]

OPPOSITION TO ABORTION

New York abortionists did garner some opposition from the medical profession. Dr. Gunning Bedford called Madame Restell "a monster who speculates with human life with as much cruelness as if she were engaged in a game of chance."[49] He wrote of one patient who told him that "Madame Restell, on previous occasions, had caused her to miscarry five times."[50] The patient also described one Restell abortion in which the aborted baby "kicked several times after it was put into the bowl."[51] Bedford wrote angrily that Restell's "advertisements are to be seen in our daily papers. . . . She tells publicly what she can do; and without the slightest scruple, urges all to call on her who might be anxious to avoid having children."[52]

But there was no opposition from the newspapers themselves, with the exception of the *National Police Gazette*, the most sensational newspaper of the era.[53] The *Gazette* typically filled three of its eight pages with ads for patent medicines and the usual run of goods and services, but none for abortion, which editor George Wilkes strongly opposed in editorials. Wilkes proclaimed in 1845 that his newspaper would expose abortionists, although other newspapers would not

> because we believe that full expositions of the infamous practices of abortionists will tend to present these human fiends in a true light before the eyes of those who may become their dupes. We shall follow up this business until New York is rid of those child destroyers.[54]

The *Gazette* proposed tough action, including police establishment of "a night-and-day watch at the doors of the slaughterhouses of the murderous abortionists of this city . . . miserable and deluded females would never incur the risks of discovery."[55]

When officials did not respond, the *Gazette* complained on Valentine's Day, 1846, that "Restell still roams at large through the influence of ill-gotten wealth and will probably still continue until public indignation drives her and her associates from our midst."[56] *Gazette* editors predicted that a "day of vengeance" would arrive for Restell and other "fiends who have made a business of professional murder and who have reaped the bloody harvest in quenching the immortal spark in thousands of the unborn."[57] The *Gazette* specifically attacked "Restell, the murderess paramount in the dark scheme of professional destruction, openly defying decency and the statute, and proclaiming to the world to stifle human life at so much per deed."[58]

Other newspapers were silent, but the *Gazette* hit hard: "We are not now demanding justice upon the perpetratess of a single crime, but upon one who might be drowned in the blood of her victims, did each but yield a drop, whose epitaph should be a curse, and whose tomb a pyramid of skulls."[59] The *Gazette* asked that laws on the books be enforced: "We call again for action from the authorities in relation to this woman. She has been for nearly ten years involved in law, and her money has saved her, as yet, from the direct penalty of a single dereliction."[60]

Authorities, unpressured by any newspaper besides the *Gazette*, did not act. Frustrated, some anti-abortionists took to the streets. At noon on February 23, 1846, a crowd began to gather in front of Restell's house. By 12:30, a crowd estimated by different observers at 300 to 1,000 was faced by 40 to 50 policemen who had stationed themselves on her doorstep. For hours, the crowd gave anti-Restell cries of "Where's the thousand children murdered in this house?" and "Hanging is too good for the monster." Restell was described as a "wholesale female strangler," and governmental authorities were attacked for not shutting down her business.[61]

It was hard for New York newspapers to avoid covering such an uprising; they did cover it, but only with quick mentions. The *Herald*, trying to minimize the importance of the abortion question, concluded its brief account with an editorial statement: "We hope that nothing will be done to endanger the peace of the city. Under all circumstances the supremacy of the law should be maintained."[62] Considering that Madame Restell was acting illegally, that was an odd statement, but it seemed that the *Herald* did not want to lose a large advertiser.

Although the press was largely inactive, the New York state legislature passed a law stiffening penalties for abortion. The *Gazette* immediately began a strong campaign for enforcement, complaining that police were engaged in "neglect of duty before the face of Heaven," and emphasizing once again that abortion is "murder . . . strangling the unborn."[63] Police finally acted, and found a woman willing to witness against Madame Restell. At the trial in 1847 Maria Bodine testified that she had been attracted to Madame Restell's house and operated on by Madame Restell without anesthesia: "She hurt me so that I halloed out and gripped hold of her hand; she told me to have patience, and I would call her 'mother' for it."[64] Found guilty, Madame Restell was given a 1-year term on Blackwell's Island in the East River. For a while, it seemed as if community pressure had won out over advertising clout.

According to later journalistic accounts, however, political connections apparently preserved Restell from any great misery. She was allowed to put aside the lumpy prison mattress and to bring in her own fancy new featherbed instead; she also brought into the "prison suite" her own easy chairs, rockers, and carpeting. Visiting hours were altered so that Charles Lohman was able to visit at will and "remain alone with her as long as suited his or her pleasure," according to Warden Jacob Acker.[65]

ABORTION PROSPERITY

Not surprisingly, Madame Restell did not advertise while she was in prison. After her release in 1848, however, she proclaimed that the trial and imprisonment were easily worth $100,000 to her in advertising. She moved to larger and better offices and was soon spending $20,000 per year on advertising (the equivalent of perhaps $1 million now). Popular pressure led to a re-arrest of Madame Restell in 1856; this time, however, her political connections were so strong that she was released at once. She was said to "have in her keeping" the secrets of leading officials, and she knew enough to keep quiet as long as she was not bothered.

Other abortionists also received protection and prospered. They advertised throughout the 1850s and 1860s. The New York *Tribune*, under the headline "MOST IMPORTANT to the LADIES," advertised "Dr. Geissner's celebrated MENSTRUAL PILLS," which "reach the various irregularities and suppressions of nature. . . . They act like a charm . . . in numerous instances producing regularity of nature after all hope had been abandoned."[66] The New York *Herald* in 1861, along with ads for "Professor Restell," notified readers that "DR. WARD TREATS ALL FEMALE DISEASES WITH UNPARALLELED SUCCESS. His great Benefactor, price $1."[67] The New York *Times* in 1863 offered a "sure remedy for obstructions" through medication that "will in a short time bring on the monthly period with regularity," and also offered other "Periodical Drops" as a "certain remedy for monthly irregularities and obstructions."[68]

Madame Restell herself was consistent. In 1865 she was running the same advocacy ads she ran in the early 1840s; she continued to proclaim her altruistic willingness to help women avoid "suffering and wretchedness" that could turn children into orphans.[69] She had many imitators: In 1867, 61% of ads in the "Medical" column of the New York *Herald* appear to have been for abortion.[70] By 1870, the results of Madame Restell's innovations could be measured in two ways: impact on society, and impact on herself.

First, the New York abortion business had grown immeasurably. Madame Restell and her colleagues had, in the words of the *British Medical Journal*, a "large and lucrative business," one in which they were "never in want of engagements." One anti-abortion doctor, J.H. Toner, noted that abortion "has become a regularly established, money-making trade." In addition, New York advertising had an impact far beyond the city limits. Weekly editions of New York newspapers, mailed across the country, had a circulation of over 100,000 during the 1850s;[71] Madame Restell and other abortionists ran lines in their ads pointedly welcoming out-of-town visitors to their premises.[72]

Second, we can measure the impact of Madame Restell's innovations on herself, economically. A millionaire in those times of hard money, when saving a penny really meant something, Madame Restell built a large bond portfolio and moved to a lavish mansion at Fifth Avenue and 52nd Street. A description of the interior written by James McCabe in 1872 indicates her style of living:

On the first floor are the grand hall of tessellated marble, lined with mirrors; the three immense dining-rooms, furnished in bronze and gold, with yellow satin hangings, and enormous French mirror in mosaic gilding at every panel . . . more parlors and reception-rooms; butler's pantry, lined with solid silver services; dining room with all imported furniture. Other parlors on the floor above; a guest-chamber in blue brocade satin, with gold- and ebony-bedstead elegantly covered . . . [many bedrooms and lounges] . . . Fourth floor — servants' rooms in mahogany and Brussels carpet, and circular picture gallery; the fifth floor contains a magnificent billiards room, dancing-hall, with pictures, piano, etc. . . . The whole house is filled with statuettes, paintings, rare bronzes, ornamental and valuable clocks, candelabras, silver globes and articles of many origins and rare worth.[73]

According to the New York *Times*, the mansion "never fails to attract the attention of the passerby, on account of its architectural beauty and magnificence."[74]

Madame Restell, once the impoverished Anna Lohman, traveled the avenues behind a patch of matched grays and a driver with plum-colored facing on his coat lapels. According to one writer, she also carried a small muff of mink in which she hid her hands, much like the ones "famous pianists or violinists used to protect their hands from harm."[75]

Chapter 2

Abortion Advances, 1840–1870

"As New York goes, so goes the nation." New York's record in abortion is like that of Maine in politics: Anti-abortion victories in New York during the late 1860s and early 1870s, and pro-abortion victories during the late 1960s and early 1970s, led the way to national change. That trend began in the late 1840s, when Madame Restell's promotional strategy was imitated by other abortionists throughout the country.

The first major American abortion advertiser outside of New York City resided just across the Hudson River. In 1840, Catherine Costello of Jersey City began to advertise her own "Female Monthly Pills," calling them "a sovereign remedy for irregularity, female obstruction, and never fails [sic] to bring on regular periods."[1] Like Madame Restell, she then promised her abortion customers a place to recover:

> Madame Costello is well aware that it is sometimes inconvenient for ladies who are laboring under a suppression of their regular illness [menstruation], to have that attention at their residences which the nature of their cases may demand, and to such she would say that she is prepared to accommodate them with board and the best of nursing at her residence. . . .[2]

By July, 1841, Costello was advertising herself as a "female physician," much as Madame Restell did, and promising "appropriate and effectual remedies for irregularity and obstruction."[3] By December, 1841, she had expanded her ad, titling it TO THE LADIES (not just to the MARRIED LADIES, which was often the heading on Restell ads), and boasting that "Suppression irregularity, obstruction &c, by whatever cause produced, can be removed by Madame C. in a very short time."[4] She also announced an office expansion in order to receive more women "who wish to be treated for obstruction of their monthly period . . . strictest regard to secrecy."[5]

Because "female monthly pills" could be readily sent through the mails, a "pill war" raged between Madame Restell and her New Jersey competitor for several years. Along with her usual ads promoting abortion, Madame Restell in December, 1841, ran an ad that attacked:

> COUNTERFEIT MONTHLY PILLS Owing to the celebrity, efficiency and invariable success of Madame Restell's Female Monthly Pills in all cases of irregularity, suppression, or stoppage . . . counterfeits and imitations are continually attempted to be palmed off for the genuine. Cheap, common pills are purchased at twelve cents a box, put up in different boxes, and called "Female Monthly Pill," with the object of selling, if possible, at one dollar. Females are therefore cautioned against these attempts to impose upon them. It is sufficient here to state that all Female Monthly Pills are counterfeits, except those sold at Madame Restell's.[6]

Over the next several months, Madame Restell continued to attack "counterfeit pills" in terms that could have been used to describe her own.[7] In March, 1842, Madame Costello fought back with an ad proclaiming that:

> Madame Costello's FEMALE MONTHLY PILL is acknowledged by the first Physicians in the United States as the very best medicine that ladies laboring under a suppression of their natural illness can take.[8]

Directly below Madame Costello's ad, however, the following ad appeared:

> CAUTION TO FEMALES. SO VARIOUS and desperate are the expedients resorted to by ignorant, though impudent pretenders, with the object of imposing upon females, that Madame Restell deems herself called upon to put them on their guard. One expedient is, to put up a miserable compound, and forthwith to call it genuine "Female Monthly Pills," with the hope therefore to effect sale for them on the reputation acquired by Madame Restell's Female Monthly Pills, and the person attempting their sale called herself, (the better to deceive the public) a "madame" or a "female physician." Females, therefore, need not be deceived by those who, though too ignorant and unskillful to discover and introduce a valuable medicine, are yet despicable and dishonest enough to palm off upon the unsuspecting or simple, miserable counterfeits."[9]

Restell, of course, had also designated herself a madame and female physician in order to deceive the unsuspecting or simple.

Costello continued to advertise herself as a FEMALE PHYSICIAN, and extended her claims for the pills she sold:

Their certainty of action has long been acknowledged by the medical profession, and hundreds that have uselessly tried various boasted remedies; indeed, so sure are these pills in their effects, that care is sometimes necessary in their use though they contain no medicine detrimental to the constitution.[10]

The reference to "care" needed in use may mean that a Costello customer had died. Madame Restell's rhetoric, in response, became even tougher. A December, 1842, ad titled "CAUTION TO FEMALES," noted that Madame Restell:

does not wish to be classed with the pretenders continually appearing and disappearing, advertising as "Female Physicians," who too ignorant and incompetent themselves are obliged to get some scarcely less ignorant quack to experiment instead.[11]

The Restell–Costello pot-calling-the-kettle-black battle continued over the next 3 years, with Costello answering Restell's charges that she was not personally involved in treating patients:

Madame C. particularly begs to impress on the minds of the delicate, that she officiates personally at every case, so that hesitation or dread need never to be apprehended.[12]

In April, 1846, however, Costello's husband, Charles Mason, was indicted for selling the corpse of one of his wife's patients.[13] The *National Police Gazette* widely publicized the trial, and some of Madame Costello's patients apparently began to talk with Jersey City police.[14] New Jersey did not treat abortionists as leniently as New York did, and Madame Costello eventually went to prison and did some hard time there.

THE SPREAD OF ABORTION ADVERTISING

That conviction might have been a small victory for anti-abortionists trying to hold down the spread of abortion — but by the late 1840s, abortion already had spread. By the mid-1840s the *Connecticut Courant* was running an ad from a female physician, Mrs. Barnes, who promised relief from "irregularity." Her pitch imitated Madame Restell's: "It is indeed a melancholy reflection that so many of the fair daughters of our land should find a premature grave, from a cause that is so easily removed."[15] Abortion advertising had spread so far that even a small Arkansas newspaper, the *Fort Smith Herald*, was running an ad telling pregnant women that they could prevent an "undesired increase of family" either through use of an instrument or ingestion of "Portuguese Female Pills."[16]

Just as New York became a regional center for abortion, so other cities became depots for their areas. New Orleans was a southern switchboard; along with a story about "drunken fish" who had consumed 100 gallons of whiskey and were swimming "blindly upon the beach,"[17] the New Orleans *Daily Crescent* in 1848 ran ads offering a "sovereign and speedy cure" for "obstructed or difficult menstruation," whatever the cause.[18] New Orleans abortion ads continued in a steady stream over the ensuing decade, with a typical 1850s ad in the Louisiana *Courier* promising to cure "periodical affections of females, however complicated they may be."[19]

Cleveland newspapers also ran abortion ads during the 1850s. A Cleveland *Plain Dealer* advertisement for Dr. Walters' pills informed potential buyers that "Married Ladies desiring an increase in family should not use them as they will certainly prevent the desired result."[20] An ad for "Dr. Ratier's Celebrated French Periodical Drops" noted that they "should not be used by ladies when in a certain condition, as they are sure to restore menses, under all circumstances."[21] Dr. H.D. Palmer offered "Female Monthly Pills" for "Ladies in want of a pleasant and safe remedy for irregularities, obstructions, &c,"[22] and Dr. Cheeseman offered a "female pill" of such potency "that even the reproductive power of nature cannot resist it."[23] Some of the ads may have been "bait and switch," because when pills did not work, operations came next for women who wanted to abort.

As in New York, ads used figleaves. An 1850s ad in the Cincinnati *Commercial* during 1858 announced that "Madame Lozier's Female Monthly Pills" were the "remedy for obstructions, irregularities, etc."; the ad ended with the capitalized words, "CAUTION: MARRIED LADIES IN CERTAIN SITUATIONS SHOULD NOT USE THEM."[24] The Indianapolis *Daily State Sentinel* advertised Dr. Hooper's Female Cordial, "a speedy and positive cure . . . for all irregularities" including suppression, and Dr. Dacier's Female Pills, which warned that "ladies in certain situations should not use these." Other pills were described as "removing stoppages or obstructions of the menses, from whatever cause."[25]

It is as hard to judge the impact of those ads around the country as it is to evaluate the marketing success of New York ads. Again, all we can go by are, first, the reports of a growing number of abortions around the country; second, the ample advertising by abortionists, who had the reputation for lucre-hunger and were unlikely to waste money; third, the certainty that those abortion ads, in an age of very small papers and ravenous readers, were seen and comprehended for what they were;[26] and fourth, the reaction to the ads of some anti-abortion individuals.

ANTI-ABORTION RESPONSE

Opponents of abortion *were* angry that abortion ads "without the slightest scruple" were calling for the "prodigal destruction of human life."[27] Members of the Massachusetts House of Representatives, for example, saw advertising as crucial to the apparent increase in abortion, and in 1847 passed a bill prohibiting advertisements for "any place, house, shop or office where any poison, drug, mixture, preparation, medicine or noxious thing, or any instrument or means whatever" was used "for the purpose of causing or procuring the miscarriage of a woman pregnant with child."[28] The Massachusetts Senate balked at censorship of newspapers and added such large loopholes that a printing press could pass through them without difficulty,[29] but the attempt did show the belief of the times that a practical way to reduce the number of abortions was to attack the mechanism seen as having dramatically raised those numbers.

The reluctance to censor advertising led opponents of abortion to demand that anti-abortion laws be enforced — but politics and law often made enforcement difficult. Politically, abortionists followed the Madame Restell mode in developing strong ties to officeholders and keeping the bludgeon of blackmail nearby. Rumors of police payoffs abounded.[30] Even if all was honest, however, legal problems of proving abortionist guilt remained. Testimony by women who had undergone abortions was extraordinarily difficult to come by, and physicians under legal seige could always claim that they merely were trying to start menstruation again, with the cause of blockage beyond their ken.

Difficulties in restricting advertising and prosecuting practice made anti-abortionists realize that their only hope was to awaken the public generally through education and exhortation. They spoke against abortion on the basis of both Biblical revelation and increasing medical knowledge concerning the beginning of human life. The early 19th century saw major scientific discoveries concerning the role of the sperm in fertilization and the beginning of life; familiar with such evidence, Dr. Hugh Hodge in 1839 could tell his class of medical students at the University of Pennsylvania that human life begins "at conception," that the child in utero "is truly a perfect *human being*, and that "its destruction is *murder*."[31]

Other doctors and medical professors joined Hodge in that statement during the 1840s and 1850s. An American Medical Association committee just before the Civil War demanded public education concerning "the slaughter of countless children now steadily perpetrated in our midst," and pledged to work "by every means in our power" to inform the public.[32]

Some of the means were books. In 1862, James C. Jackson's *The Sexual Organism, and Its Healthful Management* stated that abortion was "among the greatest of crimes."[33] In 1867, Edwin M. Hale's *The Great Crime of the Nineteenth Century* argued that abortion was both "A CRIME AGAINST PHYSIOLOGY," one that stopped "the normal course of the functions of physical life," and "A CRIME AGAINST MORALITY" that should be called by no other name than "murder."[34] C. Morrill's *Physiology of Women* in 1868, S. Y. Richard's *The Science of the Sexes* in 1870, and George H. Naphey's *The Physical Life of Women* — which sold 150,000 copies during the 3 years after its publication in 1870 — also attacked abortion.[35]

Another means of education was the reprinting of anti-abortion sermons. A "Sermon on Ante-Natal Infanticide" delivered by Indiana minister E. Frank Howe was reprinted widely.[36] Howe spoke of the "destruction of unborn children" and acknowledged that "no demonstration of the criminality of this thing will deter some of those who practice it from a continuance of the practice." He argued, however, that many women and men "have fallen into the practice thoughtlessly," particularly because news media were not communicating the truth about abortion.[37] Howe said he would try to get out the messsage as best he could: "In the ears of the thoughtless I would sound the cry of MURDER! so clearly that henceforth they cannot fail to think."[38]

Books and sermons were helpful, anti-abortionists said, but the major means of adult education was the press — yet, large city newspapers that accepted abortion ads, as most apparently did, did not cover abortion.[39] The sensational *National Police Gazette*, however, followed up its opposition to Madame Restell with an editorial that promised to criticize "any female who will have her own offspring stifled in her womb."[40] The *Gazette* continued to refuse abortion ads and charged that they were placed by "interested and mercenary wretches."[41] Under a headline "The Abortionists of New York," the *Gazette* attacked "human fiends" who were "child destroyers," and argued that "It indeed seems too monstrous for belief that such gross violations of the laws of both God and man should be accepted in the very heart of a community professing to be Christian."[42]

The *National Police Gazette* regularly reported abortion cases that *did* make it into court,[43] and it regularly emphasized protection of life from conception, "the immortal spark in thousands of the unborn."[44] The *Gazette* also exposed the practice of sending bodies of maternal abortion fatalities out of New York City, sometimes for use as cadavers.[45] It emphasized the problems of official corruption, telling of how "wretches whose skirts are red with murder . . . outface the law with their bloodstained gold."[46] In 1848 and during the next two decades the *Gazette* continued to emphasize the theme of preserving human life, with hard-hitting editorials describing "assassins' fingers" at work in women's wombs.[47] It was still hammering away at the topic of official corruption in 1867, and in that year criticized the ease by which arrested abortionists were able to put up bail money.[48] The *Gazette* asked of abortionists, "When will such unmitigated scoundrels cease to have friends at court?"[49]

ABORTION ADVERTISING IN THE 1860S

Abortionists certainly seemed to have friends, or at least pleased business associates, in many American newspaper offices throughout the 1860s. Dr. James of New Orleans promised relief from "Periodic Afflictions of Females, however complicated they might be," and offered "private rooms" for "strictly confidential" consultations.[50] The San Francisco *Daily Examiner* advertised "Dr. Gibbon's Female Pills" for "suppressions" and "irregularities." Pregnant women could read that they should "have no delicacy in calling, no difference what your troubles may be [sic]," for they could have "assurance of confidential secrecy."[51] On the same page Dr. W.K. Doherty noted that "Irregularities, suppression, etc., will receive the Doctor's most particular attention. Let no false delicacy prevent you, but apply immediately and save yourself from painful sufferings and premature death."[52]

Many of the ads argued, as had Madame Restell, that abortion could be altruistic. Doherty, for example, suggested that "All Married Ladies whose delicate health or other circumstances prevent an increase in their families, should write or call . . . they will receive every possible relief and help." Do it for the good of your family, women were told; but for those who feared discovery and social embarrassment, the final line of Doherty's ad also was soothing: "The Doctor's offices, consisting of a suite of six rooms, are so arranged that he may be consulted without fear of observation."[53]

Abortion ads continued as the United States was gripped by a bloody civil war. Dr. Cheeseman's ads in the Chicago *Daily Tribune* promised to cure "IRREGULARITIES OR OBSTRUCTIONS OF THE MENSES, whatever may be the cause of those obstructions."[54] Chicago also was home to Professor Von Veraes' offer of a "Newly Discovered Female Remedy" for "the removal of all obstructions whatever cause."[55] Other *Tribune* ads included that of Dr. John L. Lyons for his French Periodical drops, useful in altering "Suppressed and obstructed nature," with drops not to be used when forbidden in the directions.[56] Abortion ads continued in many southern newspapers as well. The Charleston, South Carolina *Daily Courier* advertised pills to end problems "that spring from irregularity, by removing the irregularity itself." Readers were told that the pills "may be safely used at any age, and at any period, EXCEPT DURING THE FIRST THREE MONTHS, during which the unfailing nature of their action would infallibly PREVENT pregnancy."[57]

Cleveland shoppers during the war could buy Madame Boivin's "Celebrated Silver Coated Female Pills," which cured "monthly difficulties" and "uterine obstructions." The ad warned in italics that pregnant women should not take the pills "during the first three months as miscarriage is certain."[58] Another Cleveland physician, Dr. King, apparently was not hurting business when he warned that his products "should not be used by Ladies in a certain condition as they never fail to restore the menses."[59]

Nor is it likely that advertisers of Percie's Pills were drastically reducing sales by noting that the pills were "designed solely as a remedy for irregularity," yet "shou'd [sic] not be used during pregnancy, as they will almost invariably cause miscarriage."[60]

Following the war, Dr. W. K. Doherty continued to run long abortion ads in San Francisco. His regular 80-line ad instructed females "in trouble" to "apply immediately and save yourself from painful sufferings. . . . All married ladies, whose delicate health or other circumstances prevent an increase in their families, should write or call."[61] Across the country, the Springfield (Massachusetts) *Republican* in 1869 included ads for Dr. Shole, whose "Lunar Mixture" promised "certainty of relief,"[62] and for Dr. Dow, who could "guarantee permanent cure in the difficult cases of suppression and other menstrual derangements."[63] The Missouri *Republican* told St. Louis residents about Duponco's Golden Pills, which stressed "removing obstructions of the monthly periods from whatever cause, and always successful," and about Mrs. Warlt, a female physician specializing in "the worst private cases" in the confidence and confinement of her home.[64]

By the late 1860s cities did not have to be large to provide a variety of abortion enticements. In Louisville, Kentucky, the *Daily Journal* in 1867 advertised Lyon's Periodical Drops as "the great cure for female irregularities," and also publicized other cures for "suppression."[65] One "female doctress" advertised a willingness to help with "obstructed menstruation.[66] An ad from the "Western Medical Office" was directed at "ladies whose health forbids too rapid increase of family"; it argued that those who suffered "stoppage of the monthly flow" could make an appointment and be "speedily cured, often in one interview."[67]

As the 1870s began, newspaper ads in a city such as Cleveland seemed to be shrinking the figleaf. Mrs. Doctress Dresden proclaimed in the Cleveland *Plain Dealer*, "Every lady that is in trouble should conduct the Doctress about her trouble and distresses. N.B. — Suppressions and irregularities will receive the Doctresses [sic] most particular attention."[68] Dr. C. A. Smith invited "troubled" ladies to visit his "Private Institute" for "Private Disease," where they could have "a safe and speedy removal of obstructions of the monthly period, with or without medicine." Smith noted that "When a woman is in trouble she should go and consult the experienced . . . physician about her troubles and diseases. Irregularities and suppressions will receive the doctor's most particular attention."[69]

In New Orleans, a typical issue of the *Daily Times* for March, 1870, had six ads concerning irregularities and suppression of the menses, with promise of confidential treatment.[70] For example, Dr. A. Urban noted that he "devotes his time to the treatment of all female complaints, let the disease be called what it may. He will attend to all diseases of the womb. Ladies afflicted with suppression of menstrual discharge will be safely and speedily relieved or no charge. . . . Everything strictly confidential."[71] Dr. Luke's ad promised "Special attention given to all Female Complaints. Ladies afflicted with Suspension of the Menses can be safely and effectually relieved. The Doctor's parlors are so arranged that patients need not see each other, thereby securing perfect secrecy in all cases where desired."[72]

Other probable New Orleans abortionists during March, 1870, included Mrs. Wardle, a "Midwife and Ladies' Physician" who had just "returned from Paris" and was ready to go to work; Mrs. D. Pownall, "a regular graduate in midwifery (of Germany) who was ready to help "all sufferers of Female Diseases"; and Mrs. Graham, who more prosaically had just "returned from the North" and was prepared to help all women "suffering from Irregularities or stoppage of the Menses."[73] In 1871 Dr. W. Bille also began promising confidentiality with a "perfect cure" for "retained menstruation."[74]

The consistent career of Dr. Lancelot Everitt indicates the longevity of many practices. On Christmas Day, 1849, he was a "Graduate in Obstetrics" telling readers of the New Orleans *Daily Picayune* that he would serve them "in accordance with the principles of the Atomology of Life and Death."[75] Everitt noted that he "gives preference to those whose cases have baffled others," but his ad lacked specificity. Throughout the 1850s and into the 1860s he continued to advertise, and by 1865 was declaring his use of "a modern philosophic [sic] practice . . . to control the various chemical actions which induce all dangerous affections of the Womb."[76] In 1870 he was more explicit yet: "Dr. Everitt never fails to eradicate from the soul and body the terrible influences and operations of suppressed or painful menses and irreg. conceptions, w/out pain or the least danger. $25.00–$50.00 or $100.00."[77]

By 1871, sounding like Mark Twain's duke and dauphin rolled into one, Everitt was proclaiming his "coronation" (sic) as a "Master of Philosophy and Fetal Evolution . . . sworn before the Lord Provost, the Senatus Academicus and Council of the Queen's Magistrates . . . to protect the honor of ladies & families, to faithfully preserve the lives of patients and forever keep sacred professional communications."[78] Everitt also was more explicit about just what he would do in cases of "irregularities" which might cause pregnancies to be "fatal to the health or honor of a patient."[79] To preserve such "honor" Everitt would journey to his patient "in any of the Southern States, incog[nito] if necessary, and in a few days . . . restore her to a condition of health & vigor."[80]

NATIONAL POLICE GAZETTE RESPONSE

The New Orleans newspapers apparently had nothing to say about such a practice. Nor, it seems, did most newspapers in other parts of the United States. Only the *National Police Gazette* ran hard-hitting editorial after editorial during the late 1860s. In one, "Our People's Shame," the *Gazette* complained that availability and publicizing of "the deadly drug and the ever alert abortionists" were convincing some women to go against the "maternal instinct."[81] The *Gazette* termed abortion "the monster, wide-spread vice of the day . . . outraging the laws of man, debasing the minds and shattering the bodies of our women."[82] In another editorial published in 1867, "THE ABORTIONISTS AGAIN AT WORK," the *Gazette* criticized men for encouraging the "vicious practice" of abortion" in order to "obviate the trouble and expense of rearing a family."[83]

The *Gazette*, however, had more readership than prestige.

Chapter 3

The New York *Times* Versus Abortion

During the 1860s, as abortion advertising continued and the *National Police Gazette* raged against it, the New York *Times* ran at least 16 small stories about 10 abortion incidents.[1] Significantly, the content and terminology of those news stories showed concern for the life of the unborn child as well as for the health of the mother, and several of the stories were about arrests following abortions in which only the unborn child died. One article noted the arrest of a doctor "on the charge of having produced an abortion"; the woman was "doing well, and is in no danger from the result of the alleged operation," but the *Times* still ran the story.[2] Another article told of a woman who decided to testify after she took her aborted child "and threw it in the river, I have been sick ever since."[3]

Still, even in the late 1860s *Times* coverage was occasional, unfocused, and irresolute—and the *Times*, like other newspapers, accepted abortion ads from Madame Restell and others.[4] For example, Madame Restell's husband "Dr. Mauriceau" ran ads under his own alias in 1867, 1868, and 1869, with guarantees of "a safe and immediate removal of all special irregularities in females with or without medicine, at one interview."[5] Ads for "Portuguese Female Monthly Pills" stated that "In all cases of stoppage or irregularity, from whatever cause, they are certain to succeed in forty-eight hours. Safe and healthy, they cannot fail in any case."[6]

The *Times* accepted such advertising even as more doctors were expressing sharp anti-abortion positions. The New York Medical Society in 1867 submitted to the state legislature a strongly worded resolution calling for tough abortion laws. "From the first moment of conception, there is a living creature in process of development to full maturity," the doctors declared: "The intentional arrest of this living process . . . is consequently murder."[7] That resolution may have had no immediate effect on the *Times*, but New York state legislation in 1869 that made all abortion manslaughter and banned abortion ads, apparently did: Following passage of the bill, abortion ads disappeared from the *Times*.[8]

The legislation by itself did not *force* the change: As usual, enforcement was lacking, at least initially, and newspapers such as the New York *Herald* continued to run thinly veiled ads without prosecution. But the New York *Times* already may have been struggling with the morality of abortion advertising; Henry Raymond and George Jones, who founded the *Times* in 1851, were professed Christian with some inconsistencies, and their double-mindedness may have been reflected in the unusual combination of abortion stories and abortion ads. When Raymond died in 1869 and Jones took over control, the passage of anti-abortion legislation that same year may have given Jones the final push he needed to give up some advertising revenue.[9]

In any case, without having to worry about pressure from the business department, the way was clear in 1870 for editor Louis Jennings, a conservative Christian, to begin a crusade against abortion. Jennings began the campaign in 1870 with a Biblically referenced editorial entitled "The Least of These Little Ones." He complained that the "perpetration of infant murder . . . is rank and smells to heaven. Why is there no hint of its punishment? Are the Police under the delusion that they are appointed merely for the purpose of dealing with open and public offenses?"[10] Jennings saw the need for public outrage, not just a tightening of laws that would go unenforced. The *Times* gave ample coverage to two more abortion cases early in 1871 but complained about "the extreme rarity of trials for abortion in this City — an offense which is known to be very common."[11] Abortionists "have openly carried on their infamous practice in this City to a frightful extent, and have laughed at the defeat of respectable citizens who have vainly attempted to prosecute them."[12]

"THE EVIL OF THE AGE"

To attack abortion, editor Jennings realized that the public had to be aroused. He also knew that exposure of the abortionists would require some unconventional reporting. In July, 1871, Jennings told *Times* reporter Augustus St. Clair to go undercover in order to gather information for an expose. For several weeks Jennings and "a lady friend" visited the most-advertised abortionists in New York, posing as a couple in need of professional services. The result was a hard-hitting, three-column article published late in August.[13]

St. Clair's story, "The Evil of the Age," began on a solemn note:

The enormous amount of medical malpractice [the common euphemism for abortion] that exists and flourishes, almost unchecked, in the City of New York, is a theme for most serious consideration. Thousands of human beings are thus murdered before they have seen the light of this world, and thousands upon thousands more of adults are irremediably robbed in constitution, health, and happiness.[14]

St. Clair then skillfully contrasted powerlessness and power. First he described the back of one abortionist's office: "Human flesh, supposed to have been the remains of infants, was found in barrels of lime and acids, undergoing decomposition." He described the affluence of an abortionist couple, Dr. and Madame H. D. Grindle: "The parlors are spacious, and contain all the decorations, upholstery, cabinetware, piano, book case, &c., that is found in a respectable home." He quoted Madame Grindle: "Why, my dear friend, you have no idea of the class of people that come to us. We have had Senators, Congressman and all sorts of politicians, bring some of the first women in the land here."[15]

St. Clair then gave figures on the economics of abortion, noting that a Dr. Evans spent $1,000 per week on advertising, received 100 letters per day requesting services, and had amassed a fortune of $100,000. St. Clair named names: Mauriceau and Restell, Dr. Ascher, Dr. Selden, Dr. Franklin, Madame Van Buskirk, Madame Maxwell, Madame Worcester. He emphasized the constant coverup, because "All the parties interested have the strongest motives to unite in hushing the scandal." He ended with a call for change: "The facts herein set forth are but a fraction of a greater mass that cannot be published with propriety. Certainly enough is here given to arouse the general public sentiment to the necessity of taking some decided and effectual action."[16]

St. Clair's article put abortion on the public's agenda, but that by itself was not enough. Newspaper crusaders know that once the basic facts are laid out and readers are becoming aware of a problem, a specific incident is still needed to galvanize the public. Tragically for a young woman, providentially for the *Times'* anti-abortion effort, the ideal story of horror arrived within the week. St. Clair published his expose on August 23; on August 27 a *Times* headline at the top of page one read, "A TERRIBLE MYSTERY."[17]

The general facts of the story were miserable enough: The nude body of a young woman was found inside a trunk in a railway station baggage room. The autopsy showed that her death had been caused by an abortion. But the *Times* provided evocative specific detail:

This woman, full five feet in height, had been crammed into a trunk two feet six inches long. . . . Seen even in this position and rigid in death, the young girl, for she could not have been more than eighteen, had a face of singular loveliness. But her chief beauty was her great profusion of golden hair, that hung in heavy folds over her shoulders, partly shrouding the face . . . There was no mark of violence upon the body, although there was some discoloration and decomposition about the pelvic region. It was apparent that here was a new victim of man's lust, and the life-destroying arts of those abortionists, whose practices have lately been exposed in the TIMES.[18]

The exciting "trunk murder" detective story received full play in the *Times* during the next several days as police tried to identify the perpetrator. A boy who had helped carry the trunk into the station tried to find a man and a mysterious lady who had delivered the trunk. Daily, readers absorbed the strategy of the detective in charge, Inspector Walling, who "issued orders which practically put every policeman in the force upon the case." The *Times* also noted that this particular tragedy was not an isolated incident: In a lead column every day on its back page (which functioned at that time as a second front page), the *Times* kept reminding readers that this particular incident showed what went on "in one of the many abortion dens that disgrace New York, and which the TIMES has just exposed as 'The Evil of the Age.' "[19]

On August 29 Inspector Walling arrested a Dr. Rosenzweig, a.k.a. Ascher, whose advertisement had been quoted in St. Clair's August 23 story: "Ladies in trouble guaranteed immediate relief, sure and safe; no fees required until perfectly satisfied. . . . "[20] The following day a *Times* editorial, "Advertising Facilities for Murder," quoted that article and noted, "What a ghastly commentary upon such an announcement is the fate of the golden-haired unfortunate who lies, [now] a mass of putrefaction, in the Morgue?" The editorial attacked "the lying notices of men and women whose profession, if it means anything at all, means murder made easy," and asked whether "the lives of babes are of less account than a few ounces of precious metal, or a roll of greenbacks?"[21]

Jones and Jennings had stood up to Boss Tweed, and the editorial now described their response to a blackmail attempts by Madame Restell's husband Lohman, a.k.a. Dr. Mauriceau: "MARICEAU [sic] found that he could not intimidate the TIMES with his filthy ravings . . . he immediately 'backed down,' and endeavored to explain away his little attempts at intimidation."[22] The *Times* kept beating the drum: "It is high time that public opinion should be fairly roused. The law must take hold of the abortionists, as it very easily can, and public opinion must set its seal of emphatic condemnation upon every agency which aids and abets the shameful trade."[23]

Four columns of the back page of that August 30 issue were devoted to a superbly written follow-up by St. Clair, and accompanying stories. "A Terrible Story from our Reporter's Note-Book" revealed how St. Clair, in his undercover research for the expose, had visited several weeks ago the accused Rosenzweig's Fifth Avenue clinic. Continuing his pattern of showing the affluence of the abortionists, St. Clair described the "fine tapestry carpet . . . elegant mahogany desk . . . piano," and so on.[24] The shocker, for those who had been reading the previous day's stories, was inserted subtly:

> As we entered the room a young girl emerged therefrom. She seemed to be about twenty years of age, a little more than five feet in height, of slender build, having blue eyes, and a clear, alabaster complexion. Long blonde curls, tinted with gold, drooped upon her shoulders, and her face wore an expression of embarrassment at the presence of strangers. She retreated to the end of the hall, and stood there for a moment, and then went to another part of the house. In a few moments the Doctor made his appearance.[25]

St. Clair then described his discussions with Rosenzweig, including the doctor's demand for $200. When St. Clair asked what would happen to the aborted infant, Rosenzweig was quoted as replying, "Don't worry about that, my dear Sir. I will take care of the *result*. A newspaper bundle, a basket, a pail, a resort to the sewer, or the river at night? Who is the wiser?" When St. Clair asked more questions, Rosenzweig became suspicious and began to shout, "I'll kill you . . . you spy, you devil, you villain." According to St. Clair's account Rosenzweig's hand then "moved to his breast pocket," and St. Clair had to draw a revolver to make good his escape.[26]

On his way out, St. Clair glimpsed once again the beautiful young woman he had seen on his way in. This time, as a fitting conclusion to his story, he drove the point home:

> As I passed through the hallway I saw the same girl who had left the parlor when I made my first visit to the house. She was standing on the stairs, and *it was the same face I saw afterward at the Morgue. I positively identify the features of the dead woman as those of the blond beauty before described.*[27]

With one of its own reporters giving a first-hand account, the *Times* sometimes seemed to be convicting Rosenzweig in the press; however, although quoting Inspector Walling's views, the newspaper refrained from editorials demanding punishment for a specific individual still presumed innocent until proven guilty. Other developments vigorously reported by the *Times* also kept public attention focused on the abortion story. The young lady was identified as Alice Mowlsby, a poor orphan who lived with her aunt in Paterson, New Jersey. Her "seducer" was identified as Walter Conklin, son of a mill-owner. As facts of the case continued to be revealed, Conklin admitted responsibility for arranging the abortion and committed suicide.[28]

EXTENDING THE CRUSADE

The *Times* kept at it, reporting on September 6 "ANOTHER ABORTION MUR-DER" of "a beautiful girl twenty-two years of age."[29] On September 8 the *Times* gave prominent play to a judge's discussion before a grand jury of Rosenzweig's alleged crime, one:

> most foul in its character, making the heart grow sick at the contemplation of such fiendish depravity. . . . Let the warning word this day go forth, and may it be scattered broad-cast throughout the land, that from this hour the authorities, one and all, shall put forth every effort and shall strain every nerve until these professional abortionists, these traffickers in human life, shall be exterminated.[30]

Anti-abortion doctors seized the opportunity. Although the *Times* crusaded, the American Medical Association circulated a report emphasizing "the safety of the child" and denouncing "the perverted views of morality" underlying abortion. In extremely strong language the AMA doctors denounced physicians who performed abortions: "We shall discover an enemy in the camp. . . . It is false brethren we have to fear; men who are false to their professions, false to principle, false to honor, false to humanity, false to God." The doctors described physician-abortionists as "these modern Herods," "educated assassins," and "monsters of iniquity" who present "as hideous a view of moral deformity as the evil spirit could present."[31]

The AMA language went further than that of any newspaper, but the doctors were resolute:

> If our language has appeared to some strong and severe, or even intemperate, let the gentlemen pause for a moment and reflect on the importance and gravity of the subject. . . . We had to deal with human life. In a matter of less importance we could entertain no compromise. An honest judge on the bench would call things by their proper names. We could do no less.[32]

A district attorney also engaged in a heated denunciation of Madame Restell and her ill-gotten wealth, with lines such as "Every brick in that splendid mansion might represent a little skull, and the blood that infamous woman has shed might have served to mix the mortar."[33] The press from this point on was not pushing an agenda on uninvolved leaders, but was also reflecting the heat around it.

With judges, doctors, and lawyers aroused, New York newspapers other than the *Times* could not neglect the story. For example, the New York *Tribune* ran a hard-hitting editorial entitled "THE ROOT OF THE EVIL,"[34] in obvious homage to the *Times'* "EVIL OF THE AGE" theme of abortion as big money-maker. The *Tribune* attacked "an infamous but unfortunately common crime — so common that it affords a lucrative support to a regular guild of professional murderers, so safe that its perpetrators advertise their calling in the newspapers, and parade their spoils on the fashionable avenues."[35] The *Tribune* editorial concluded with a flat statement that "abortion at any period is homicide."

Rosenzweig's trial, which began in a crowded courtroom on October 26, received wide coverage; as the *Times* noted, "Notwithstanding the period which has elapsed since the perpetration of the terrible tragedy, public attention has never been diverted from this extraordinary case."[36] The *Times* had been instrumental in focusing that public attention, of course. On October 29, Rosenzweig was found guilty of causing death through medical malpractice and was sentenced to 7 years imprisonment. The judge told him that he was getting off easy, for "You sent two human beings to their last account, deliberately, willfully, murderously."[37] The judge said he would join with others in recommending to the Legislature harsher penalties.

The *Times* kept up the crusade. Early in December it reported that one medical board reported stiffer penalties for abortion, and also noted that "The Press and the Judiciary were thanked for their determined opposition to this crime."[38] One week later the *Times* gave front-page coverage to another medical group's statement that "the fetus is alive from conception, and all intentional killing of it is murder."[39] That committee wanted judges to be given discretion to assign sentences of life imprisonment in abortion cases; it also suggested that passage of new legislation would be possible because New York was "grievously shocked . . . by the terrible deeds of certain abortionists lately exposed."[40]

The *Times* continued the campaign during the rest of 1871 and into 1872, noting that "The time is opportune to strike quickly, and to strike home."[41] The *Times* emphasized that the fight against abortion was a fight against money and power: "Great mansions on grand avenues are occupied by disgusting 'practitioners' who continue to escape prosecution."[42] It recommended passage of a bill "far-reaching enough to catch hold of all who assist, directly or indirectly, in the destruction of infant life," and gave its recommendation one additional populist thrust: "The people demand it."[43] With the *Times* pushing, the New York legislature of 1872 passed tough new antiabortion laws, with easier rules of evidence and a maximum penalty of 20 years imprisonment.[44] Enforcement also was stepped up.

The "trunk murder," with the emphasis given it by the *Times*' crusade, may have had some impact on abortion policy outside of New York. The sensational tale of the beautiful blonde and the evil abortionist received play in newspapers across the United States; there was no shirking from use of the words "abortion" and "abortionists." The San Francisco *Daily Examiner* discussed "the mystery enveloping the case of the young girl whose body, evidently murdered by abortionists, was found in a trunk."[45] The Chicago *Tribune's* New York correspondent wrote of the young lady "who came here to procure an abortion."[46] The New Orleans *Daily Picayune* reported that evidence against "the abortionist" was increasing.[47] The Galveston (Texas) *News* reported "a deep feeling of indignation" in New York, where "the number of abortionists is known to be large. [The *Times*] is demanding a general cleaning out of these establishments by the police. It is believed that the indignation of the public will result in securing some action in this direction."[48]

Coverage of abortion by the *Times* and other newspapers probably contributed to the general tightening of abortion laws throughout the United States during the 1870s, and to increased pressure on the press to cover the work of abortionists. Attacks on "advertising murder" may have hit home, as many states passed bans on either performing abortion or advertising for abortion. For example, the 1873–1874 California legislature passed a law stating that "Every person who willfully writes, composes or publishes any notice or advertisement of any medicine or means for producing or facilitating a miscarriage or abortion . . . is guilty of a felony."[49] The New York legislature linked contraception and abortion (a linkage that would be controversial in the 20th century) and tried to be comprehensive in its restrictions on:

A person who sells, lends, gives away, or in any manner exhibits or offers to sell, lend or give away, or has in his possession with intent to sell, lend or give away, or advertises, or offers for sale, loan or distribution, any instrument or article, or any recipe, drug or medicine for the prevention of conception, or for causing unlawful abortion, or purporting to be for the prevention of conception, or for causing unlawful abortion, or advertises, or holds out representations that it can be so used or applied, or any such description as will be calculated to lead another to so use or apply any such article, recipe, drug, medicine or instrument, or who writes or prints, or causes to be written or printed, a card, circular, pamphlet, advertisement or notice of any kind, or gives information orally, stating when, where, how, of whom, or by what means such an instrument, article, recipe, drug or medicine can be purchased or obtained, or who manufactures any such instrument, article, recipe, drug or medicine.[50]

Such laws did not knock out abortion advertising, however, as chapter 4 shows; nor was there a sudden rush to cover abortion. Newspapers often continued to avoid battle against abortionists with political clout and advertising dollars. Some editors may have been squeamish or have felt that newspapers read by the whole family should not go into detail about the destruction of families. But courageous editors such as those on the *Times* argued that "It is useless to talk of such matters with bated breath, or to seek to cover such terrible realities with the veil of a false delicacy. . . .

From a lethargy like this it is time to rouse ourselves. The evil that is tolerated is aggressive; if we want the good to exist at all it must be aggressive too."[51]

THE SUPREME COURT'S FAULTY HISTORY

The *Times* throughout its coverage showed that the "evil" consisted in the death of unborn children as well as in the hazards to mothers. A century later, the historical summary in *Roe v. Wade* depended heavily on two articles by New York lawyer Cyril Means, Jr., who contended that the purpose of mid-19th century anti-abortion legislation was solely to protect the health of the mother.[52] Means argued that because early abortion now is physically safer than giving birth, furthering of the purpose of the 19th century legislation required overturning of its specific prohibitions.[53] Pro-abortion lawyers in their brief before the Supreme Court used the same argument: "In keeping with modern medical practice, this court would reinforce the purpose of early abortion legislation if it invalidated the statute."[54] But if press coverage was in any way representative of the public and legislative mood, the pro-abortion historical argument is completely erroneous.[55]

The *Times*, in short, cared about unborn children, those "thousands of human beings . . . murdered before they have seen the light of this world."[56] With such concern, the *Times* went after the murderers, including Madame Restell herself. *Times* coverage of abortion helped to turn her into an object of general hatred in New York City. Occasionally, her carriage would be chased down Fifth avenue by a volley of rocks, and by shouts of "Madame Killer."

Madame Restell was very discreet in her abortion activities from 1871 on. In 1878, however, at age 65 but hardly in retirement, she slipped. The *Times* was able to report in a front-page headline, "MME RESTELL ARRESTED" for "selling drugs and articles to procure abortion."[57] The *Times* noted that "The residence of Mme Restell is one of the best known in New York. . . . Her wealth is entirely the proceeds of her criminal profession. Her patrons are said to belong to the wealthiest families."[58] This time, however, Madame Restell's patrons were not able to protect her from arrest under very hostile circumstances, or from reporters who followed every detail of her arraignment and trial.

Some of the developments were low comedy. Madame Restell could not immediately raise bail from her own funds, because her investments in bonds and real estate were not liquid. Bondsmen, however, said they would put up sufficient funds only if the judge would order reporters not to print the bondsmen's names in the newspaper. The judge refused and the bondsmen refused. Madame Restell's lawyer turned to one bondsman and asked him to help out, saying "Will you not allow a Christian feeling to govern you?"[59] But there was nothing Christian about Madame Restell, the *Times* suggested, as it quoted the bondsman refusing not from opposition to abortion but from dislike of publicity: "I've got a wife and a family of girls, and I'll be hanged if I'm agoing [sic] to have my name in the papers as a bondsman for an abortionist."[60]

Madame Restell eventually left jail while awaiting trial, but she could not leave behind newspaper attacks. She had lived by the press and was now dying by it. She asked her lawyers if there was some way to suppress the newspapers, but was told that nothing could be done, for the press was "without standards." One of Madame Restell's colleagues complained angrily, "Money! We've plenty of that. But what good is it with the newspapers against us?"[61] Madame Restell's lawyer asked both judge and editor to have mercy on his client, a "poor old woman," but he was laughed at. Madame Restell could not seem to understand the causes of the judgment she was facing: "I have never injured anybody," she complained: "Why should they bring this trouble upon me!"[62]

Madame Restell at age 65 became an avid newspaper reader, but she found no peace. The New York *Tribune* described how she was "driven to desperation at last by the public opinion she had so long defied."[63] At night she paced her mansion halls like a latter-day Lady Macbeth, looking at her hands and bemoaning her situation. Finally, the night before her trial was scheduled to begin, Madame Restell was discovered in her bathtub by a maid, with her throat cut from ear to ear, an apparent suicide.

The *Times* announced this denouement at the top of page one: "END OF A CRIMINAL LIFE. MME RESTELL COMMITS SUICIDE."[64]

Chapter 4

Danger and Dollars, 1878–1898

The New York *Times*, following the death of Madame Restell, continued its attack on the other abortion madames of New York. It hit hard at a Madame Berger when she was arrested following the death of both mother and child during an abortion operation, and applauded when she was sentenced to 12 years in prison.[1] It attacked Mrs. Annie Morris, known as Madame Romaine, who had been protected by her husband, a policeman.[2] Increasingly, however, doctors came to dominate the abortion industry, and the *Times* gave front-page coverage to the arrests of Dr. M. E. Smith, Dr. Edward Pynchon, Dr. George Kellogg, and Dr. C. H. Orton.[3]

The list continued, physician after physician, in 1880 and 1881: Dr. John Buchanan, Dr. George L. Brook, Dr. Vincent Haight, Dr. William Fayen, Dr. Willoughby, and others.[4] As the titles indicate, most of the abortionists who came under police investigation and press attack were doctors. Their medical techniques apparently were standard for the period, but they had little hope — in the absence of antibiotics — of stopping infections.

CONCERN FOR THE UNBORN

During the 1880s, the New York *Times* continued to show concern not just for the health of mothers, but for the lives of unborn children as well. It gave top placement on page one to the discovery of "TWENTY-ONE MURDERED BABIES" in Philadelphia. The lead noted that "the bodies of 21 infants who had been killed before birth" were found in a house formerly occupied by a Dr. Isaac Hathaway: "Only a few spadefuls of earth had been thrown up when Detective Wolf's implement struck something that made a grating sound. The spade had crushed through slender, thread-like bones, as thin and bleached as paper. . . . A few inches further down another skull and more tiny ribs and leg bones were found."[5]

Times front-page coverage of the trial was vivid: Hathaway, 83, "a shabby-looking old man, stooping and weak, attired in a very dirty shirt, and with hair and voluminous beard dyed in raven black," looked on as the district attorney held a cigar box with the bones of the "21 infants . . . Whenever the box was moved, they rattled like hard withered leaves. There were many bits of skulls among them, some almost complete."[6] Hathaway's wife acknowledged that he had done 400 to 500 abortions, burying some bodies in the basement and burning others in a stove. Hathaway was sentenced to 7 years at hard labor, which at his age was akin to the death penalty; neighbors gossiped that Hathaway had kept two dogs in the basement to feast on the corpses of the unborn children.

The *Times* noted more doctor arrests later in the decade. A story in 1884, "Two Physicians in Trouble," noted that two of the "best known physicians in Providence, R.I." were on trial "for alleged illegal practice."[7] A typical story in 1886, "DOCTOR INDICTED," detailed abortion charges against a well-known New Haven physician, Dr. Gallagher, who had operated on a woman known for "wide acquaintance with the bloods of the town and the Yale students."[8] The *Times* emphasized Gallagher's prominent status and noted that lawyers were surprised to see him in court.[9] A similar story about a well-connected doctor noted the abortion arrest of Philadelphia physician David Otway.[10]

The *Times* often contrasted the power of abortionists with the powerlessness of unborn children and the vulnerability of their mothers. When the abortion trial of Dr. Herman W. Gedicke began in 1880, the *Times* noted that "the trial excites considerable interest from the fact that the accused is wealthy and is a member of the board of Aldermen" of Newark, N.J.[11] Actually, the *Times* made a factual error, because Gedicke was a former alderman, but it reported correctly that the woman on whom Gedicke had operated, Mary Cunningham, charged that Dr. Gedicke "had given her medicine and used instruments to produce an abortion. When she made that charge he had her arrested and indicted for perjury. She was acquitted, now he is on trial."[12]

Gedicke had more problems when evidence that he had paid $2,000 to bribe the jury came to light; he was eventually found guilty of criminal abortion. The *Times* quoted Judge McCarter's characterization of the conviction as "a most signal triumph of the law over power and influence."[13] However, Gedicke was sentenced to only 2 years at hard labor, and later received a pardon for reasons that the historical record does not clarify.[14]

The *Times* seemed to seize opportunities to play up human interest stories involving abortion. For example, it reported discovery of the corpse of a 5-month-old, recently killed unborn child floating in a cigar box in the water. Inside the cigar box, alongside the body, were a soap dish and a match box. The body, crushed out of shape, was wrapped in a piece of paper. Detectives, drying the paper and finding a hotel inscription on it, learned that a woman in one of the rooms was very ill. When the husband, George Davidson, was called out of the room and confronted with the evidence, he first offered bribes to have the case suppressed, but then gave a full confession: Davidson, it seemed, was a wealthy man married to the daughter of a former New Jersey Supreme Court judge, and thought to avoid embarrassment by paying his family doctor $2,000 to perform the abortion. The doctor was summoned to the hotel and arrested. The *Times*, willing to confront wealth and power, gave full coverage to the incident.[15]

The availability of abortion, in short, was seen as an opportunity for the strong to oppress the weak — particularly unborn children, and women victimized by employers who doubled as seducers. In January, 1884, the *Times* told on its front page the tale of a wealthy man who seduced the daughter of a court-house janitor and took her to Philadelphia for an abortion.[16] That same month another story, "A Victim of Malpractice," told of a young woman impregnated by her employer's son and forced into an abortion that became fatal to both mother and child.[17] A later story, "Fannie Briggs' Death," told how "Fannie Briggs was an attractive girl of 19 years and had been employed in the dry goods store of George A. Hettrick." Hettrick impregnated her and demanded that she have an abortion. She did, and she died.[18]

ABORTION AS OPPRESSION

The newspaper that most emphasized abortion as oppression, and then urged sympathy for pressured mothers and unborn children was the *National Police Gazette*. It called abortion "THE CRIME AGAINST NATURE," and criticized abortionists "Willing to Prostitute Talent, Education and an Honorable Profession to Step Into Restell's Shoes."[19] The *Gazette* emphasized the effect of abortion on both mother and child, and in some stories was not clear as to whether abortion or infanticide had been committed; as reporters would learn during the Edelin and Waddill trials described in chapter 13, a thin line divided the two. For example, a story from Indianapolis described the corpse of a mother killed during an abortion operation headlined as "A DAMNABLE DEED." The story noted how

Between her lower limbs, lying upon his back, were the remains of a newly-born infant of the male gender, the umbilical cord showing the child to have been forcibly torn from its mother while yet alive, while upon its skull is the mark of a cruel blow, as if the helpless one had been swung by its heels against an unyielding surface, and its skull crushed until life was extinct.[20]

The *Gazette* emphasized the life of the child as well as the health of the mother. An editorial in January, 1880, "Slaughtering the Innocents," called abortion a "crime that stands pre-eminent in the list of human infamies." Abortionists, the *Gazette* noted, "have not hesitated to advertise their brutal avocation openly in the daily press. . . . Those who are supposed to ferret out and eradicate such ulcers from the body social, have tacitly winked at and allowed this practice to go on uninterrupted until some hideous revelation of infanticide makes action necessary." Yet, "the life of one little innocent should be a suffucent incentive . . . it is the duty of the police to at once institute stringent measures for their [the abortionists] extermination."[21]

Concern for unborn children also was evident in 1880 when the *Gazette* published an indictment that jumped off the page in headline letters half an inch high: "HORROR! The Astounding Revelations Made by a Denver, Colorado, Physician. THE CURSE OF AMERICAN SOCIETY. The Terrible Sins Which Vanity and Fashion Led Their Devotees to Commit." The *Gazette* quoted an unnamed "eminent physician" of Denver in an attack on those who "kill their offspring secretly without the slightest compunction."[22] The doctor was quoted as saying that many abortions are done for "extravagance" and "love of ease," but he noted that abortion is "Child murder . . . a brutal and revolting act, and the law provides a punishment for it when it can be proved." A killer of an unborn child is "as much a murderess as one who kills it a few minutes after it is born."[23] The interview ended with a question, "What is the best means of preventing this great crime?" The doctor was quoted as saying:

> Publicity. Let the people know what is going on around them. There is no remedy for a great social secret sin like exposure. Drag it out into the lurid light of day. Do not cover it up and hide it beneath an assumed modesty so shallow that every eye can peep through it and see the false morality beneath.[24]

The *Gazette* did its best to drag abortion into day's lurid light. It called one abortionist "HELLISH EARLL." A Monster Whom it Would be an Insult to Humanity to Call a Man. A LONG RECORD OF INFAMY. Living on the Lives of Innocent Babes and Heartless Erring Mothers."[25] The *Gazette's* story began with vigor: "The civilization of today is opposed to babies, and its basest product is the abortionist. He is the human hyena, and the living, quivering flesh of foolish or unfortunate womanhood is the grave from which he tears his prey. He lives upon the crushed and mangled bodies of tender, breathless infants." The article ended with a vision of final judgment of the abortionist, "when the spirits of all the women and babies he has wronged will rise up in testimony against him."[26]

The *Gazette* usually portrayed the mother as victim rather than perpetrator.[27] The crime of the abortionist was emphasized in headlines such as "MURDEROUS MALPRACTICE. Another case of the Abortionist's Deviltry Brought to Light by the Silver Lake Mystery. Vickie Connor's Fate. Shocking Case of Illicit Love and Medical Murder with a Beautiful Girl as the Victim."[28] The *Gazette* often tried to view the story from the perspective of the unborn child; in one "Shocking Revelation of Betrayal, Abortion and Death Which Horrified a Quiet New Hampshire Neighborhood," the *Gazette* told of how a doctor was charged with murder after performing an abortion on a young woman, for "the child was alive."[29]

The *Gazette* also publicized the possible repercussions to the mother herself of such unnatural actions, as in an article headlined "THE PENALTY For Outraging Nature—An Abortionist's Victim—Dying Alone, Cursed With the Results of Defying Humanity." The story, from Chicago, noted that "Some weeks ago a young woman placed herself under the care of Dr. Thomas N. Cream." Later, "a sickening stench came from the rooms she had occupied. The police were notified, and upon breaking in the doors a horrible spectacle met their gaze. On the bed lay the body of a young woman, rapidly decomposing. Her face had turned black, the cheeks and neck were swollen and covered with mold, the arms lay across the breast, and the left leg was drawn up and the sheets drenched with blood."[30]

The New York *Times* covered that same incident in similar fashion. "CHICAGO—A fatal and revolting case of malpractice was discovered here this morning," its story began: Police "found the body of the woman lying in a bed saturated with blood, rapidly decomposing, and bearing unquestionable evidence of the operation which had caused death." The *Gazette* account was somewhat more vivid, but there was no great difference between abortion coverage by the respectable *Times* and its sensational counterpart. Both newspapers hit abortion hard, apparently in the belief that ignoring abortion would merely lead to a false peace with continued oppression of unborn children and women.

Both newspapers also saw that the main culprits were not back-alley quacks but regular physicians seeking extra money. The *Times*, as noted, ran story after story about abortions committed by doctors; *Gazette* stories featured alliterative headlines such as "BLOOM'S BRUTALITY," concerning Dr. Harris Bloom, and "THE ABORTIONIST'S ART," concerning the Greensburg, Indiana, trial of Dr. C. C. Burns.[31] A Dr. Gaylord was featured in a Massachusetts abortion story,[32] and an article from Kansas noted the arrest of a Dr. H. J. Bennett.[33] An Iowa story concerned the arrest of a Dr.

Gottschall, an Ohio story that of Dr. J. W. Wright, and a Chicago story that of a Dr. Cook.[34] After an abortion in Pennsylvania, police were "looking for a physician in good standing, who is charged with the crime."[35]

The *Gazette* also was like the *Times* in viewing abortion as a device of the powerful to avoid prosecution. The *Gazette* headline on a story concerning a womanizing Cincinnati hospital superintendent was, "PATIENTS DEBAUCHED By the Superintendent and Then Furnished With Means to Produce Abortions."[36] A *Gazette* story from Columbus, Indiana, "Sensational Seduction Suit," told of how "Malinda J. Arnold, aged twenty-one, a poor friendless girl, whose father is dead, brings the suit against William Springer, a prepossessing young man, son of Edward Springer, one of the wealthiest and most influential citizens of this county." According to Malinda, William promised to marry her and she "submitted to his desires on divers occasions." When she became pregnant "he refused to make good his promise of marriage, and he procured an abortion on her."[37] Such stories of betrayal and abortion were a recurring *Gazette* motif.[38]

The single longest *Gazette* story concerning abortion came after the same horror story covered by the New York *Times*, the mass murders by Dr. Isaac Hathaway of Philadelphia. *Gazette* editors, like their counterparts on the *Times*, had a sensational headline: "THE DEMON DOCTOR. Blood Curdling Discoveries in a Philadelphia Physician's Cellar. The Remains of Twenty-one Murdered Infants Unearthed by the Police, and More Horrors Promised."[39] The story described the findings in the cellar: "The men had hardly dug down six inches when they struck the skull of a babe . . . 23 infant craniums and a lot of thread-like bones were turned up by the spade." The *Gazette*, like the *Times*, reported neighbors' gossip:

> It is said that the doctor kept a pair of fierce and ferocious hounds in the cellar . . . and that these beasts subsisted wholly from the infant remains thrown to them by the doctor. After the bones had been licked clean by the dogs they were covered up with a little dirt.[40]

The *Gazette* gave vivid coverage to abortion throughout the early 1880s,[41] and expressed bitterness when abortionists were treated leniently: When a convicted abortionist released after 5 years in prison was arrested 3 months later for another abortion, the *Gazette* complained that "Judicial clemency will doubtless make things easy for her again. Judicial honesty, however, ought to hang her."[42] Until the mid-1880s, the *Gazette* showed regular concern for both unborn child and mother.

So did some other newspapers of the 1880s. For example, the Springfield *Republican*, in an editorial entitled "Child Murder in Massachusetts," attacked "child-murdering" by "respectable physicians."[43] The *Republican*, which had dropped its abortion ads, saw a continuity in life from conception through birth and beyond, and criticized "the disposal made of infant life, both before and after birth."[44] It even noted that "the prevention of birth (we refer to the destruction of incipient human life by any of the various means of abortion, medical or surgical) has extended widely among married people." A *Republican* editorial ended with a call for "other newspapers and especially the medical journals [to] bear an honest testimony in the matter—without fear, favor, malice, or hope of reward."[45]

Other New England newspapers covering abortion incidents included the Boston *Journal*, the Manchester (New Hampshire) *Union*, and the Boston *Globe*. Elsewhere in the country, the Washington *Post* ran a small story headlined "Funeral of the Murdered Girl," noting that Henrietta Carl was "murdered by abortionist Earll,"[46] and the Cleveland *Plain Dealer* editorialized about the problem.[47] But many newspaper news pages were silent.

ADVERTISING CONTINUES

Advertising pages of many newspapers, however, were not. Laws against abortion advertising generally were unenforced. The U.S. Congress in March, 1873, included a ban on abortion-related ads in its "Act for the Suppression of Trade in and Circulation of Obscene Literature and Articles of Immoral Use," commonly called the Comstock Act. That law had a temporary effect on newspapers such as the New York *Herald*: A typical *Herald* issue in February, 1873, included nine abortion ads, but a typical issue in April had none. Anthony Comstock's March 13, 1873 diary entry, 10 days after the law's signing, reads, "Today *Herald* has stricken out the objectionable parts of their [sic] advertisements. This is a great victory."[48] But as early as 1875 enforcement was lax enough for the *Herald* to reinsert some veiled abortion ads.

Advertising worked. The New York *Times* in 1875 quoted the dying statement of a 24-year-old woman following an abortion, when a prosecutor tried to get her to blame the abortionist; she said, "I went of my own accord from what I saw in the *Herald*."[49] The *Times* editorialized following the incident, "It is something peculiar to our later civilization to find women openly advertising their readiness to commit murder." The *Times* argued against acceptance of such ads, because "the trade of the advertisers in question is that of simple murder, either of mother or child."[50] But the *Herald* continued to advertise abortion whenever it could get away with doing so—and with anti-abortion laws generally unenforced after initial excitement wore away, it could do so often.

The New Orleans *Picayune* also was a holdout.[51] In its pages Dr. E. Berjot, a "specialist in menstruation" who claimed that "irregularities [were] always relieved," regularly offered "rooms for confinement and operation;

strictly confidential."[52] Dr. W. Bille, "a pupil of Professor Ricord, Paris," argued that patients should come to him, for "Difficulties of menstruation always relieved."[53] Dr. J.B. Perez sold "Dr. Perez Female Regulating Pills" and vouched that he personally would cure "female irregularities" if necessary.[54] Their ads, each costing 75¢ a day, continued through the late 1890s,[55] and were joined by ads for abortifacients including French Tansy Wafers[56] and a compound called "Apioline" advertised as "Recommended by the leading French Specialists for diseases of women; Superior to Tansy, Pennyroyal and injurious drugs."[57]

The San Francisco *Examiner* was a third holdout; during the 1880s and 1890s it ran an average of nine abortion ads daily, with about eight lines per ad. In 1889 Mrs. Dr. Strassmen was writing that "All Female Monthly Irregularities are restored, from whatever cause, by my genuine remedies; real process, without medicine, never fails to regulate in one day."[58] In 1890 Dr. E. Vice advertised a "process" by which "monthly periods [are] restored in one or two days without medicine."[59] Others offered an "INFALLIBLE REMEDY FOR IRREGULARITY" or the "only safe and sure cure for all female troubles."[60]

Similarly, Mrs. Dr. Gwyer in 1893 advertised "A sure, safe and speedy cure for all monthly irregularities (from whatever cause)." She promised "consultation free and confidential," and suggested a willingness to do what some other physicians (probably male) might refuse do: "All ladies that are in trouble, sick and discouraged should call on the Doctor and state their case. They will find her to be a true friend to her sex."[61] Other ads also appealed to "All ladies wanting instant relief for monthly irregularities, from whatever cause," and some directly proposed what today is called a first trimester abortion: "ARE YOU WORRIED AND NERVOUS? Are you troubled because your periods are irregular? If you have not neglected attending to them over three months you can speedily be relieved without the least danger or inconvenience . . . Dr. J. V. La MOTTE."[62]

Amidst all the abortion ads, one small one of a different character could be found: "Women who have fallen and wish to reform can find a Christian home and friends by addressing Rev. J. W. Ellsworth, 1014 Washington street."[63] But a message like that probably was overwhelmed by abortion advertisers promising their own brand of compassion: "We will see you through your business, no matter what the cause; no bad after effect."[64] Fast service was available from an abortionist who "Restores monthly periods from any cause in one day."[65] Egalitarian service was available: "ALL LADIES SHOULD CONSULT MRS. DR. LA PHAME: relief at once to those who are in trouble; have arranged my home to suit rich and poor; business strictly confidential."[66] Service in the middle of the night was available from "DR. ANTHAN, THE RELIABLE PHYSICIAN! All ladies assured quick relief of suppression any time or cause."[67]

The Chicago *Tribune* was a fourth newspaper that opened its arms to abortionists. In the *Tribune* during January, 1876, "Mrs. Landto" advertised her remedy for ladies with "Suppressed or Disturbed Menstruation,"[68] and "Dr. Stone, Confidential Physician," proclaimed his desire to treat "All female difficulties.' "[69] In July of that year Dr. Clarke pledged confidentiality: "IF IN TROUBLE you are advised to consult him . . . FEMALE DIFFICULTIES treated with safety and success. Celebrated Female Pills, $1.50; extra strong, $5 per box."[70] Dr. James, Dr. C. Bigelow, Dr. Kean, and Dr. Lyon also were there to help those "IN TROUBLE."[71]

Some of the advertisers were long-lived, others came and went. In August, 1876, Clarke, Kean, and James were still advertising, but Lyon and Bigelow were gone, replaced by two others, Dr. A. G. Olin and a Dr. Roberts, who guaranteed "permanent and speedy cures in all Private and Special Diseases."[72] Often, ads were carefully nuanced; for example, Olin perhaps felt that his ad was too vague and not pulling in enough customers, because by November he had added a sentence to his copy: "LADIES requiring delicate attention, call or write."[73]

Occasional abortion ads could be found in other newspapers as well. The *Missouri Republican* included an ad for "Dr. Smith, Ladies' Physician, treats females only. If you are in trouble consult the doctor. . . . Womb difficulties a specialty."[74] The Galveston *Daily News* included one brief ad in 1884.[75] These ads of New Orleans, San Francisco, Chicago, and other cities, it should be noted, were all for illegal services; but the anti-abortion laws, like laws against prostitution and some forms of pornography today, meant nothing without enforcement. With most newspapers silent, abortion was not on the public agenda unless some group put it there.

PHYSICIANS AGAINST ABORTION

The medical journals tried their best. For example, Dr. J. E. Kelly in the *Journal of the American Medical Association* in 1886 noted that the unborn child from conception "is human, and at all periods differs in degree and not in kind from the infant and the adult. Therefore we must regard it as a 'human being' with an inalienable right to life, and that its destruction is homicide." Kelly suggested that acceptance of abortion because of the "undeveloped condition" and "dependent and defenseless state" of the unborn child was "an argument with which equal propriety may be advanced against the rights of many adults, most children and all infants." He proposed that "Mental deficiency might be pleaded with equal justice in defence of the murder of many of our fellow creatures, as the imbecile, the insane, and even the comatose, but, far from extenuating the act, their condition only aggravates any violence which is offered to them."[76]

Kelly went on to suggest that in abortion, "The physician undertakes an operation which is necessarily destructive of one human life, and, owing to its dangerous nature, most hazardous to another, and possibly, as in case of multiple conception, the operation may result in the death of three, or even a greater number, of human beings." Kelly argued that the abortionist was using his own judgment that the unborn child should not live and then killing the victim, much after the manner of a man during the Irish rebellion of 1798 who was known for fiendish cruelty. That murderer had as his epitaph: "Here lies that brutal Hempenstall,/ Judge, jury, gallows, hangman, all," and Kelly concluded, "I cannot discern how he differed from the physician who produces abortions."[77]

Some publishers also were active, regularly issuing books with antiabortion messages. *Eve's Daughters* noted that some "ignorant women" still "are apt to believe that the child does not live until the life is felt by the mother; that all attempts to destroy and dislodge the loathed intruder prior to that time are sinless."[78] Author Marion Harland quoted a clergyman's wife who upbraided her doctor for refusing to abort her unborn child: "And you, who call yourself a humane man, sworn to do your utmost to alleviate the miseries of the human race, condemn me to months of suffering, to the perils of accouchement and subsequent loss of valuable time rather than crush a contemptible *animalcule*?"[79] She quoted another as ready to murder "her unseen, but *living* child" to promote her career.[80] Harland concluded that "Sharp and severe measures are imperatively indicated for consciences thus diseased and twisted."[81] Education was vital, and newspapers could play a major role. But would they?

Chapter 5

Driving Abortion Underground

Although authors during the 1880s and 1890s were calling for more coverage of abortion and its evils, the two leading anti-abortion newspapers were pulling back, for different reasons.

In 1884 the *National Police Gazette* was apparently doing well. It boasted that "as a national advertising medium the Police Gazette is unrivaled. It is read by fully a million readers every issue." Three of its eight pages were usually filled with ads, at an ad rate of $1 per line.[1]

But slowly, a new kind of advertising began to appear. Readers were told they could purchase a "racy" set of "Ten Beautifully Illustrated Fancy Cards," including one of a "Parlor Scene at 12 P.M."[2] Other ads appeared: "Get the Set of Twelve Pretty French Girls, highly colored and in interesting positions, 50¢,"[3] or "Naked truth and secrets of nature revealed. . . . Engravings from nature."[4] Soon there were more: Ads for photos entitled "In the Act" and "Caught at It,"[5] ads for "The Three Sisters, their naughty doings, 96 pages, 50¢," ads for "Japanese Women Before Their Bath, set colored pictures, 50¢," ads for "The Female Form Divine, 5 photos, no tights, 50¢."[6] Ads for items such as "The Magic Revealer" also showed up: "Any gentleman wishing to see or learn the mysteries of nature as revealed through a direct importation from Paris, can do so."[7]

As more ads for what we now call soft-core pornography appeared, advertising for condoms also emerged. "Gentlemen only," one ad read, "We have common sense article made of fine rubber which is invaluable."[8] Other ads screamed, "GENTS' PROTECTORS best rubber, never fail, pliable, safe and durable, affording absolute security. By mail, 25¢ each."[9] A few ads simply noted the availability of "A Very Useful Rubber Article for Gentlemen."[10]

And then, amazingly for a newspaper that had opposed abortion for 40 years, the ads for abortifacients pushed through the cracks in the sidewalks. "Ladies. Dr. Lejean's pills have been used in France for nearly fifty years with the most gratifying results," one ad proclaimed. "They do not injure the system, and they *never* fail. Price $1.00 per box."[11] Other ads claimed the efficacy of an old standby, tansy, as in "LADIES. Tansy Pills are perfectly safe, and never fail; sent sealed, with directions, for 25 cents,"[12] or "PILLS OF TANSY are Perfectly Safe and always Effectual,"[13] or "LADIES Try the old reliable and you will not regret it. Caton's Tansy Pills are perfectly safe and never fail."[14] Attempts to package the drugs in more palatable ways were played up; one ad in March, 1886, read "LADIES. If you are in trouble send for the French Medicated Lozenge; acts like a charm; is Sure, Speedy and Safe."[15]

Even as those ads proliferated, some remnants of anti-abortion coverage remained. A headline in May, 1886, told of "A SAD STORY. The Horrible Secret Revealed by the Death from Malpractice of a Popular Boston Church Singer."[16] Other coverage critical of abortion could be found as late as July, 1887.[17] But the old coverage could not last for long; no 19th century newspaper that accepted abortion ads consistently ran anti-abortion articles. The *National Police Gazette*'s coverage of abortion became steadily softer as its pornography became harder. By 1887 a column advertising photographs included phrases like: "12 pictures of beautiful women, full view, very spicy. . . . Two immense highly colored pictures, man and woman (together). . . . In the Act, all different positions. . . . Private Bed-Room Photos. . . . Don't Be Bashful. You want 'em [sic]; 5 rare photos and 14 spicy illustrations . . . 36 photos, naughty girls. . . . Get the set of four pretty French girls, highly colored and in interesting positions. . . . At It! Racy scenes showing how they do it at the ages of 7, 16, and 60."[18]

Why did the *Gazette* change? None of its executives apparently left explanations, but the appeal of money should not be overlooked. The *Gazette* of the mid-1880s was unlike its predecessors; the latter-day version seemed to leave no sin unturned in its search for advertising dollars, and even added a personal section with not-too-subtle come-hither notices such as "Lady and Gent, each possessed of fine form, would pose as model," or "Young Lady, 18, will correspond with gentlemen or sell my photograph (not in tights) at 25 cents."[19] The *Gazette*'s new advertising policy brought in tens of thousands of dollars. It would have been philosophically inconsistent and historically unprecedented for the *Gazette* not to transform its news policy when its advertising procedures changed.[20]

ATTACKING THE VULTURE

The New York *Times* did not make such a drastic change during the 1880s.

In 1890 it vividly covered the activities of an arrested abortionist, Dr. McGonegal, who "has the appearance of a vulture. . . . His sharp eyes glitter from either side of his beaked nose, and cunning and greed are written all over his face."[21] The *Times* reporter described McGonegal's accomplice, Fannie Shaw, as "wholly repulsive in appearance, vice and disease having made her a disgusting object."[22] The reporter journeyed to McGonegal's neighborhood in Harlem to learn how he was regarded by the people he said he was trying to help. The reporter concluded, "To the good people of Harlem, and especially to the poorer class, this grizzly old physician had long been an object of intense hatred. They were certain of his unholy practices, although he had escaped conviction, and when he drove through the streets in his old-fashioned, ramshackle gig, they hooted and jeered at him in derision."[23]

Times coverage of abortion continued through the early 1890s. It appeared that in New York at that time abortionists were becoming better organized and forming groups to carry out their practice; for example, the *Times* reported in 1894 the arrest of 5 physicians and 10 midwives arraigned on charges of illegal practice.[24] As during the 1880s, the *Times* reported the arrests and trials of many doctors: Van Ziles, Lee, Thompson, and Kolb were just a few of the physicians names in the headlines.[25] Doctors' offices, not back alleys, dominated the business.

Suddenly, however, the coverage fell to a trickle and then stopped: One story in 1897 listed in the New York *Times* index, one in 1898, and then none at all during any of the next 18 years.[26] Assuming that the index does reflect reality for these years,[27] the change seems sudden, but there is a probable cause. George Jones, who owned the *Times* throughout the 1870s and 1880s when it was strongly opposing abortion, died in 1891. Editors appeared to continue his policies until 1896, when Adolph Ochs assumed ownership of the *Times*. Two months after Ochs took over, the *Times* introduced a slogan that would become famous, "All the News That's Fit to Print." The *Times*, a morning newspaper, also developed this advertising slogan: "It Does Not Soil the Breakfast Cloth."

When *Times* editor Elmer Davis wrote the official history of the newspaper in 1921, he explained the sloganeering as an effort to tell the public that the *Times* would be free of "indecency" or "sensationalism," with "contaminating" material left out.[28] During the two decades after 1896 the *Times* apparently defined abortion as something not fit to mention, because it definitely did soil the breakfast cloth. In the 1870s, the *Times* argued that evil is aggressive and "the good must be aggressive, too. In the 1880s, it suggested that readers needed to be educated to the heinousness of abortion, or else natural inclinations plus the economic interests of those who profit by it would allow the act to keep creeping in. But in the 1890s the *Times* retired from the battle, and praised itself for doing so.

Others carried on. Doctors with strong anti-abortion viewpoints may have been shut out of some nervous newspapers, but some showed strong journalistic talents as they published vivid books and popular articles. For example, Dr. J. R. Black made an impact with *Ten Laws of Health*, which sounds very much part of today's abortion debate in its attack on those who try to:

> convince themselves and others that a child, while in embryo, has only a sort of vegetative life, not yet endowed with thought, and the ability to maintain an independent existence. If such a monstrous philosophy as this presents any justification for such an act, then the killing of a newly-born infant, or of an idiot, may be likewise justified. The destruction of the life of an unborn human being, for the reason that it is small, feeble, and innocently helpless, rather aggravates than palliates the crime. Every act of this kind, with its justification, is obviously akin to that savage philosophy which accounts it a matter of no moment, or rather a duty, to destroy feeble infants, or old, helpless fathers and mothers.[29]

Perhaps the most popular of doctor-journalists was J. H. Kellogg, author of several popular books during the 1880s and 1890s. In one, *The Home Hand-Book of Domestic Hygiene and Rational Medicine*, he defined the killing of a child before quickening as *abortion*; "the destruction of the child after the mother has felt its movements" he called *infanticide*. Both were parts of a "terrible crime" for which husbands as well as wives and abortionists were responsible, because "in many instances husbands are the instigators as well as the abettors of the crime, and in their hands lies the power to stay the sacrifices to this horrible modern Moloch."[30]

Kellogg was not optimistic about ending abortion because he saw men filled with "false ideas of life and its duties," and women influenced by "the enticing, alluring slavery of fashion." He knew that laws by themselves were ineffective: "Only occasionally do cases come near enough to the surface to be dimly discernible; hence the evident inefficiency of any civil legislation."[31] But Kellogg urged that "An effort should be made, at least," and he praised a minister who said in a sermon, "Why send missionaries to India when child-murder is here of daily, almost hourly, occurrence; aye, when the hand that puts money into the contribution-box to-day, yesterday or a month ago, or to-morrow, will murder her own unborn offspring?"[32] But Kellogg also noted the existence of "apologists for this horrible crime," probably including some on newspapers, who worked hard "to convince themselves and others that a child, while in embryo, has only a sort of vegetative life."[33]

IGNORING COMSTOCK

Abortion did seem to be holding its own around the country during the late 1890s and the first several years of the new century, with few newspapers tackling it on the news pages but many ads promoting it. The *Rocky Mountain News* in 1896 had ads for a pill that "restores all irregularities from whatever cause," and for a doctor who will cure "female complaints, irregularities."[34] Alongside ads promoting "fortunes in Cuba" and teeth-pulling for 50¢, the Washington *Post* in 1898 ran an apparent abortifacient ad aimed at women without children, with the implication that they should respond to the ad if they wanted to stay that way.[35] The Houston *Post* in 1902 advertised the Dr. White Medicine Company, with a Houston post office box number; the company offered "DOUBLE STRENGTH PILLS — Pennyroyal, tansy and cottonroot. $2 per box; for relieving cases of suppressed menses."[36]

In Texas other ads for abortifacients appeared, including one from Madame Guillaume, who "relieves all ladies suffering from suppressed menstruations with her French Regulating Pills."[37] The Dallas *Morning News* ad contended that those pills "never fail giving instant relief . . . no matter how obstinate, long standing and under what circumstances the case may be [sic]."[38] The ad even included a confession: Madame Guillaume advertised her services as "the treatment of irregular menstruation by a woman . . . who has been there herself."[39] The Houston *Post* ran more abortifacient ads;[40] elsewhere in the South, ads for Tansy Pills, Pennyroyal Pills, and other abortifacients appeared in the Atlanta *Constitution*.[41]

Abortion ads seemed to be spreading again in New York. The New York *Journal* in 1895 typically ran at least seven abortion ads each day. Dr. Conrad prided himself on his "scientific, skillful treatment of all female complaints and irregularities."[42] Other ads noted "skillful treatment of all female complaints and irregularities" and emphasized that all services were "confidential."[43]

In Chicago at the end of the century, nine newspapers were running abortion ads. For example, the Chicago *Times Herald* ran abortion ads that probably brought in well over $3,000 per year. A typical issue in 1899 contained 87 lines of obvious abortion advertising under the "Medical" section, at a price of 10¢ a line; ads stressed "irregularities of women," clearing up "the most complicated cases," and giving "confidential advice and correspondence," with pills sold for $2 a box.[44] The ads tried to insinuate ideas and not just announce products or services. On New Year's Day, 1900, one of the nine ads under the medical heading noted that reinstitution of menstrual flow "has brought happiness to hundreds of anxious women . . . longest cases relieved in two to five days."[45] Another ad suggested that its "monthly regulator has saved thousands of women from suicide in the last

60 years. Don't fret and worry."[46] By February, 1901, the ad price had gone up to 15¢ a line, but at least eight abortionists were still there, claiming to "relieve and cure most stubborn cases of irregularities, obstructions, suppressions."[47]

Unless someone took action, abortion seemed likely to break out of its confines and to become quasi-acceptable once again. Theological restraints were diminishing as modernism began to overwhelm staunch Biblical beliefs in many churches; immigration was creating rapid urban growth; new communications media such as telephones and movies were emerging. New versions of the theological, social, and technological change that provided fertile ground for the growing practice of Madame Restell in the 1840s appeared. At this point, however, a leading innovator arose on the anti-abortion side rather than among the abortionists.

ANTI-ABORTION PRESSURE IN CHICAGO

Dr. Rudolph Homes, a Chicago physician, decided that books and articles by individual doctors were no longer enough, and resolutions by medical societies were too easy to ignore. With newspapers not investigating abortionists, he decided that the Chicago Medical Society itself should investigate, and even hire detectives if necessary. With Holmes' urging, a Committee on Criminal Abortion was established by the Chicago Medical Society on November 23, 1904.[48] Holmes, who became chairman of the committee, pushed it to agree that the best approach lay in "influencing the daily press to discontinue criminal advertisements or inducing them to edit the most flagrant violators."[49]

Holmes and his committee members visited James Keely, managing editor of the *Tribune*. They did not ask Keely merely to remove from his newspaper abortion ads; they knew that thinly veiled ads would soon re-emerge. Instead, they demanded that Keely accept no medical ads, and Keely agreed. As Holmes reported the victory, Keely "ordered that no more medical advertisements should be accepted by his paper after July 1, 1905, whose purpose was to attract women exclusively or which had the expressed purpose of treating female irregularities or female ailments."[50]

The next step, according to Holmes, was "to influence other papers to follow the lead of the *Tribune*." The committee "visited all the daily papers of Chicago" and told editors they had to give up abortion advertising in any form or face public attack and eventual prosecution by the Medical Society. "Four other papers joined us by agreeing to refuse all advertisements of a criminal nature," Holmes reported, even though "one of the papers lost $50,000 a year by so doing." But four other editors held out: "Two papers announced they always had carefully supervised their advertising columns and for years had accepted no such notices as we described; when we sent them clippings from their papers no comment was forthcoming on their part. The representatives of the two remaining papers heaped upon us the most vituperative insults."[51]

To rope in the recalcitrant the medical society hired a detective agency. The detectives were to gain proof that advertisers under question did perform abortions, so that public pressure and sections of legislation could be brought to bear. According to Holmes, "a detective appealed to each advertiser for the purpose of having abortion produced on herself or on a friend. With two exceptions, all the parties visited either agreed to perform the necessary operation, or to sell a medicine which would correct the female irregularity." The Medical Society confronted the newspapers with that evidence and also informed postal authorities, who issued a "stop order" against mail delivery of the publications that contained abortion ads.[52]

A check of the Chicago press showed that Holmes' strategy worked. For example, a typical issue of the Chicago *Tribune* in March, 1905, contained 17 abortion ads promising to take care of "all difficult female complaints," or "all diseases and complications peculiar to women."[53] Advertisers such as Ida von Schultz were on the list of those visited by detectives and found to be performing abortions. By the end of the year, however, there were no noticeable ads for abortionists in the Chicago *Tribune*, and most other newspapers also had emptied their columns of such "medical help."

Some editors who had ridiculed Holmes and his fellow doctors held out until 1907, hoping the pressure would end. But on April 21, 1907, a directive from the U.S. Postmaster-General made the stop order on those newspapers found to have run abortion ads "permanent." This, as Holmes noted, meant "that any paper which published [abortion] notices after the order was entered would be refused the privileges of the mails." He checked the advertising columns and reported that "from April 21 all the papers in Chicago have been free from advertisements suggestive of criminal operations."[54]

Pressure also was applied in other cities, with generally similar results. But Holmes was experienced enough to know that nothing is "permanent" in the abortion wars. He told the Chicago Medical Society:

> Now that the advertisements are removed the work of the Committee in the future will be to see that they are kept out; in the course of time they undoubtedly will reappear in a new guise, for the abortionists' clearing house certainly is planning to circumvent the order.[55]

Efforts of the doctors were given additional support in 1909 when Congress toughened Comstock Act provisions by passing a law prescribing a fine of up to $5,000 and/or imprisonment for up to 5 years for anyone using the mails to give advice for producing abortion.[56]

That same year saw a change in newspaper coverage, as the press once again responded to medical groups that seemed to have the most power. The New York *Journal*[57] began paying more attention to abortion; for example, beneath a headline, "PHYSICIAN ARRESTED IN HOMICIDE CHARGE," the *Journal* in 1909 told the story of "Dr. Isidor Stein, a well-to-do physician, with a fine office."[58] It reported Coroner Harburger's dramatic account of his conversation with a woman who just had an abortion:

When I arrived at the hospital, I saw that the woman was dying. Then word was brought to me by an assistant that he had heard that the doctor who had performed the operation had arrived at the hospital to seek an interview with his patient. I gave orders that under no circumstances should he be allowed to see the woman alone. . . . Then I proceeded to take the woman's antemortem statement. She had rallied for the moment and proved to be the bravest woman in the face of death I have seen for a long time.

"Do you believe you are about to die?" I asked. "Yes I know I am going to die very soon," she answered. . . . She told me the doctor had performed three operations upon her. . . . [Then] somebody said, "There's Dr. Stein who is accused of performing this operation." I stepped over to him and said: "Dr. Stein, I want to confront you with your victim." Then I said to the woman, "Turn. Look at this man. Who is he?" "That is Dr. Stein . . . the doctor who attended me."[59]

The *Journal* reported that the woman died, and abortionist Stein was arrested. The undercurrents of the story were typical for the era: A wealthy, established abortionist (not a back-alley amateur) oppressing a victimized woman.

SENSATION IN SAN FRANCISCO

Another Hearst-owned newspaper, the San Francisco *Examiner*,[60] reported a similarly compelling situation the following year. Six of the seven columns on page 1 of the September 24, 1910, San Francisco *Examiner* — and almost all of pages 2, 3, 4, and 5 — were devoted to the story of Eva Swan, a schoolteacher who died after having an abortion and was buried in a doctor's cellar.[61] The wording was circumspect: Eva Swan wanted to be saved from the "consequences of indiscretion," and "Dr. Grant, the police have information, attempted to perform an illegal operation."[62] But the details themselves were like those of the New York *Times'* "trunk murder" in 1871: Eva Swan died and Grant "packed the body of the girl in a trunk."[63]

The *Examiner* included details of how Grant and an assistant carried the trunk at night to a house the doctor rented, tore up a section of the

wood flooring of the basement, dug a hole, and saturated the earth with
nitric acid: "Then they took the body of the girl from the trunk, wrapped
it in a blanket and flung it into the hole. They covered it with loose earth
and poured in more nitric acid. Then over the grave they had dug they
built a cement floor four inches thick."[64] The crime came to light only
when Grant's assistant, with troubled conscience, talked about the incident
to another Grant employee, Ben Gordon. Gordon went to the police after
he quarrelled with Grant over $18 Gordon said the doctor owed him: "Crime
Hidden Months Revealed by Boy as Act of Revenge," the headline concerning that aspect of the story proclaimed.[65]

Accompanying the main articles were large pictures of Eva Swan, Dr.
Grant, and other principles of the tragedy, along with a picture of men
"digging at the spot where the body was found" and a diagram of the interior of the house where the body was buried."[66] The *Examiner* also ran
a first-person story by Gordon along with headlines that showed moral outrage: "Buried Like an Animal. Brutality of Deed Shown in Way Girl's Body
Was Thrown Into Hole Dug in Cottage Cellar."[67] The *Examiner* continued to play the horror very large during the next 3 days, with stories
covering most of the first four pages of September 25, the first three pages
of September 26, and the first three pages along with page 5 on September
27. After slipping to page 13 on September 28, the story roared back to
the first two pages on both September 29 and September 30, before dying
down to page 3 on October 1 and page 39 on October 2.

Throughout that coverage, the *Examiner*'s tale was of murder most foul,
with numerous references to the "hacked and acid-eaten body" of Eva Swan,
and ill-gotten gains, with the abortionist said to have "spent money very
freely" and "owned a big automobile."[68] The *Examiner* revealed that
Grant's real name was Robert Thompson, that he was a graduate of Dart-
mouth and Baltimore Medical College, and that he appeared heartless; when
booked for murder, Thompson "squeezed a puffed cheek with pudgy hand
. . . never blinked an eyelid . . . chew[ed] gum as he heard the charge read
against him."[69]

The Eva Swan story played large outside San Francisco as well. An Associated Press (AP) account offered sensational detail, noting that "Gallons
of nitric acid had been poured upon the body, which had been crushed into
a shallow grave in the basement."[70] AP also reported the confession by
Thompson's nurse that Thompson had "packed the girl's body in a trunk,
first cutting off the legs at the ankles."[71] When the AP reported the verdict of the coroner's jury it noted that, "Thompson performed a criminal
operation upon the young woman, which resulted in her death . . . the jury
requested the authorities to take steps to stop malpractice in medicine 'so
common at present' and prevent the display of signs advertising 'this criminal practice of abortion.'"[72] AP and other wire service reports were used in

the Washington *Post* and other newspapers across the country,[73] and the New York *Herald* also covered the story.[74]

Some West Coast newspapers also sent their own reporters to cover the criminal investigations. Los Angeles was still a small city in 1910, but a special Los Angeles *Times* reporter was present at the inquest to report that Thompson had "the appearance of a vulture" and sat "practically unmoved" during the hearing, with "his cruel mouth twisted into a cynical smile."[75] Thompson's nurse testified that she saw him "saw off the young woman's legs with a common wood saw, and then jam her mutilated and blackened body into the trunk."[76] The nurse "detailed the ten days of suffering of the young patient and ended by telling of the girl's death, alone among strangers. No one was in the room when the unfortunate victim breathed her last."[77] Thompson, according to the article, was silent in the face of his barbarism, but the press was not.

The Swan murder led to the expulsion of abortion advertising from San Francisco newspapers. Even after passage of the 1909 federal law, and despite the long existence of the California law forbidding abortion advertising, a "Physicians" heading in the *Examiner* included about 10 each day from those seeking to treat unspecified women's concerns. For example, Dr. Alice Bell, "regular graduate physician," said she could cure "all women's ailments," and suggested that women "call and have a confidential talk WITHOUT COST." She ended her ad, "Don't be afraid to call on DR. ALICE BELL. THERE IS NO MALE DOCTOR CONNECTED WITH THIS OFFICE."[78] A male Dr. Dale spoke directly to the woman "worried about your condition," suggesting that she consult with a "a SPECIALIST . . . who is always SUCCESSFUL and GUARANTEES RESULTS in all female ailments. No matter how obstinate your case may be," Dale advised, "come to me in privacy, where you are sure of IMMEDIATE RELIEF."[79]

Other San Francisco doctors, such as Brink, Lewis, Day, Abbott, Gray, and Emerson, also took out ads emphasizing strict confidentiality and using some of the old code words, such as "obstinate cases" and "worried about your condition."[80] One of the longer ads through September 23, 1910, ran as follows:

Dr. J. E. and Dr. Mary Grant GRADUATE PHYSICIANS FEMALE SPECIALISTS FOR 15 YEARS GUARANTEE to cure the longest and most obstinate female cases in 24 hours by STRICTLY up to date, ANTISEPTIC, SAFE and painless METHODS without delay from home or work. TRAVELERS can be treated and return home the same day. We have never had a failure. Confinements and adoption arranged. PATIENTS unsuccessfully treated elsewhere will obtain relief at once. HONORABLE, RELIABLE, SCIENTIFIC TREATMENT GUARANTEED. Consult us freely and confidentially; it will save you time and money. 1293 Golden Gate Ave.[81]

Significantly, on September 24, with the name of Dr. J. E. Grant on the front page for a gruesome murder, the Grant ad was gone from the classifieds. Possibly, Grant's advertising contract just happened to expire on September 23; however, none of the other likely abortionist ads were removed that day. It seems more likely that an *Examiner* employee knocked out the Grant ad to try to save his or her newspaper from community hostility: the guarantees of safety in the ad were particularly hard to take.

For the next 10 days ads from Grant's colleagues remained in the *Examiner* without change, and on October 3 the categories in the classified section still proceeded in their usual order: Educational, Business Colleges, Millinery, Physicians. On October 4, however, the "Physicians" section vanished without explanation, and the listings were for Educational, Business Colleges, Millinery, and . . . Maternity Homes. The latter category included only one ad, for the San Francisco Lying-in Home. Under undoubted pressure, the *Examiner* banished Lewis and Day, Abbott and Gray, and all their ilk — and none of them were seen in the *Examiner* advertising sections again. The *Examiner* neither mentioned its own Grant ad nor its change of policy.

Overall, sensational newspapers such as the New York *Journal* and the San Francisco *Examiner* took the lead in abortion coverage early in the 20th century. "Serious" newspapers, such as the New York *Times*, were silent. But one missing aspect of the *Examiner's* massive coverage of Eva Swan's death needs to be pointed out: Never in all the pages of detail was it expressly noted that Thompson had killed both Eva Swan and her unborn child.[82] Thus, although the removal of abortion advertising and the return of abortion coverage signified that anti-abortion forces were victorious in Abortion War I, one crucial part of the story was beginning to be left out — and that omission would play a crucial role in the eventual rallying of pro-abortion forces.

PART II

SPIKING THE UNBORN CHILD, 1910–1965

A Denver physician in the *National Police Gazette*: "There is no remedy for a great social secret sin like exposure. Drag it out into the lurid light of day. Do not cover it up and hide it beneath an assumed modesty so shallow that every eye can peep through it and see the false morality beneath.

The New York *Times*: "All the News That's Fit to Print"

Chapter 6

Sounds of Silence

Despite federal regulations and physicians' campaigns, isolated ads for abortifacients could still be found in some city newspapers during the years just before World War I. For example, the Los Angeles *Times* ran a tiny ad for Chichester Pills,[1] and the Atlanta *Constitution* informed readers that 50¢ sent through the mail would still bring "Dr. Edmondson's Tansy Pennyroyal and Cotton Root Pills, a safe and reliable treatment for painful and suppressed menstruation or irregularities and similar obstructions."[2] But such ads became increasingly rare, and a few of another kind emerged: An ad in the San Francisco *Examiner* in 1911 noted that "any girl in sorrow or perplexity needing a friend or adviser is invited to write or call on Miss Tanner, Salvation Army."[3]

Except for implicitly anti-abortion notices of that sort the advertising pages were clear of any concern for the issue, and few abortion stories made the news pages either. The *New York Times* was still worrying about "soiling the breakfast table," but the reason why months of microfilm reading of sensational newspapers like the New York *Journal* and its counterparts across the country produces so little is not clear. Birth control activist Margaret Sanger wrote in her autobiography that on Saturday nights she saw lines of 50 to 100 women standing "with their shawls over their heads waiting outside the office of the five-dollar abortionist"—but journalists, both those working on newspapers and those with more independence, did not write about such lines.[4] The pathetic stories Sanger told about "Sadie Sachs" and other maternal victims of abortion went untold in the general press.

Sanger probably exaggerated to some extent; even a historian very sympathetic to her noted that Sanger "often distorted her past to serve her own ends."[5] No one really knows how many abortions were occurring during this period. Calculations based on the number of women visiting birth control clinics suffer from the self-selected nature of the population sample. Assumptions that the percentage of women seeking abortion during this period was as high as that of the mid-19th century, when abortion was advertised widely, or that of the late 20th century, are based on the dubious view that demand for abortion remains constant.[6] Yet, whether the number was in the thousands or tens of thousands, enough abortions were performed in New York City during the 1910s that the sad phenomenon should have received press exposure.

SUPERFICIAL COVERAGE

The entire first half of the 20th century is often called the "silent era" of abortion; this volume shows that the silence was frequently broken. During the decade of the 1910s, however, even where there was an occasional brief article concerning an abortion incident, newpapers dropped coverage just when it was getting interesting. In 1916, faced with a story of official corruption, the New York *Times* finally broke its two decades of abortion silence and told how Dr. Andre Stapler confessed his connection with the death of Mrs. Louise Heinrich following an "illegal operation."[7] The *Times* also complained that "former officials of the coroner's office concealed the real causes of death" after abortions, usually for bribes of $200 and up.[8] But one short story was all the *Times* ran: The next day, there was nothing. If any more abortion stories were written, the practice of *spiking* them — sticking stories onto a spike on the editor's desk for eventual disposal — apparently was standard.

Coverage in the sensational press was a bit fuller. The New York *American*[9] ran a gripping headline: "Confession Bares Trust of Illegal Physicians/ Dr. Andre L. Stapler, Convicted of Manslaughter, Tells of Widespread Malpractice/ Gives Names of Twelve Doctors in New York City and Also Man in Office of Coroner."[10] The story noted bribes of $200 to $5,000 and explained that Stapler:

> gave the names of twelve physicians who are the principal malpractitioners in New York. . . . He gave in detail the methods which are used by the members of the trust to conceal the true causes of death in cases where illegal operations were performed. He showed how false certificates of death are obtained and the Board of Health is deceived. He referred repeatedly to dealings with certain officials in the Coroner's office, who aided in concealment. He also told of instances in which the police aided in the concealment of deaths from malpractice.[11]

The next day the *American* kept at it with a headline, "Doctor Held; May Exhume Many Bodies/ William McCracken, Accused of Criminal Practice, is Arrested in Eighteenth Street Office/ Charge is First to Follow the Disclosures of Dr. A. L. Stapler, Convicted of Manslaughter."[12] The story noted that the bodies of at least 10 women who may have died following abortions would be exhumed, and quoted the city coroner's statement that "there is undoubtedly a very large illegal practice in this city." The *American* noted that "many women who patronized these illegal establishments are said to have been socially prominent," and that deaths had been covered up by falsification of death certificates.[13]

The *American*'s headline, "Doctors Offering Evidence to Stop Malpractice," indicated public and physician response to the news stories.[14] According to the *American*, interest was widespread:

> Offers of help in eliminating criminal medical practice in New York yesterday flowed into Assistant District Attorney Dooling's office from unexpected sources. Some of those who offered information that would lead to the conviction of malpractitioners were eminent physicians. Others were laymen who had been victimized.

But the *American*, instead of investigating on its own the "large illegal practice" and the falsification of death certificates, waited for the police to take the lead in examining "the charges of Stapler that the police are implicated in hiding criminal practice in New York." The police evidently did nothing to clean their own house, and the press let the matter drop.

Lack of coverage by the sensational press did not stem from an unwillingness to cover unpleasant questions involved with death, sex, and other matters. Although the New York *American* was letting the Stapler matter drop, it was running headlines such as "At Pistol Point Takes Wife of Uncle by Force," and captioning a photograph of Americans killed by Mexican bandits with the words, "Note the bloodstains."[15] The battle for birth control also received attention, with headlines such as "150 Fete Mrs. Sanger on Eve of Her Trial/ Prominent Men and Women Champion Cause of Advocate of 'Birth Control' Publicity."[16] (The New York *American* noted that Sanger partisans at her trial included male representatives of radical groups and many women in fur coats, with 20 liveried chauffeurs waiting outside the courthouse.) But abortion received little coverage.

Again, several speculative reasons for the lack of coverage are worth considering. There probably were fewer abortions than in the past, and fewer readily visible abortionists. But it also may be that the idea of abortion had become so discredited that newspapers, forgetting the New York *Times* dictum about tolerated evil becoming aggressive, saw no reason to crusade. After all, loopholes in abortion laws were being closed during this period,[17] and even Margaret Sanger was telling clients at her first birth control clinic (opened October 16, 1916) that

> abortion was the wrong way — no matter how early it was performed it was taking life; that contraception was the better way, the safer way — it took a little time, a little trouble, but was well worth while in the long run, because life had not yet begun.[18]

In any case, newspapers outside New York apparently were silent, and another New York abortion story did not appear until 1919, when police arrested Greenwich Village abortionist Dr. Frederick Van Vliet.[19] The *Times* mentioned the story very briefly; the New York *Journal*, under the headline "Doctor and 11 Women Taken in Police Raid," did much more, telling how the women who were arrested and asked to be witnesses "pleaded to be released, saying their reputations were at stake; that their husbands did not know where they were and would not understand."[20] The *Journal* indicated sympathy for the women but not for Van Vliet, who had been arrested before for malpractice and was out on bail when he was arrested again.[21]

In 1920 the New York *Times* continued its pattern of very light coverage of abortion, compared with that of the New York *Journal*. For example, each newspaper ran several stories on the trial of Dr. Julius Hammer, charged after one of his abortion operations led to death for both mother and child.[22] Each newspaper reported that the trial was halted amidst charges of bribery and then resumed. But the *Journal* reported on public interest in the abortion case: "Many prominent physicians and fashionably gowned women waited in the courtroom until the verdict was returned. Two policemen were stationed at the doors to help keep the large crowd orderly."[23] The *Journal* gave the result front-page coverage: "Dr. Hammer is convicted of Manslaughter,"[24] and tried to place the case in context: "Thousands of women every year risk death to avoid the responsibility of motherhood."[25] The *Times*, however, dropped the story onto page 9.[26]

The *Journal* also noted an argument during the Hammer trial that would later play a large role in abortion debates. Hammer's attorney contended that Hammer had exercised his professional judgment in performing the operation and should not be penalized. The prosecutor saw it differently: Hammer had made a practice of performing illegal operations, thus indicating that his professional judgment did not meet ethical expectations. Was there an impending conflict between medical ethics and claims of physician autonomy? The New York *Times* did not mention any such questions in its typically brief coverage of another abortion: "Dr. Kerr Held in $3000."[27]

Newspapers in other cities also gave very brief coverage to abortion arrests in the early 1920s. In San Francisco, a typical *Examiner* story reported without much detail that a jury had found Dr. Galen Hickok guilty of "performing an illegal operation" on the wife of a San Francisco restaurant owner.[28] In Los Angeles, the *Times* periodically reported abortion arrests, as in one story under the headline "Physicians Accused by Girl Dancer/ Missing Maid Located in Hospital After Asserted Illegal Operation."[29] But by the mid-1920s, four new elements were emerging: The influence of the Soviet example; changing sexual customs of the "roaring 20s"; the beginning of some pro-abortion sentiment within the birth control movement; and a developing split on abortion within the medical profession.

The significance of the first two elements is interesting to discuss but hard to prove. Some magazines had material about the Soviets, and some political romantics hoped to imitate in American the Soviet "liberation" of women, yet the influence of the hard left in the United States was limited during the 1920s, and by the time that influence grew in the 1930s, Soviet abortion policy had changed. Press discussion of new mores supposedly brought about by fast cars and loose living *was* widespread during the 1920s, but it is unclear how that translated into action; there is no indication of a sizeable abortion upsurge during the 1920s.

The potential influence of the birth control movement was far greater, particularly when it began to receive a more favorable press during the 1920s. Speakers at the first conference of the American Birth Control League, held in New York in 1921, distinguished between consent to contraception and advocacy of abortion. For example, Dr. John C. Vaughan, a firm advocate of birth control, argued resolutely against abortion, except when absolutely needed to save the life of the mother:

> Once fertilization has taken place, then all the possibilities of a new soul, a new individual, are opened up, and an individual life is started that should be covered by the same protective laws that cover all human beings. The same laws that protect adults protect children. It is no less a crime to kill a baby than it is to kill an adult. Why should it be any less a crime, why should it be more moral or legal to destroy a life in its intra-uterine stages than it is after these stages are over and the baby has been born? And I say again that from the time the ovum is fertilized until the infant passed out of the uterus any destructive interference with it must be considered abortion, and that abortion should never be necessary, can never be moral, and must rarely be legal.[30]

Others shared Vaughan's position. Yet, as Germain Grisez has noted concerning the birth control advocates of the era, "The official policy was against regarding abortion as a method of birth control, but the movement had a dynamism of its own."[31] Margaret Sanger in 1928 wrote of abortion as a "desperate remedy," one inferior to contraception but not necessarily wrong, because the unborn child was only an "immature fruit."[32] With an emphasis not on the lives of unborn children but on, in Margaret Sanger's words, "mothers in bondage," it was likely that advocates of liberation from pregnancy would begin to praise abortion as a useful backup.[33]

In many ways the most crucial change to develop in the 1920s was that among physicians. Ever since the American Medical Association's 1859 committee report condemning abortion, doctors had maintained a united front, at least in public. During the 1920s, however, some editorials in the *Journal of the American Medical Association* began to portend a return to the old quickening distinction dropped by that AMA committee. One editorial, for example, noted that "In a strictly scientific and physiologic sense, there is life in an embryo from the time of conception,"[34] but then suggested that doctors abide by the looser view that "it should be less of an offense to destroy an embryo in a state in which human life in its common acceptance has not yet begun than to destroy a quick child."[35]

The New York *Times*, like the AMA, began giving out some mixed signals during the 1920s; sometimes, the *Times* even seemed to be sympathizing with abortionists. For example, the *Times* portrayed one arrested abortionist, Dr. Hadley Cannon, as a family man collapsing in a police station, to the sorrow of his wife and their two children.[36] The New York *Journal*'s coverage was different: It gave more detail concerning the crime, reported that Cannon had fled his previous home in upstate New York because of a previous malpractice case, and noted that his wife divorced him there and was given custody of their children.[37] The *Journal* kept on the story after the *Times* dropped it.[38]

MOLOCH'S TEMPLE

A larger difference in coverage emerged in 1925 when New York City newspapers presented the biggest abortion story since the 1890 arrest of Harlem physician McGonegal. The New York *Times* gave sparse coverage to the arrest of Henry L. Mottard, alias Dr. H. L. Green, but the New York *Journal* played the story at the top of its front page, with pictures and text emphasizing the search of Mottard's farm on Long Island "for surgical instruments and bodies of infants."[39] As Mottard confessed to crimes, the *Journal* expressed horror and amazement: "The blandness with which Mottard uttered his remarkable professions leads the authorities to believe that . . . he has been a veritable Moloch in his destruction of infants' lives."[40]

The *Journal* also implied that abortion was a pagan ritual when it described Mottard's farm as a "temple . . . where women came in considerable numbers to sacrifice."[41] It emphasized Mottard's wealth by captioning a photograph of the interior of Mottard's house, "One of the Luxurious Rooms in Mottard's Home."[42] According to the *Journal*, the house was "lavishly furnished and has especially handsome furniture in the music room. . . . Hunting trophies adorn the walls and two skulls rest on tables at the entrance to the front door." Mottard's chicken farm had "more than 1,700 hens of varied fine breeds."[43] The *Journal* described Mottard's "fully equipped operating room," complete with "countless photographs of pretty women — some of them known on the stage — who ventured to inscribe their pictures with various terms of affection, such as to 'our dear benefactor and friend.' "[44]

The following year brought another big story, this one reminiscent of the "trunk murder" of 1871. Coverage emerged slowly, with a story at the bottom of the New York *Journal's* second page about a body cut into pieces and packed into two boxes. "The packing was done by a trained surgeon," the reporter noted, and cited police belief that the boxes were dropped accidentally while being sent to medical students for research.[45] The next day, however, a front-page headline "Clue to Slain Girl in Box," attracted attention to four photographs and a story emphasizing death following "an illegal operation."[46] The New York *Times* briefly covered the death on page 26,[47] the *Journal* went all out. It graphically described the body cut into eight pieces and put in the box, along with a "blood-soaked bundle containing a tablecloth, several towels and female apparel"; the legs of the corpse still had stockings on them.[48] The *Journal* story continued the next day with identification of the "pretty 18-year-old victim of the box tragedy" as Edith Green, whose fiance confessed that he had taken her "to Doctor Walsh's office for an operation to forestall approaching motherhood."[49] The *Journal* played up the horror in a page 1 story the following day under the headline "Vital Organs Found in a Raid on the House of Physician Accused in Girl's Murder."[50] Follow-up stories including pictures of Edith Green with the caption, "Death Ends Smile,"[51] and the arrest of a second physician, under the front-page headline "Arrest Here in Torso Murder."[52]

The coverage difference between the *Journal* and the *Times* on those three stories of 1924, 1925, and 1926 was typical of their differences in abortion coverage during this entire period: The *Journal* (and its sister newspaper, the *American*) made readers inescapably aware of the danger of maternal death through abortion, but the *Times* merely touched on the matter. Similarities in coverage also deserve comment: The newspapers noted the deaths of unborn children only rarely, and neither presented an overall examination of the abortion problem. But readers of sensational newspapers would learn a bit more about abortion in New York than readers of the *Times*.[53]

ROBERT THOMPSON RETURNS

Furthermore, sensational newspapers such as the *Journal* or *American* and their major competitor, the New York *Daily News*, sometimes practiced investigative journalism similar to that of the *Times* in 1871.[54] Such enterprise arose when Robert Thompson, the abortionist (under the name James Grant) whose activities received such enormous coverage in the San Francisco *Examiner* during 1910, pushed his way back into the news. Thompson had been convicted of murder and sentenced to 20 years in San Quentin Prison, but he received parole after 9 years and moved to Boston. Once there, he again opened an abortion business, this time under the alias "Stanton A. Hudson." In August, 1922, he was arrested on the charge of procuring an abortion, but was discharged. In December, 1922, he was sentenced to 3 months in jail for violating the state medical practice act. He was freed in February, 1923, only to be soon rearrested on the charge of advising and prescribing instruments to procure abortion.

Thompson was not convicted of that charge, but he moved to New York City. In September, 1927, Thompson — using the alias "Robert Malcolm" — was charged with attempted abortion and possession of narcotics, but the case was dismissed by a local magistrate, with Thompson then boasting that "he could beat any police case because he had the pull."[55] That was provocation enough for the New York *Daily News* and one of that tabloid's aggressive reporters, John O'Donnell. With the best investigative work since that of Augustus St. Clair and the New York *Times* in 1871, O'Donnell (with sources in the city board of health) found that 30 physicians were sending patients to Thompson "in return for generous commissions," and private hospitals were supplying narcotics and drugs for Thompson's operations.[56]

Police, pushed by public opinion and the board of health, eventually raided Thompson's office. The raid was botched, probably intentionally, with the *Daily News* charging "that policewomen had been bribed by Thompson to destroy evidence of the clinic's criminal operations and had assisted the quack doctor in spiriting away his semi-conscious women patients."[57] The policewomen actually helped the key witnesses into taxi cabs, according to the *Daily News*, which quoted Thompson's nurse as saying, "My God, some of these women are too sick to be moved," but then rushing them out anyway.[58] Lack of evidence allowed Thompson to be tried only on practicing medicine without a license, which he had lost after his California sentencing, but the *Daily News* made the most of it; O'Donnell wrote that "The ghost of little Eva Swan, whose carefully dissected body was found eighteen years ago . . . rose to face the head of Manhattan's criminal surgery ring yesterday."[59]

At the trial's opening, O'Donnell described how Thompson "laughed at the law . . . cursed and swore at newspapermen."[60] O'Donnell noted that

Thompson "often boasted he couldn't be prosecuted because 'What I know about the girl friends of some officials will burn them up.'" The *Daily News* played the story like a fictional serial, asking in italics at the end of one story, "*Has the law sprung its trap sufficiently well to hold 'Dr.' Thompson this time, or will he again laugh at it? Read newest developments . . . in* THE NEWS *tomorrow.*"[61] Such soap opera coverage was considered unprofessional, but it kept the story alive and pointed to a major reason why abortion continued in New York: Thompson's belief, apparently justified as long as his profile was low, "that his knowledge of prominent politicians' love affairs would prevent legal interference with his so-called death clinic."[62]

In January, 1929, when Thompson was given a 1-year prison term, the *Daily News* expressed joy that seemed out of keeping with the brevity of the sentence: "New York rid itself for all time of America's arch criminal surgeon yesterday."[63] O'Donnell did quote the New York Board of Health's statement that "This is the most outstanding victory over criminal surgery in New York in this generation," and noted that "Thompson and his syndicate were exposed by the *Daily News.*"[64] But in a period of evident bribery and blackmail by abortionists that was beginning to resemble the high times of Madame Restell, that "most outstanding victory" was not worth much. Within a year, Thompson was out of jail, and his temporal fate would not scare many.[65]

Others also wanted to celebrate as best they could. The *Daily News* was commended for its work by the *Journal of the American Medical Association (JAMA)*. *JAMA* commented on "the failure on the part of the forces of law and order properly to control an individual whose record has been one of major crime," but noted the "encouraging" fact "that publicity, when backed with action by officials who are persistent and incorruptible, can bring the most insolent and self-confident criminal to justice."[66]

The last abortion story to receive major sensational coverage during the 1920s arose in 1929 when Dr. Edwin Carman, a health officer at Hempstead, Long Island, for 18 years, was arraigned on charges of "performing an illegal operation."[67] Carman was known to reporters: His wife was acquitted in 1911 after a front-page trial for allegedly murdering a woman visitor to her husband's office, and Carman himself participated in a 1922 racetrack scam.[68] The New York *Journal* emphasized that Carman was a "socially prominent physician . . . from a prominent old Long Island family" who had fallen upon hard times.[69] The New York *Daily News* wrote, "He is said to have lost thousands of dollars in fake stock swindles. . . . On one occasion he established what he announced would be a model dairy farm near Freeport and purchased a herd of infected cows to supply the milk. Health authorities condemned them."[70]

Carman's abortion trial brought "sensational revelations," according to the *Daily News*, and his attorney was forced to put forward a somewhat contradictory double defense. The first part pointed to what would become a familiar abortionists' plea in later years: Carman performed illegal operations only when "necessary to save his patients," so he was actually an altruist. The second part showed the disgrace in which abortion still was held: The attorney said that 17 years before, when his wife was on trial, "Dr. Carmen remained staunchly by his wife's side, and brought all the powerful influence of his high standing in the community to bear in her favor"; that "ordeal" led to a "slow process of derangement," and the good doctor eventually became so batty that he did not quite know what he was doing.[71]

The jury bought neither part of the defense and found Carman guilty, but the judge handed him a suspended sentence, contingent on his retiring from medicine and abortion.[72]

Chapter 7

Greed and Corruption, 1930–1939

At first, press coverage of abortion in the 1930s was no different than that prevalent during the 1920s. The first big story of the new decade came in March, 1930, when Dr. Maurice Sturm went on trial for abortion amid reports of bribery. The New York *Evening World* emphasized the corruption angle with a headline, "DR. STURM PUT ON TRIAL AFTER 'FIXING' CHARGES."[1] The *World* noted that Dr. Sturm was said to have "declared to friends in New Jersey that his political pull in New York was so strong that he never would be tried."[2] The New York *American* wrote of how Sturm had sent the chief assistant to the District Attorney "a $1,000 bank note 'in appreciation of his courtesy to me.' "[3] The *American* noted that "During an investigation Assistant District Attorney William D. Ryan resigned, amidst charges of a $10,000 bribe solicited from Sturm by Ryan."[4]

Sturm already was known to editors with long memories. He was party to a highly publicized lawsuit shortly before World War I when accused of stealing a tuberculosis vaccine from its inventor, Dr. Friedrich Franz Friedman. Sturm's defense was that he was an altruist at heart: Yes, the vaccine could make him "the biggest man in America," but his goal was to prevent "a monopoly of the cure." During the trial, a court-appointed referee charged Sturm with "moral instability" and a "disposition to state anything as a fact which seems most convenient, or for his interest at the time," but the issue became moot when the "cure" turned out to be a fake.[5]

Newspapers also reported that Sturm had been arrested for both felonious assault on "a pretty English widow" and attempted grand larceny: "Mrs.

Laura Baird . . . exhibited a broken nose . . . and contended that Dr. Sturm
had tried to keep $25,000 in jewelry, stocks, certified checks and cash that
belonged to her."[6] This may have been trial by newspaper, but the implication in the popular press was clear: An abortionist was assumed to be
a person of moral turpitude with a tendency toward greed, fraudulent behavior, lying, and abuse of women.

The New York *Times* continued to downplay abortion incidents, burying on inside pages the same stories placed by the New York *Journal* on
page 1.[7] Both newspapers, however, indicated that most abortions were
performed by regular physicians—Dr. George Rothenberg, Dr. George
Haley, Dr. Mulholland, Dr. William Gibson, Dr. Gilbert Ashman, Dr. Edward Mandell, and so forth—and not back-alley butchers.[8] (Sometimes
officials helped to cover up the crimes, and sometimes the doctors were the
officials; Gibson, for example, was a county coroner.[9]) The newspapers
also suggested that abortionists proceeded out of greed, not altruism. For
example, the New York *Journal* quoted one judge's comments about abortionist Dr. Jacques Alper: "This man's eagerness for money caused him to
go into this racket. Why he was such a fool, I do not know. Doctors who
do such things have no place in the medical profession."[10]

Although New York remained the abortion capital, other newspapers
occasionally gave minor coverage to their own local activities. On the West
Coast, for example, the Los Angeles *Times* ran brief articles on abortion
arrests and convictions: "Two local physicians . . . have been arrested [and]
charged with performing an illegal operation," a typical lead began.[11]
Such stories generally emerged when a woman suffering after an abortion
operation went to a local hospital, hospital authorities notified the police,
and crime beat reporters relayed the story.[12] Major newspapers did not use
the word "abortion," however; frank usage was left to small publications
such as Margaret Sanger's *Birth Control Review*, which headlined one story. "Demand for repeal of the law against abortion was general."[13]

The article, a report of the Sexual Reform Congress held in Vienna in
1930, proclaimed that "Physicians, sociologists, poets were unanimous" in
favoring worldwide legalization. "Physicians spoke of the danger to wom-
en of abortions performed by unskilled quacks," the *Review* noted, whereas
"sociologists defended the right of parents to determine the number of their
children according to their desire."[14] The Congress, along with a panel on
abortion held that same year at the International Birth Control Conference, signalled the beginning of the first openly pro-abortion public relations stirrings in the United States since the days of Madame Restell.

ABORTION PUBLIC RELATIONS IN THE 1930S

The campaign of the 1930s involved three separate tactics. The first involved a call to Americans to emulate Soviet pro-abortion practice; at the Sexual Reform Congress, "Russia was frequently mentioned as having attained high ideals in regard to sexual rights."[15] Soviet legalization of abortion received favorable attention not only in journals of the left but even in the sedate *American Journal of Public Health*, which proclaimed that "good specialists" were performing abortions in the Soviet Union, and that "Legalized abortion is the only means for women's emancipation because there are not yet any contraceptives that prevent pregnancy with certainty."[16] But the Soviet Union turned against abortion for a time during the mid-1930s, and a Soviet recommendation became less significant in any case as purges of unborn children were replaced by purges of old Bolsheviks.

The second tactic was a frontal assault on laws restricting abortion. Dr. William J. Robinson, the leader of the straight-shooters, began the first chapter of his book, *The Law Against Abortion*, with non-negotiable demands: "I shall not beat about the bush. I shall not shilly-shally, I shall not equivocate. [I present] A DEMAND FOR THE COMPLETE AND TOTAL ABROGATION OF ANY LAW AGAINST ABORTION."[17] Robinson acknowledged the objection against repealing anti-abortion laws simply because they were difficult to enforce: "We might as well, the objector will continue, abolish the laws against burglary, arson, and murder, because the crimes are being daily committed in spite of the laws against them."[18] He then gave a response to such objections that would not become typical until the 1960s: "People who put abortion on the same level as burglary, arson and murder . . . are people of such a mental caliber that any discussion with them would be futile."[19]

Robinson influenced some people but won few friends. The third pro-abortion tactic of the 1930s — the gradualist approach — worked better. The panel on abortion at the International Birth Control Conference proposed that abortion advocates hide their desire to make all abortion legal, and instead campaign for a broadening of medical indications: "One must start with the attainable, if one is to reach the unattainable."[20] The goal would be to legalize abortion to protect not just the life but the "health" of the mother, for if the latter could be extended to include "mental health," the door could be opened wide. Other pro-abortionists during the 1930s proposed "socio-economic indications for legalization" — abortions for the poor — as a way to get out of the Depression.[21]

Even Robinson, with all his fervor for an immediate abortion great leap forward, acknowledged the usefulness of slower public relations methods[22] of gradually winning people to the pro-abortion side. "If complete abrogation is impossible at this time, then at least a very radical modification," he wrote: "I have always believed that half a loaf is better than no bread."[23] To woo the public, Robinson proposed using the argument that "The law against abortion has not done away with abortions — about two million of them are performed in the United States annually — but it has

driven them into dark places" and "has made them expensive."[24] Robinson pulled that number out of nowhere, but it sounded nicely round and
impressive.[25]

Robinson, however, was a known radical without patience for the long
haul; the effective pro-abortion spokesman of the 1930s was Dr. Frederick
J. Taussig of St. Louis. Taussig, in his book *Abortion*,[26] attacked the
"ridiculous, ofttimes incomprehensible, and harsh statutes on our books."[27]
He recommended that abortion be legal when "the mother is physically
depleted by childbearing and poverty" or "clearly irresponsible."[28] He argued that the primary concern of doctors should not be the life of the unborn child along with the life of the mother; instead, Taussig suggested a
"freedom from religious bias" that would lead to "consideration for the
health of the mother," including mental health, and concern for the welfare of the family as a whole.

Socioeconomic and mental health rationales for abortion were radical
steps that, when taken, could open wide the doors of abortion businesses.
Taussig embedded such proposals, however, in a suggestion that the number of abortions, legal or not, would always be high, and that the only way
to reduce the number of non-doctors performing illegal abortions was to
allow more legal ones. Furthermore, Taussig argued that when the poor
did not have as much access to abortion as the rich, society was at fault;
the poor should receive abortion subsidies, or at least have obstacles to their
use of "good" abortionists removed.

To buttress those positions, Taussig emphasized his medical profession-
alism and provided a mass of statistics. Basing his calculations on the records
of a New York City birth control clinic, Taussig decided that one abortion
took place for every 2.5 confinements in urban areas; he did not note that
visits to still-controversial birth control clinics were hardly typical jaunts.[29]
He also postulated a rural total of one abortion for every five confinements
throughout the United States; his evidence for that were estimates by some
physicians in "the rural districts of Iowa."[30] Dubious techniques yielded totals of 403,200 abortions in urban areas and 278,400 in rural areas, for a
nationwide annual total of 681,600.[31] Taussig put on a show of even greater precision in estimating 8,179 maternal abortion deaths annually nationwide.[32]

Taussig's proposals and questionable numbers received a tremendous
boost when a full-page review in *Time* magazine pronounced his book
"authoritative" and accepted the statistics he arrived at after "careful figur-
ing."[33] *Time*, which was famous for snide attacks on individuals its editors
did not like, simply described Taussig as "a handsome man" with a "great"
family and an emphasis on "strict and meticulous clinical work."[34] Editors
also accepted Taussig's contention that the cause of maternal deaths in abortion was not the general inability of doctors to stop infections at that time,

but the "secretiveness growing out of laws which declare abortions criminal unless performed to preserve the health or life of the mother."[35] Furthermore, *Time* relayed Taussig's encouragement of abortions when there were "eugenic reasons," "suicidal tendencies," and "economic reasons in women of high fertility."[36]

PACIFIC COAST ABORTARIA

Although boosting Taussig, *Time* showed no concern for the unborn child. It also left out ethical questions in its report in 1935 of an "amazingly widespread and efficient chain of Pacific Coast abortaria," with offices in Seattle, Portland, San Francisco, Oakland, San Jose, Los Angeles, Hollywood, Long Beach, and San Diego.[37] News about the chain was unavailable because its principals had been arrested, but *Time* seemed most interested in the efficiency of the operation:

> Reginald L. Rankin, a onetime Washington lumberman, conceived the idea of a great businesslike abortaria chain .to accommodate the thousands of California, Oregon and Washington women who wished to avoid the logical result of conception . . . Mr. Rankin, who apparently thought of everything, also organized a Medical Acceptance Corporation to finance installment payments for abortions in precisely the way other finance companies finance the purchase of motor cars, automatic refrigerators, vacuum cleaners. Fees for abortion were to be $35 for a pregnancy of six weeks or less up to $300 for a seven-month affair.[38]

Time described how Rankin had hired as manager "a skilled operator, Dr. George Eliot Watts of Los Angeles, graduate of the University of Oregon Medical School . . . noted for his competency in performing abortions."[39] Rankin's main mistake, the *Time* story suggested, was that he had become greedy and allegedly bribed a state medical examiner to put pressure on other abortionists "to subjugate themselves to Rankin dominance or get out of business."[40] *Time*'s coverage differed from that of the Los Angeles *Times*, which treated the story of "abortaria" not as new business but old slime. The *Times* gave the Los Angeles trial of Rankin and others regular crime coverage, and noted that the judge gave the strongest allowable penalties — 10 to 25 years in San Quentin — to Rankin, three doctors, and the medical examiner.[41]

In 1938, on the 100th anniversary of Madame Restell's introduction of widespread abortion advertising, press sympathy for abortion in some hard cases emerged in coverage of the trial of a prominent British physician, Alec Bourne. Bourne wanted to change interpretation of Britain's abortion law so that it would allow abortion to preserve not just the life but the physical and mental health of pregnant women; he found the perfect test case when he performed an abortion on a 15-year-old girl who had become pregnant as the result of rape.

The London *Times* reported both sides of the argument, but American press coverage was all for Bourne. For example, an Associated Press report of the trial did not mention the British attorney general's insistence that, regardless of sympathy everyone felt for the girl, there was still "a fundamental difference between preserving life and preserving health."[42] Nor did the AP story explain how a death on top of a rape would strengthen the mental health of the maternal victim; instead, it played up a pro-abortion judge's comment that Bourne had performed "an act of charity," and emphasized reaction from Bourne's friends: "Cheers from the crowd, including leaders of the British medical profession and socialites, greeted the verdict."[43]

Thus, apology for abortion in some situations gained a press foothold. Some articles in smaller magazines, such as one by A. J. Rougy in the *American Mercury*, even began arguing for legalization of abortion in all cases; Rougy argued that it would take too much effort to enforce anti-abortion laws that, in any case, were the result of "religious taboos."[44] Other writers began to justify abortion by reverting to the early 19th century argument that the unborn child is not human. Louis Kelley, in a 1938 *Forum* article, asked, "If there are those who choose to destroy an unformed protoplasm jeopardizing the welfare of the already living . . . how can we then condemn them?"[45] Abortion, Kelley wrote, is the "lesser of two wrongs."[46]

Along with their advances in publishing and press coverage, abortionists and pro-abortion forces seemed to be making a comeback in practice during the mid-1930s, at least in New York City. Newspapers did not run ads, but abortionists circulated handbills; with arrest unlikely and conviction rare, abortionists were scheduling appointments in advance at their own offices, confident that police would not intervene. In 1937, however, a plea from an anguished father set off a sequence of events that for several years threatened to put abortionists back on the defensive.

NEW YORK WAR ON CORRUPTION

The father's plea, as reported in a New York *Journal-American* article in July, 1937,[47] told of one plea that even look-the-other way police found impossible to refuse. The father telephoned the Brooklyn district attorney's office and said: "My 16-year-old daughter is going to have an illegal operation this afternoon. For God's sake please stop it."[48] The father said the abortion would take place at Dr. Louis Duke's office in Brooklyn. Police raided the office, stopped the abortion, and arrested Duke.

Duke, however, was no run-of-the-abortion-mill doctor: A former president of the Brooklyn Civic Club, he had excellent political ties with the dominant Democratic Party. Newspapers on the lookout for political corruption began exploring the relationship of Duke's political connections with his ability to do abortions with such alacrity. The New York *Daily News* and the New York *Daily Mirror*[49] led the way by noting that a local judge, Mark Rudich, had freed Duke once before under suspicious circumstances.[50] The *Daily Mirror* also revealed that a previous indictment against Duke had been pigeonholed, coming to light for the first time following Saturday's raid," and that no one in the district attorney's office "could explain why Dr. Duke had not been tried on the earlier indictment."[51]

State officials, under pressure from the tabloids, began investigating undue "political influence" in Brooklyn. John H. Amen, a special assistant attorney general assigned to uncover corruption, pushed Duke and other accused abortionists hard.[52] He offered abortionists immunity if they would provide evidence concerning what the *Journal-American* called "a politico-criminal alliance."[53] Rudich quickly came under sharp attack, both on grounds of judicial temperament and financial temptation. The *Journal-American* commented on Rudich's bad jokes, noting that he had once told a man arrested for public intoxication in a cemetery, "It is a grave situation to be found intoxicated in a cemetery. In the future, stay away from spirits."[54] But the abortion bribery charges were serious, and they stuck: Rudich was removed from the bench on March 25, 1939, and disbarred on April 20.[55]

The New York *Times* became interested in the scandal when it involved Solomon Ullman, a Deputy Attorney General for New York with statewide responsibility for enforcement of anti-abortion laws. It turned out that Ullman, during his 14 years at that position, had turned into a fox guarding the chicken coop, as he allegedly agreed to protect abortionists from prosecution in return for thousands of dollars in bribes.[56] The *Times* made his arrest its lead: "Ullman is Seized on Bribery Charge in Medical Racket."[57] The *Journal-American* also reported charges that Ullman "connived in permitting Brooklyn to become an abortion center."[58] But it put the Ullman case in a wider context by emphasizing evidence that abortionists:

> had an elaborate system of protection. An investigator cited one instance of a case being thrown out for lack of evidence although a woman was found dead on the doctor's operating table by police raiders . . . Higher-ups are alleged to have directed the hands-off-the-abortionists policy and harvested their share of gold.[59]

The *Journal-American* did the most thorough job of explaining how a "socially and politically prominent" doctor such as Louis Duke could build himself a "sumptuous establishment" and perform abortions without great

concern in a "richly-furnished Bedford Avenue office"; the key was his "political influence."[60] There was nothing inevitable about the spread of abortion, because there were not that many people professionally involved in
it; the *Journal-American* reported that:

> For a number of years, a small but influential group of doctors, numbering
> about 20, controlled the Brooklyn abortion business, earning illicit fees aver-
> aging from $100 to $500 an operation. . . . Powerful political connections
> helped them escape the law when police raided their offices and arrested them
> . . . . Bank accounts of the abortion group have been examined and it has
> been discovered that large withdrawals from certain doctors' accounts were
> made at the time of their arrests. Part of these amounts were paid to officials
> as bribes.[61]

The goal would be to wipe out that small group and keep the pressure on
its potential successors; there was no need to give up.

For a while, John Amen in the government and editors in the city room
kept the heat on. When Judge George Washington Martin, a deep-in-debt
racetrack loser accused of taking abortionists' bribes, was indicted, the
Journal-American played up the story with headlines like "MARTIN $1,000
BRIBE, SAYS DR. DUKE," and "Paid Two Officials Dr. Duke Testifies."[62] So
did other New York newspapers: "Doctor Tells of a $1,000 Bribe,"[63] "DOC-
TOR TESTIFIES HE ADVANCED $1,000 TO PAY MARTIN,"[64] and "DUKE SAYS HE
PAID 10% FOR PROTECTION."[65] Stories gave details; the *Journal-American*
noted that, "While $60,000 in debt, King's County Judge George W. Mar-
tin called Assistant District Attorney Francis A. Madden to discuss the abortion charge the jurist is accused of dismissing for a $1000 bribe."[66]

Scandal coverage showed how abortionists systematically paid off prosecutors and police. Dr. Duke was said to regularly set aside 10% of his gross
income for 'protection.' "[67] The New York *World-Telegram* noted that
Duke even took deductions on his income tax returns of 1935, 1936, and
1937 for these essential business expenses.[68] The scandals also brought the
word "abortion" out into the open. The New York *Times* moved past the
"illegal operation" euphemism when it reported that Madden, the assistant
district attorney who was supposed to prosecute "abortion" cases, allegedly
had been bribed to save abortionists from prosecution.[69] The *Journal-
American* repeatedly highlighted new charges against Madden, including
one that he "demanded $20,000 to sidetrack prosecution of an alleged abor-
tionists, but finally agreed to accept $5,000."[70]

Duke's testimony gained additional credibility when another abortionist,
Dr. Henry Blank, turned state's evidence and corroborated what Duke was
saying.[71] Their admissions led directly to the conviction of William
McGuinness, an assistant District Attorney, for accepting bribes. For many
months Amen hoped that McGuinness would confess and help him nail

down the accusations against Martin and Madden, but McGuinness refused and received an 18-month prison sentence. The New York *Mirror* reported the outcome: "Six felons on the same trip to nowhere stood by sheepishly yesterday as William F. McGuinness, former Assistant District Attorney of Brooklyn, wept for his wife and child before starting for Sing Sing."[72]

New York newspapers treated Amen as a hero. The son-in-law of Grover Cleveland, and educated at Philips Exeter, Princeton, and Harvard Law School, Amen was portrayed as the upper class gentleman sacrificing the wealth he could gain through private law practice in order to fight for justice.[73] The New York *World-Telegram* editorialized,

> A public shocked by disclosures of the abortion racket as an addition to the racket list is bound to be doubly shocked by charges that a public prosecutor, until recently on the Attorney General's staff, accepted $13,000 in bribes to protect an alleged abortionists-physician and furthermore conspired to obstruct justice and the inquiry . . . Mr. Amen has made a strong start on his big job. We hope he will go on with equal energy, regardless of persons, powers or influences that seek to restrain him.[74]

For Amen, however, the sensational New York newspapers — he particularly praised the *Journal-American* — were the heroes. Just before Christmas, 1939, *Editor & Publisher* reported that Amen "publicly thanked" New York journalists for their help in providing information and leads that "proved very valuable."[75]

The press had helped to restore the abortion issue to New York public consciousness as it had not been since the *Times* coverage of the 1870s and 1880s. The question at the end of the 1930s was whether the clean-up would continue and advance, or whether the rug would be pulled over the dirt pile once more, with a few more lumps than before.

Chapter 8

Building the Abortion Rationale

The anti-abortion drive of the late 1930s in New York lost momentum in the early 1940s, for several reasons.

First, New York abortionists used all their resources to slow down the press and legal attack. Newspapers reported that a policeman was poisoned 1 week after he volunteered to testify against an abortionist.[1] Other witnesses suddenly developed amnesia. Reporters' contacts became closemouthed. When one witness refused to talk any more to investigators, the New York *Daily Mirror* noted that "what was to have been the strongest link in the chain Mr. Amen has been forging . . . apparently has been weakening."[2] Abortionists also cashed in political IOUs. The *Journal-American* reported that "Local politicians are scheming to get Special Prosecutor Amen a Supreme Court judgeship — which would take him out of the Brooklyn investigation, where he is embarrassing too many people."[3]

Second, public officials under investigation for corruption developed a routine way of fighting testimony of abortionists who turned state's evidence: The officials said the testimony should be disregarded because it came from "a murderer who killed hundreds of unborn children — the lowest type of scoundrel."[4] Officials who had collaborated with abortionists were hypocritical to use such an argument as a defense, but prosecutor Amen faced a Catch-22 long before that term became familiar: He could not get evidence about corruption unless he made a deal with abortionists, but if he offered immunity the testimony would be seen as unreliable.[5]

A third factor, of course, was the beginning of American involvement in World War II. The life-or-death abortion battle became secondary to a life-or-death war; Amen himself enlisted in 1942. Calls to spend more resources on abortion-fighting fell off as the war effort demanded time, money, and attention. Many newspapers commended Amen when he left the Attorney General's office to join the army; the *Journal-American* editorialized that Amen had "done a magnificent job of housecleaning in Brooklyn,"[6] but journalists did not note that the house was still dirty.

A fourth factor, however, may have been press response to the Amen campaign even before Pearl Harbor, but after the campaign had been in progress for 2 years. Essentially, much of the press seemed to become bored. One attorney in 1939 equated press coverage to a "Roman holiday" — but such festivals were often followed by hangovers. As H. L. Mencken had noted, many newspapers avoided discussion of issues and instead conducted "emotional wars upon errant men: they always revolve around the pursuit of some definite, concrete, fugitive malefactor, or group of malefactors . . . the impulse behind them is always far more orgiastic then reflective."[7] Sometimes, Mencken wrote, the Roman holiday atmosphere would lead to a reaction, with press and public eventually turning on the reformer, "butchering him to make a new holiday."[8]

Nothing so dramatic as a new butchery resulted this time. The short-term results of the Amen onslaught were negative for abortionists. Some, along with their bribed protectors, went to jail, and others became more concerned about arrest.[9] The operation itself began to be accurately named in newspaper headlines, with the word "abortion" included, as in "Six Are Arrested in Abortion Raid" or "Two Doctors Held in Abortion."[10] The 1938–1941 campaign showed that Taussig and Robinson were wrong to say that the only way to cut down on illegal abortion was to make abortion legal; campaign results indicated that a concerted attack on abortionists could make a difference, if prosecutors, press, and others were willing to expend the necessary resources, and unwilling to accept abortion as a legitimate activity.

And yet, events and articles during 1942 showed that the long-term effect was still very much in doubt. The New York *Times* during that year ran many short articles about the arrest of physicians, with headlines such as: "2 PHYSICIANS SENTENCED," "3 DOCTORS GUILTY IN ABORTION CASE," "BRONX PHYSICIAN INDICTED," "MANHATTAN DOCTOR HELD IN $150,000 BAIL," "2 DOCTORS INDICTED IN ABORTION DEATH," "DOCTOR INDICTED AS AN ABORTIONIST," and "DOCTOR, 56, INDICTED."[11] The *Times*, however, tended to report these stories neutrally, without disparaging abortion. Because the *Times* was not quite so objective in its treatment of alleged murderers of children already born,[12] it was clearly drawing a line between the treatment of children unborn and those readily visible.

ABORTION PUBLIC RELATIONS IN THE 1940S

Also in 1942, the National Committee on Maternal Health held a confer-

ence on abortion at the New York Academy of Medicine and proposed four
ways of handling the public relations problems that a pro-abortion position presented. First, Sophia Kleegman charged that restrictions on abortion were "formulated largely by the "theological dogma" of "one particular church."[13] Second, conference speakers argued that when abortion was
a possibility for a woman, "the ultimate decision should be hers."[14] Third,
conference speakers emphasized the desirability of national uniformity in
abortion and proposed "a model abortion law which could be accepted by
all the states of this country."[15] Fourth, Algernon Black of the Ethical Cul-
ture Society returned to the medically discredited "quickening" distinction
when he opposed the view that "abortion is the destruction of a human being," and other speakers followed along that line. Black contended that an
unborn child "has not the selfhood [sic], the relationships, or the consciousness of human personality — save potentially."[16]

The proposals are worth examining because they were the first formula-
tion at a U.S. conference of positions that would underlie pro-abortion public
relations for the following three deca⦁es. Taussig suggested a platform of
gradualism, but now specific planks were being laid: Anti-abortion laws
violate church–state separation, hurt women, and attempt to save that
which is not yet human. All these were tied to the basic position, enunciat-
ed by Dickinson and Dr. Anna Kross, that illegal abortion was unstoppable except through legalization.

Abortion public relations in 1942 not only built on Taussig's work but
found its most skillful spokesman for the three decades to come: Dr. Alan
Guttmacher, then an associate professor at John Hopkins University School
of Medicine, later the head of Planned Parenthood. The New York *Times*
gave Guttmacher favorable publicity early in 1942 when, under the headline "SUGGESTS DOCTORS RELAX 'HYPOCRISY,' " the *Times* quoted Guttmacher's view that more abortions should be performed legally in order
to "cheat the criminal abortionist."[17] Guttmacher also justified some abortions for eugenics reasons when he spoke of "heredity blemishes [sic] on family trees which make it safer not to garner the fruit, or perhaps at the
most just an apple or two."[18]

The *Times*' movement toward neutrality was not followed by other
newspapers immediately. The New York *Journal-American* continued to
portray doctors involved in abortion as rich profiteers. "A wealthy physician was charged with homicide in Felony Court yesterday for an alleged
abortion on a Bronx girl," one story began.[19] "A well-to-do physician on
the upper West Side," according to another story, was operating out of a
"luxurious five-room office."[20] The New York *World-Telegram* played up
a raid on "a luxurious doctors' suite just off Park Avenue in the 60s, where
the befurred patients arrived by limousine." According to the newspaper,

"a woman showed up at the address in her limousine with a uniformed chauffeur," and "the mink coat clientele came from as far away as West Virginia."[21]

All New York newspapers stressed the influence and political connections of abortionists; for example, the arrest for abortion of a former Westchester County supervisor and Board of Education member received wide coverage.[22] Yet, the lives of unborn children were never an explicit consideration in any of the newspaper stories — and, with those victims rendered invisible, a press tendency to adopt their mothers' perspectives began to emerge. The New York *World-Telegram* ran a story offering justification for abortion; One of its reporters interviewed "a pretty young married woman of 26" who said she decided on an abortion because " 'My husband doesn't earn much. . . . When I discovered I was pregnant, I said, 'We can't afford this.' He said, 'I know we can't.' " The story was written very sympathetically, from the woman's point of view, with no specific mention of what the "this" that was fatally unaffordable actually was.[23]

Across the country, newspaper articles on abortion still were rare, but some magazine writers were suggesting that the only way to stop illegal abortion was to legalize it. Jane Ward in the *American Mercury* opposed abortion but suggested that until abortion laws were liberalized, "criminal operations" would inevitably take their toll.[24] Vera Connolly suggested the same in *Collier's*[25] and *Time* exuded sympathy for a convicted doctor when it told how "one of the best abortionists in the United States," Alice Chairman, was jailed even though she was a "good practitioner."[26] Planned Parenthood spokesman Abraham Stone was cited as an expert in several articles when he said that the "unscrupulous abortionist," not abortion itself, was the main problem.[27]

Stone's comment pointed out another development of the 1940s that would be critical for press coverage of abortion: a growing ambivalence toward abortion among advocates of birth control. Margaret Sanger consistently campaigned for birth control by saying it would end abortion.[28] A New York *Times* story in the midst of the Amen anti-abortion probe publicized Sanger's birth control campaign and differentiated it from pro-abortionism: "Campaign Opened for Birth Control; Wide Distribution of Scientific Knowledge Urged at Dinner of Group Seeking $310,876 . . . Mrs. Sanger Says Abortion Rings Menace Women"[29] And yet, there are signs that Sanger's anti-abortionism may have been for public relations purposes; for example, in 1933 Sanger privately began instructing her clinic manager to link up clients seeking abortion with doctors who might find ways to operate on "therapeutic" grounds.[30]

Regardless of Sanger's own stance,[31] it was predictable that increasing acceptance of birth control would lead to a greater push for abortion. After all, Sanger's philosophy and rhetoric — "No woman can call herself free who does not own and control her body. No woman can call herself free until she can choose consciously whether she will or will not be a mother — clearly was, and would be, of use to the pro-abortion movement.[32] As birth control became widely accepted in the 1940s and 1950s, those who did not distinguish between birth control before conception and killing an unborn child already conceived, would move on from one social innovation to the next.[33]

The greater press acceptance of contraception and some abortions was evident in 1944 when a conference recommending increased use of both received favorable publicity.[34] Furthermore, the New York *Times* policy of neutrally reporting abortion arrests of reputable physicians deepened in 1943 and 1944: It noted without comment that Dr. Anthony Renda received $3\frac{1}{3}$ to 7 years at Sing Sing,[35] that three other doctors joined him there,[36] and that Dr. Aloysisus Mulhollard was sentenced to 6 to 12 years in 1944.[37] Other arrests, reported straightforwardly, included those of Dr. Dukoff, Dr. Morris Weiss, the father-and-son physician team of Leslie and Leslie, and Dr. Alice Chairman.[38]

"GOOD" AND "BAD" ABORTIONISTS

Increasingly, other newspapers also began to present the new perspective proposed by abortion conferees: The problem is not abortion but the "unscrupulous abortionist." The New York *Daily News*, at the height of its economic success in the late 1940s, ran one long article attacking "practitioners of medicine's black art — disreputable midwives, disgraced nurses and quack doctors" who were employees of "chain-store abortion enterprises."[39] Then, as if in contrast, the *Daily News* ran a long, sympathetic article about "an outstanding physician" who allegedly performed a few abortions on the side.[40] The story suggested that some abortionists were altruistic, and ended with the notion of "debating the question: Medals of honor or lamp posts and gallows for abortionists?"[41] The story implied that "good" abortionists should be praised, and only unscrupulous ones punished.

Newspapers in other cities also began presenting such ideas. The San Francisco *Examiner*, which had played large the abortion case of Robert Thompson in 1910, had a dramatic opportunity to examine abortion issues in 1946 during the San Francisco trial of Dr. Charles B. Caldwell, a well-established physician accused of committing an abortion that led to a maternal death. The evidence seemed ample: Two women testified that he had committed abortions on them; Caldwell's office receptionist testified that she had watched him doing four abortions; the deceased woman said on her deathbed that Caldwell had done the abortion; California prosecutors charged that Caldwell's business "has been almost entirely that of performing illegal operations."[42] The *Examiner*, however, praised Caldwell's competence and merely reported that his former receptionist was allowed "to testify in somewhat lurid detail regarding operations which she claimed to have witnessed in Dr. Caldwell's offices."[43]

Stories of abortionists began to be reported straightforwardly and succinctly; only abortionists considered unscrupulous received the antagonism once aimed at all abortionists.[44] The New York *World-Telegram* noted that one office where abortions were performed was similar to "a regular hospital."[45] The better medical conditions did not in themselves lead these publications to endorse abortion, but their reporting of "clean" abortionists tended to be neutral in tone, with scathing sarcasm reserved for freak shows such as that evident in the trial of Erminia L. Pugliesi. Her trial and sentencing to 2 to 4 came in a cellar because Mrs. Pugliesi, who weighs 412 pounds, could not reach an upstairs courtroom. (She came to the courthouse in a specially built car, remodeled to have one large door in place of two.)[46]

One of the most colorful abortionists of the era was Dr. Leopold Brandenburg, arrested on abortion charges for the third time in 1947. Brandenburg had once gained notoriety for a fingerprint-removing operation on Roscoe (Cocoa) Pitts, an Alcatraz alumnus trying to avoid connection with his past entrepreneurial activities; Brandenburg, after slicing the skin from Pitts' fingers, inserted the raw ends into "pockets" cut into the flesh of Pitts' chest. As the New York *Journal-American* reported, "It took six very uncomfortable weeks for each hand before the flesh of the fingers and chest grew together so that the hand could be cut away."[47]

The story did not have a happy ending, as a few telltale whorls remained; Pitts, arrested in Waco, Texas on a motor violation, was identified as the person who had dynamited a safe in North Carolina. When police asked Pitts for the name of a physician who would operate with such creativity, Pitts was understandably irritated enough at the failure of the operation to recommend Brandenburg. Brandenburg also was indicted when $10,000 taken from a U.S. mail truck in North Carolina showed up in his bank account, but the doctor went free because there was no evidence that he knew the money had been stolen.[48]

Clearly, there was enough here for reporters to attack Brandenburg sharply—but they did not. Instead, his medical abilities were emphasized. After two abortion arrests, the New York *Daily News* called him "a huge, jovial fellow, puttering happily among his pills and his instruments," and showing reporters around, saying "I operate here . . . I have better equipment than most hospitals."[49] After Brandenburg's third arrest, the *Daily News* emphasized that he was held without bail on the abortion charge while "still in his white surgical suit."[50] The *Journal-American* also noted that he was "still dressed in the white surgical suit he wore when arrested."[51] His doctor's status seemed to leave him immune from considerable criticism. *Time* magazine reported Brandenberg's arrest but also took it easy on him, noting that his abortion patients were getting the same drugs and precautions that they would in a hospital.[52] The New York *Times* was also neutral in its coverage.[53]

Other abortion stories of the late 1940s continued on the neutral course set after the conferences earlier in the decade; only the *Journal-American* seemed opposed to abortion generally, judging by its references to abortion "rackets" and its willingness to attack even reputable physicians when they were charged with "illegal surgery" and active in "illegal rings."[54] The *Journal-American* emphasized the material wages of sin, noting that two doctors had performed abortions in "luxurious surroundings."[55] Other newspapers also tried to estimate the wages of those arrested for abortion: The New York *Times* reported that one doctor had earned $200,000 for performing abortions,[56] the *Daily News* reported that one doctor arrested six times previously "is building a $100,000 home" on Long Island,[57] and the *World-Telegram* reported that a doctor sentenced to 2–4 years in prison "had bank books showing deposits of $70,000 between January and November."[58] (These figures should be multiplied by about 7.5 to make them comparable to 1988 dollars.)

Most of these stories were as small as abortionists' earnings were large.[59] Reporters sometimes sounded special notes, as in the death of an heiress (money could not buy either love or an absolutely safe abortion) and the subsequent suicide of an abortionist.[60] Sometimes the excellent educational backgrounds of some abortionists received attention; for example, one arrested doctor was a medical school graduate of Johns Hopkins and a former physician to Rutgers University.[61] Charges of corruption came to the surface occasionally. One man was arrested in 1948 for allegedly offering to fix an abortion case for $5,000.[62] By the late 1940s in New York, however, doctors who paid protection money could once again count on continuing their practices unhindered and unheadlined. The same newspapers that had pushed for investigations a decade earlier now let the stories drop.

Ironically, the big story of the 1940s was missed in the press entirely. The introduction of penicillin quickly reduced the number of maternal deaths due to abortion by over 90%;[63] had the story of rapid decline due to medical innovation been reported then, the myth that legalization of abortion was needed to reduce maternal death might have been cut down. But that story was ignored, and the foundation for a pro-abortion push was laid.

It was only a foundation. Little explicitly pro-abortion organizing activity was evident in the late 1940s, perhaps because the country as a whole was embarking on a strongly pro-natal decade, and perhaps also because the birth control battle was not yet over. The press movement toward abortion neutrality in the 1940s suggested, however, that when pro-abortion forces began their attack, reporters would not be in the way.

Chapter 9

Heading Toward the Moon, 1950–1959

Major stories about abortion began to emerge in newspapers across the country during the early 1950s. For example, Houston newspaper readers on a Saturday in 1950 could wake up to a headline and picture bannered across the top of page 1: "Eyewitness Describes One Midwife Operation."[1] The story was sensational because, much as in Philadelphia during 1883, bones of unborn children were dug up on the property of an accused abortionist, Mrs. Diane Banti. A man who had done yard work for Mrs. Banti:

> said women would come to the Banti house and after Mrs. Banti took them into the back room he could hear them screaming. Within about 10 or 15 minutes Mrs. Banti would bring a package out to him, he said, and he would bury it. He pointed out the place where the skeleton of a premature baby was found Thursday and said he is pretty sure he buried one of Mrs. Banti's packages there about three months ago.[2]

The *Post* included a photo of some 24 people standing on the Banti garage. According to the article, "Officers were continually chasing people off the garage in back of the house," but the "curious" kept coming back.[3] If the curious came back to the Houston *Post* the next day they were disappointed, however: There was no follow-up story, nor were there any more stories about that bizarre incident.

Other newspapers across the country began to cover in detail abortion-related maternal deaths—although, much like New York newspapers 15 years earlier, some did not use the word "abortion." For example, the Los Angeles *Times* in 1952 gave the top left quarter of its second page to a headline, "Wealthy Woman Dies in Mystery," and two accompanying pictures.[4] The lead told how "Miss Patricia Layne Steele, 32, wealthy and attractive Los Angeles woman, was found dead yesterday in a downtown areaway between garages. Police said she was the victim of an illegal operation."[5] According to her doctor, she was 4 months pregnant, and was very seclusive; according to one of her friends, "She was simply a fine person. Quiet. Always in good taste."[6]

The Los Angeles *Times*, perhaps worrying about its own taste, did not follow up on the Steele story. Other newspapers ran shorter stories and also let them drop.[7] New York newspapers continued the occasional reporting of affluence and death: One story began, "A wealthy physician was charged with homicide in Felony Court yesterday for an alleged abortion on a Bronx girl,"[8] and another told of "a well-to-do physician on the upper West Side" performing abortions in his "luxurious five-room office."[9] But even stories of corruption did not lead to any investigative reporting. A story of official city physicians charged with performing abortion received brief mention.[10] Indictment of a former detective on charges of extorting $3,600 from a Bronx doctor, under threat of arrest unless the doctor paid off, received brief mention.[11] Suspension of another detective for allegedly protecting a major abortion business also received brief mention.[12]

At first glance, then, abortion coverage in the early 1950s is puzzling: There is more of it than before, but newspapers seemed detached from it. When a hospital administrator revealed that he was not reporting abortion cases to the Brooklyn district attorney, as he was legally required to do, no one in the press seemed to care.[13] Instead of attacking abortion generally, newspapers simply tended to distinguish between the activities of "bonafide doctors" and others.[14] For example, Dr. Henry Blank, when rearrested and taken away for 2 years in Sing Sing, went with the accolade of one newspaper that he was considered "one of the best in the business."[15] In press treatment of abortionists, having "an elaborate layout of surgical instruments and drugs" seemed to cover a multitude of sins.[16]

The puzzling detachment can perhaps be explained by comparing early 1950s abortion coverage to a voyage to the moon. At a certain moment, when the spacecraft approaches lunar orbit, the gravitational pull of the more distant earth beneath and the moon ahead are equal. Metaphorically if not meteorically, the spacecraft could be seen as hanging in space for an extended second — but the direction of movement is still pressing it firmly away from earth. With earth as the anti-abortion base of decades past and lunar dust as the destination, that was what abortion coverage was for a time shortly after mid-century.

And then the lunar pull took over. Columnists ignored deaths of unborn children but commented on maternal deaths following abortion; for example, Max Lerner in the New York *Post* wrote of "between 5,000 and 6,000 deaths a year." (That was an estimate from 20 years before, pre-penicillin.)

When one woman died, Lerner wrote, "It is you and I who must share the blame for Gertrude Pinsky's death, and the five or six thousand other women who die each year." Ignoring the pails and jars and shrouds in which unborn children were placed, Lerner turned his wrath on "the cruel cloak of darkness and furtiveness" that made abortion-seeking a task not to be entered into easily.[17]

ABORTION PUBLIC RELATIONS DURING THE 1950S

With anti-abortion evidence left out of the press, pro-abortion forces took the opportunity to begin pressing their case. Alan Guttmacher was an active pro-abortion spokesman and a leading participant in many conferences and convention sessions that provided abortion with an academic cover. Guttmacher's abortion platform was the same as that developed at the "Maternal Health" conference in 1942: Abortion is liberty, abortion is a woman's right, anti-abortion laws are unfair impositions of biblical morality on others, unborn children are not really human, illegal abortion is unstoppable except by legalization. The difference in the 1950s, however, was that abortionists were successful in targeting three particular groups of leaders: physicians, liberal theologians, and lawyers.

One example of the appeal to doctors came in the work of Dr. Harold Rosen, psychiatrist at Johns Hopkins Hospital in Maryland. With Arthur Mandy, Alan Guttmacher, and other pro-abortion doctors, Rosen participated in a panel discussion of abortion at the annual meeting of the American Psychiatric Association in Atlantic City in 1952. From those discussions he edited a volume published in 1954, *Therapeutic Abortion*, which argued that religious "taboos" against abortion stood in the way of psychiatrists and other doctors improving maternal mental and physical health.[18]

Part of the appeal to liberal theologians came in a second book published in 1954, the Rev. Joseph Fletcher's *Morals and Medicine*.[19] Fletcher, a professor at the Episcopal Theological School in Cambridge and a Planned Parenthood activist,[20] justified abortion on the grounds that the unborn child lacks freedom and knowledge and is thus not truly a person. As some ministers tried to slip away from the Biblical position on abortion — some already had slipped away from other Biblical positions — Fletcher's thinking became very attractive.

Part of the appeal to lawyers came in the third of the crucial 1950s pro-abortion books, Glanville Williams' *The Sanctity of Life and the Criminal Law*.[21] The book, based on lectures given by the British law professor at the Columbia University School of Law, argued that unborn children should be protected only for "reasons relating to the well-being of [already born] human beings."[22] Williams could not find any reasons, and proceeded to argue that abortion prior to an arbitrarily determined date—perhaps viability, perhaps the beginning of brain functions—should be legalized, with no questions asked.[23]

Williams rounded up the usual arguments: Anti-abortion laws were said to be hard on physicians, unfair to the poor, deadly for women, theologically biased, and unenforceable. But Williams, noting that the public was opposed to abortion, added a Machiavellian twist to Taussig's strategy of arguing for legalization in specific situations (rape, incest, mental health, some socioeconomic concerns, etc.). Williams sagely observed that such halfway measures would be difficult to administer: If the press would label such measures "unfair" to those kept from abortion, the end result would be public weariness and eventual acceptance of across-the-board abortion. Williams' analysis implied that pro-abortionists should fight for short-run reform with the understanding that such changes would increase tension.

Books by Rosen, Fletcher, and Williams all had influence. In many ways the most crucial intellectual event of the period for the pro-abortion movement, however, was a conference in 1955 held at Columbia University's Arden House. It brought together many of the same individuals who attended the 1942 conference sponsored by the National Committee on Maternal Health—but by 1955 many of those individuals had gained power within medicine. Dr. Earl Engle, for example, was Professor of Anatomy, Obstetrical and Gynecological Service at Columbia-Presbyterian Medical Center. Dr. Frederick H. Falls was Professor of Obstetrics and Gynecology at the University of Illinois College of Medicine. Dr. Iago Galdston was executive secretary of the Medical Information Bureau of the New York Academy of Medicine. Dr. Sophia Kleegman was Clinical Professor of Obstetrics and Gynecology at New York University College of Medicine. P. K. Whelpton was director of the Scripps Foundation for Research on Population Problems at Miami University.[24]

The conference was sponsored by Planned Parenthood and chaired by Alan Guttmacher; its proceedings were edited by Mary Calderone and published as *Abortion in the United States*. The conference and book included denunciations of anti-abortion law by Dr. Theodore Lidz of Yale University and Dr. Robert Laidlaw, chief of the psychiatric division of New York's Roosevelt Hospital. Lidz argued that restriction on abortion "foments crime by bringing the underworld at times into what should be a medical problem . . . the abortion laws should be changed."[25] Laidlaw, past president of the American Association of Marriage Counselors, appealed to doctors' desire for autonomy: "If we had a law which said that under certain circumstances you might operate on a ruptured appendix and in other circumstances you might not, we would feel shackled in the exercise of our medical judgment there, just as we now feel shackled in connection with the abortion problem."[26]

In 1955, Dr. Harold Taylor, who had chaired the 1942 meeting, was Director of the Obstetrical and Gynecological Service of Columbia-Presbyterian Medical Center. He tried to get conference participants to decide whether their goal was to have abortion legal only in cases of rape, incest, fetal deformity, and major maternal health problems, or to legalize abortion entirely in order to put illegal abortionists out of business. He said that allowing abortion for "medical reasons" would help women in need but would only knock out a small part of the illegal abortion business — unless doctors hypocritically provided supposed medical justification, perhaps on grounds of "mental health," for any patient who wanted an abortion. "In which area are we working?" he asked conference participants: "If you are going to find medical reasons for aborting 750,000 women, then there is a medical reason for aborting anybody. Let's face that!"[27]

Other conference participants, however, did not want to acknowledge that clear distinction: Because "abortion on demand" would be a hard sell but abortion for reasons of rape or deformity might be more popularly acceptable, they did not want to follow Taylor's lead in separating the two issues. Dr. Sophia Kleegman, who had argued at the 1942 meeting that anti-abortionism was theological bondage, responded to Taylor's point by suggesting that the conferees had to keep public relations needs in mind; she asked whether pro-abortion spokesmen should "be equally truthful with all groups of people."[28] Galdston, a professional public relations official for the New York Academy of Medicine, also saw image as crucial: "We must not even allow for the remote impression that we are indiscriminately in favor of abortion."[29]

Lidz proposed that the conference should not present a platform of abortion on demand, but should contend

> that abortion is preferable to the birth of a child that might be injurious to the well-being of the mother and perhaps to other children in the family as well as to the specific child to be born, because the mother and the family, for emotional, physical, social, and economic reasons, are not in a position to take care of another child.

Lidz suggested that such a position would combine the opportunity for widespread abortion — "a broader base on which to make decisions" — with a satisfactory public relations position.[30] The emotional reasons alone could lead to abortion for almost 50% of women, Lidz contended: "At any given moment, about 7 per cent of a population is psychotic and about 30 to 40 per cent is seriously disturbed emotionally. This gives us a basis for estimating the number of mothers who may be unable properly to raise their children."[31]

Taylor contended that adoption of such broad indications would amount to virtually unlimited abortion, with physicians accepting "as a psychiatric indication the simple wish of a woman not to go through with a pregnancy."[32] Rosen, however, thought the radical position could be adopted, without it being labeled as such, if doctors stressed "the emotional health and well-being of a potential mother, a potential father, already existing siblings, *and* the potential child."[33] Public relations was seen as crucial; after more discussion, conferees decided that a "carefully worded statement" be issued to sociologists and social workers, and that other statements should be made to inform the general public.[34]

The eventual conference statement noted, without providing evidence, "the mounting approval of psychiatric, humanitarian, and eugenic indications for the legal termination of pregnancy," and demanded legal changes.[35] Thirty-one conference participants signed; Taylor and several others did not.[36] There was no minority report, however. When the proceedings emerged in book form, reviewers typically did not look behind the scenes or even read the book closely, but exulted over its existence: *Time* publicized the book, and Lester David in a popular magazine of the period, *Coronet*, called it "the most comprehensive and authoritative book of information ever compiled on the vital subject of abortion."[37]

The pro-abortion public relations strategy was extraordinarily successful. Throughout the late 1950s, pro-abortionists spoke publicly of broadening the list of "medical indications" for abortion. They pleaded for "compassion" toward women in cases of rape or fetal deformity. They publicized maternal deaths at the hands of "back alley butchers." They played up the number of illegal abortions and the need to put quacks out of business. They never suggested, however, that their goal was to legalize all abortion. Anti-abortion forces slept, confident in the belief that legal barricades to abortion had been imbedded so long they could not be moved — or, if they were moved slightly, it would not matter.

"SAFE" VERSUS "UNSAFE" ABORTIONS

In the mid- and late-1950s, as if they were following the public relations agenda set by conference participants, many newspapers distinguished ever more sharply between abortions conducted by regular physicians and those performed by "butcher quacks." The New York *World-Telegram* and *Sun* gave equal time to abortion pleading under a headline "How Do Doctors Justify Abortions?"[38] In 1956, the New York *Herald Tribune* attacked "illegal abortionists" involved in the Christmas eve operation on, and subsequent death of, 20-year-old fashion designer Jacqueline Smith: Her "body was cut into fifty pieces, placed in Christmas wrapping paper and dumped into various trash cans."[39] The New York *Times* ran six stories on the death and its aftermath.[40]

Another big story of back-alley butchery came the following year under a New York *Daily Mirror* headline, "Dig Up Body of Girl, 17, on Long Island." The article told how "the body of a pretty blonde, 17-year-old bank clerk, missing 10 days from her home, was dug out of a rubbish heap yesterday near the Jamaica racetrack. Police said she had died after an abortion."[41] The *Daily Mirror* and other New York newspapers explained that the girl had put together $300 to pay an abortionist that her boyfriend had found for her. He went with her, and she died. When the boyfriend demanded a refund he was given back $160 to "give the kid a decent burial" — but he dumped her body in the rubbish near the racetrack.[42]

Such stories helped to create a concern about abortion — but the stories were skewed in that the unborn child was not mentioned, and then skewed even more when "good abortionists" received favorable press treatment. A United Press story published in the New York *Herald Tribune* described one physician whose "operating room and procedure were very sterile . . . only one woman in 1,000 might have had any trouble."[43] The story noted that "the doctor and his two assistants were wearing medical masks when the raiders broke in," and that the operating room "contained an obstetrical table, standard operating room lights, anesthetics and an instrument table."[44] The Washington *Post* described that abortionist as "a practicing physician since 1924 . . . The county medical examiner said that his examination indicated the operations were performed with high surgical efficiency."[45] A United Press story from Detroit admiringly described Dr. Raymond Maurer's "clinic" with its "21 beds and the latest scientific equipment."[46]

None of the newspaper stories mentioned unborn children; the only problem seemed to be risk to the mother. Beneath the headline "Life Gamble Lost by Ex-Swim Star," the Los Angeles *Times* told how "A former woman world's champion swimmer gambled her life against the promise of a motion picture career here and lost."[47] The story explained that Virginia Watson had an "illegal operation . . . in order to accept the promise of a minor screen role with actor Johnny Weissmuller"; the story implied that had she won her gamble, all would be well.[48] A story from Philadelphia told of how a mother set up the abortion that killed her daughter: " 'When you love your child, you will do anything for that child,' grief-stricken Mrs. Gertrude Silver said today as she told of setting up the abortion that killed her beautiful heiress daughter." There was no mention of love for unborn sons or daughters.[49]

Massive numbers of abortions began to be portrayed as inevitable. An

Associated Press article reported on the trial of an Akron doctor who defended himself by saying, "This has been going on since earliest recorded history among both the savages and civilized people, and it will always go on."[50] The reporter did not indicate that abortion was not common among some civilized people, including those in America before the 1830s. In many newspapers official corruption concerning abortion also was portrayed as inevitable. In 1957, the New York *Journal-American* reported that the Brooklyn and Queens district attorneys had begun "an all-out war to stem the rising rate of abortions" and strike at "death-dealing traffickers in abortion."[51] The New York *Times* and other newspapers paid no attention to this attempt to repeat the Amen anti-abortion campaign of 1938–1942, and the crusade soon fizzled.

Newspapers began generalizing, often incorrectly, about patterns of abortion. The *Journal-American* stated that in "a typical case" abortions are performed by a woman "totally without any medical training," in a "dirty, smelly apartment," and "on the bed, as a rule, under totally non-sterile conditions."[52] This was not true; even the pro-abortion Kinsey Institute acknowledged that at least 85% of abortions were done by regular doctors under clean conditions[53] — but the press accounts gave a very different impression.[54]

Sometimes the generalizations were given a supposed statistical base. A New York *Times* article stated that Americans had 750,000 "criminal abortions" each year.[55] The New York *Journal-American* stated, "It is estimated that between 1 million and 1,300,000 abortions take place in America every year,"[56] but did not indicate the origins of that estimate. Press comments about an "epidemic" of "back-alley abortions" became typical, along with the recurrent suggestion that the only way to stop illegal abortion was to make it legal. *Time* magazine even stated that no one knew the exact number of abortions, but "the number must be astronomical."[57] All of those star-gazing numbers had mysterious origins and no statistical validity, but they certainly served the public relations need of pro-abortion forces.

Some of the exaggerated figures embarrassed even Planned Parenthood researcher Christopher Tietze, who acknowledged that the available numbers indicated a range of anywhere from 200,000 to 1.2 million illegal abortions annually, and noted that there was no scientific reason to choose any specific number in between.[58] Because legalization and legitimation of abortion since *Roe v. Wade* produced a total of about 1.5 million abortions annually, and because the 1950s was a pro-family, pre-sexual-revolution decade with abortion still illegal and culturally illegitimate, it seems unlikely that a figure 80% as great as the 1980 total would be reached in 1955; the actual figure probably was much closer to the bottom of Tietze's range. Even a pro-abortion writer such as Harold Rosen endorsed a figure of 330,000,[59] and estimates of 100,000 also were made.[60]

Facts notwithstanding, publicity for high estimates continued. Another pro-abortion conference in 1958, this time under the auspices of the Society for the Study of Sex, received media attention.[61] Toward the end of the decade pro-abortion spokesmen continued to choose their words carefully so as not to arouse too much opposition. Alan Guttmacher, for example, told the New York *Tribune* that "the termination of pregnancy was a desirable end" for pregnant women threatened with "life-long misery"; he did not define "misery" and he did not even use the word "abortion."[62] The New York *Post* ran other Guttmacher interviews, provided publicity for Planned Parenthood publications, and quoted the Planned Parenthood view that "illegal abortions are a 'disease of society.' "[63]

Pro-abortion efforts among leadership groups had an impact. The big breakthrough came in 1959 with the American Law Institute (ALI), a prestigious society of judges, lawyers, and professors that published influential "model codes" for state legislatures to write into their laws. That year a group of ALI members and guests (including Glanville Williams) published a draft of a revised statute on abortion to include in the organization's "Model Penal Code." The proposal removed abortion from "homicide" and made it an "offense against the family."

According to the ALI proposal, a doctor would be justified in performing an abortion in cases of rape, incest, or serious deformity, and also whenever the doctor "believes there is substantial risk that continuance of the pregnancy would gravely impair the physical or mental health of the mother." Williams and his colleagues were masterfully precise in the imprecision of such language. Many states already had laws allowing for abortion in many cases of that kind, but the ground for exception had to be present: the ALI proposal, however, allowed abortion whenever the physician said he *believed* the conditions to be present. That clause would make prosecution of abortionists even more difficult.[64] This was a radical change — "the thin edge of the wedge on which the movement could begin to hammer," one pro-abortion leader called it[65] — but newspapers such as the New York *Times* reported it as a small move toward sensibility.[66]

Chapter 10

From Murder to Liberation

In three ways 1962 was the year of the great leap forward for pro-abortion forces.

First, in that year pro-abortion books and broadcasts designed for the general public, rather than elite audiences of doctors, lawyers, and liberal theologians, began to emerge. A paperback semi-autobiography, *The Abortionist*, portrayed an abortionist as a kindly but victimized public servant who risked his or her freedom for the sake of many. It suggested widespread hypocrisy in its tales of "the lawyer who brought his wife for an abortion — and two days later his mistress," or "the policewoman whose lover, a high police official, offered to let the operation be performed on the steps of police headquarters — with a cordon of police for protection."[1] The message of that one book was spread to millions when an episode of the CBS television drama *The Defenders* gave an abortionist a similar halo.

Second, the summer of 1962 brought with it a story of a double abortion murder that perhaps even topped in gruesomeness the trunk murders and headless corpses of the past. Newspapers across the country reported how a woman who died during an abortion operation was cut up piece by piece, with bones and pieces of flesh stuffed down a sewage line.[2] When the line became clogged the crime was discovered, and newspapers provided gory details as in the past — but this time, the reason for the crime was said to be not abortion, but *illegal* abortion, with the implication that if abortion were legalized and abortion businesses were open for inspection, such things would not happen.

The third advance was the most significant. "PILL MAY COST WOMEN HER BABY,"[3] the headlines screamed: " 'BABY CASE' PAIR HEAD FOR SWEDEN."[4]

The story, as it played in the press, resembled an episode of "The Perils of Pauline," with a heroine tied to tracks, a train coming over the horizon, cut to heroine, cut to train, cut to heroine struggling, cut to train barreling along . . . but this was the real saga of Sherri Finkbine, a Phoenix television performer, and her unborn child.[5]

At age 29, Sherri Finkbine was the "pretty mother of four healthy children," and the wife of a high school history teacher. [6] As Miss Sherri, she starred in the Phoenix version of *Romper Room*, a nationally syndicated program for children. She seemed to have an all-American life—but she had unwittingly taken the drug thalidomide, then surfacing as a cause of birth defects in Europe and Australia. Known in England as "The Sleeping Pill of the Century," thalidomide was used by European mothers beginning in 1958 to relieve the nausea of early pregnancy. It was distributed to children as a pacifier and termed "West Germany's Baby-Sitter." Tragically, doctors soon learned that women who took thalidomide during their second month of pregnancy ran the risk of bearing children with phocomelia (flipperlike limbs) or without any limbs at all.[7]

Due to the heroic efforts of Dr. Frances Kelsey, a Food and Drug Administration pharmacologist, thalidomide was not cleared for use in the United States.[8] Thalidomide did come to America, however, through roundabout routes. During the summer of 1961 Robert Finkbine was chaperoning 50 rambunctious students on a tour of Western Europe when he felt in need of a tranquilizer and went to a British physician. The physician prescribed two bottles of Distaval, which contained thalidomide. One year later, when Sherri Finkbine was in the first trimester of her pregnancy and had trouble sleeping, she found the Distaval in a medicine cabinet and took some pills. In the succeeding weeks of her second month of pregnancy she used Distaval again, and again.

On July 16, 1962, Sherri Finkbine read a newspaper story about babies born in Europe with serious birth defects after their mothers had taken thalidomide. She called her doctor to ask about the tranquilizers with the unfamiliar name.[9] The doctor checked and found out she had been taking thalidomide. The doctor, who probably had been affected by the increase in pro-abortion thinking during the 1940s and 1950s, then dispensed some advice. As Sherri Finkbine later explained, he "showed us pictures in a British medical journal of children born to mothers who had used the drug—horrible pictures . . . the arms . . . legs . . . fingers and toes . . . He told us, these are not odds to gamble with." The Finkbines said they wanted an abortion.[10]

Here the plot thickened. Arizona law at that time allowed an abortion only when the mother's life was in danger. That would ordinarily have been no barrier for Sherri Finkbine, because committees of three doctors appointed by the Arizona Medical Society regularly stretched the law to give approval for abortion in special situations. In this case, a Finkbine abortion was approved by a three-member medical panel on July 23, just 3 days after Sherri Finkbine first approached her doctor; the grounds were psychological danger to the mother. The abortion was scheduled for July 25 or 26, and apparently would have taken place then had not Finkbine told a Phoenix newspaper about her story, in order to "alert others" to thalidomide dangers.[11]

Once the story hit the press, hospital administrators feared protest and prosecution, and refused to perform the abortion doctors already had approved. Hospital officials joined the Finkbines in demanding a declaratory judgment saying the Finkbine abortion would fit the statutory reasons for abortion and therefore would be legal, so that the hospital would be guaranteed immunity from prosecution. The judge ruled that the case was not properly before the court because no one had filed a complaint against the Finkbines or the hospital; he noted that both state and county attorneys had said in open court that if the facts of Mrs. Finkbine's plight were as presented, Arizona law would be no bar to the abortion.[12] The Maricopa County deputy district attorney insisted that if doctors found the abortion necessary, "It is not a crime."[13] Hospital officials, however, wanted a further judicial pat on the back, in advance, before proceeding.

With Sherri Finkbine cast as the Pauline amidst perils, and thalidomide as the train about to run her over, the legal and judicial system became Oil Can Harry. Although the judge was ruling *only* that the case was not properly before his court, newspaper reporters generally accepted without question the Finkbines' statement that the judge was opposed to "medical and psychiatric opinion" concerning the "recommended treatment."[14] The Washington *Post* inaccurately headlined its page 1 story, "JUDGE BALKS AT LEGAL ABORTION FOR VICTIM OF DEFORMING DRUGS."[15] The Los Angeles *Times* charged that the judge refused to "legalize" an abortion for Finkbine, a claim accurate only in that the judge felt no legalization was necessary and was not allowed to bless operations in advance.[16] A headline in the New York *Times* read, "MOTHER, REBUFFED IN ARIZ., MAY SEEK ABORTION ELSEWHERE."[17]

Later news stories in other newspapers paid no attention to the complexities of the legal case.[18] One of the public relations themes developed at pro-abortion conferences of the 1940s and 1950s — the idea of a narrow and inhumane legal system — was now on the public agenda. Sherri Finkbine made frequent public statements to that effect, with comments such as "here in the U.S. the decision is made by the courts rather than medical men."[19] Planned Parenthood's Alan Guttmacher immediately seized his opportunity and commented, "The Phoenix case shows the idiocy of the situation. They [the laws] just haven't kept up with medicine."[20]

Had journalists probed beyond such statements, other complicating information would have arisen. Pro-abortionists had pushed for abortion in cases of fetal deformity, but even if that logic was accepted it was unclear whether thalidomide did have an effect in most cases. Dr. Frances Kelsey, responsible for keeping thalidomide from American markets, noted that "statistics published in Germany, where the incidence of deformity has been highest, show that Mrs. Finkbine has a 20% chance of bearing a deformed child."[21] Other estimates varied widely. When the Finkbines decided to travel to Sweden for an abortion, the Associated Press mentioned that all seven Swedish women who had applied for an abortion because of the use of thalidomide had their requests granted, although X-rays revealed deformities in only two of the cases.[22]

Reporters could have covered the story in this way: "She has a pleasant home, adequate finances, and a supportive husband, but plans to kill her baby." Or this way: "Woman insists on abortion even though there is only a 20% chance of deformity in child she carries." A sensation-minded newspaper, in an era when large families were typical, could have proclaimed, "Four children say, 'We want one more,' but television star refuses." A more solemn newspaper could have emphasized the statistics and provided examples of babies born with phocomelia whose parents were determined to help them lead normal lives.

Those emphases did not make it out of the linotype machine in major American newspapers. The Kelsey statistic appeared only in one of the eight newspapers examined, and was not followed up.[25] All the newspapers reported the information from Sweden, but it appeared as the last paragraph in most stories, and none of the newspapers followed up on it.[24] Instead, the Los Angeles *Times* was typical in its emphasis on "pretty Sherri Finkbine," the perfect suburban housewife and mother, a "deeply tanned brunet [sic] wearing a sleeveless dress of white linen who tapped the toe of an orange spike heeled pump."[25] Soft style buried hard questions.

During July and August, 1982, hundreds of newspaper reporters, instead of investigating further, hung on the Finkbines' every word as they first considered Japan and then went through the process of securing visas and making travel arrangements to Sweden.[26] Reporters suggested that those who might criticize the Finkbines' decision were heartless. The Atlanta *Constitution* wrote that Sherri Finkbine "had to go to Sweden to find a more civilized attitude toward her plight," and that Americans "ought to have a look at their abortion laws in light of what they did to her."[27]

Reporters accepted the Finkbine contention that the "operation" would be performed for the good of the baby. The New York *Journal-American* quoted Sherri Finkbine as saying, "We weren't concerned for ourselves but we were concerned for our unborn child. We couldn't, in all conscience, bring into the world a child whose chances seem so utterly hopeless."[28] Although many people throughout the United States offered to adopt the child if born, the Finkbines were said to be continuing abortion plans for altruistic reasons; a Washington *Post* reporter told Finkbine of one such offer and noted that she burst into tears, saying, "It doesn't change our minds. It wouldn't be fair to the child."[29] The New York *Times* quoted Finkbine as saying, "I burst into a rage when a San Francisco couple offered to adopt the baby. If it were born, the last thing I would want to do would be to place the burden on someone else."[20]

As these last quotations show, even Sherri Finkbine referred to the being in her womb as a "child" or "baby." So did most journalists, at first. Headlines used the word "baby" and came up with euphemisms for abortion: The New York *Times* reported, "COUPLE MAY GO ABROAD FOR SURGERY TO PREVENT A MALFORMED BABY,"[31] and a Los Angeles *Times* headline stated that the Finkbines planned "BABY SURGERY."[32] Sometimes the constructions were ludicrous: A columnist wrote of Sherri Finkbine's desire to avoid the possibility of "mothering" a drug-deformed child,[33] and the New York *Journal-American* described an operation to "lose the baby."[34] But at least the existence of a "child" was acknowledged.[35]

With Sherri Finkbine such a sympathetic character, however, the standard terminology for reporting what she was about to do did not seem appropriate; aborting a "child" suggested murder, and the Finkbines did not seem like murderers. Consequently, the word "fetus," which had been used only when reporters focused on the medical aspects of the situation, began to replace the words "baby" and "child."[36] Journalists may have started to use the word "fetus" to seem more scientific and medically accurate, but the usage certainly alleviated the tension of juxtaposing implicitly antiabortion language with a favorable portrait of a woman about to kill her "baby." George Orwell's dictums about political language serving to defend the indefensible by softening the force of some images could be extended to this new nomenclature also.[37]

Reporters, although dehumanizing the baby by exchanging English for Latin, also lapped up descriptions of the unborn Finkbine as a non-human "living death."[38] The New York *Post* described a child "doomed to grotesque deformity," and posed the question: "What right, one might even ask, does anyone have to bring into the world a creature cursed from birth with an affliction so gruesome that it must loathe its own image and cry out against those who might have spared it this suffering?"[39] Instead of stating that the unborn child might be born without hands or arms, the *Post* had him or her faced not with "the prospect of handicap but of monstrosity."[40] Although even thalidomide babies who suffer phocomelia still have normal intelligence and life spans, thalidomide was said to have "killed the essence of some even in their mother's wombs so that they were fortunate enough to be born dead."[41]

None of the newspapers focused on the probability that the baby would not be deformed, or its prospects for a nearly normal life even if it were. Instead, the stress was on Finkbine's supposedly unselfish willingness to sacrifice her privacy to promote "more humane" abortion legislation. The Los Angeles *Times* quoted her as saying, "I hope that in a small way we have contributed toward achieving a more human attitude toward this problem . . . the main thing is to do what is right for the baby."[42] Sherri Finkbine was viewed as moral woman up against immoral law, a socially responsible adult refusing to steal candy from a baby and thus having no choice but to "interrupt" her pregnancy: "For its sake I don't feel it morally right to bring a deformed child into the world," she said. "Interrupted pregnancy seems to me to be the only kind and loving thing to do for my unborn baby."[43] None of the major newspapers analyzed or even commented on such thinking.

Clearly, the pro-abortion conferences and publications of the 1940s and 1950s were bearing journalistic fruit: Abortion was receiving front page justification across the country, and restrictions on abortion were portrayed as cruel and unusual punishments. Coverage was always from Sherri Finkbine's perspective; in Sweden, upon receiving the news that her abortion had been approved, she is said to have "dropped the telephone receiver and buried her face in her hands weeping. 'I can't tell you how relieved I am. I don't know what I would have done if it had not been granted.' "[44] Earlier, she had said what she would have done: 'If we should have an abnormal child we would love the child, and give it the best care in the world."[45] But, as the story developed, journalistic identification with Finkbine was so intense that alternatives were ignored.

Overall, Sherri Finkbine was the heroine and the legal system was villainous. Reporters ignored or did not stress facts not fitting that story structure. No major newspaper studied emphasized the fact that only two of seven babies aborted in Sweden for thalidomide were known to be deformed, or the statement of Frances Kelsey that only 20% of German thalidomide babies were deformed. Not one of them seriously examined the lives that the 20% who were deformed could still expect to have. On August 18 the Finkbines' unborn child died from abortion in Sweden, and coverage dribbled off with some final praise for Sherri Finkbine's assumedly compassionate decision.

During the last week of August a question on abortion for the first time was included in a Gallup Poll. The poll asked whether Sherri Finkbine did right or wrong "in having this abortion operation." Of those responding, 52% thought she had "done the right thing," 32% felt she had done wrong, and 16% had no opinion.[46] The poll did not indicate public support for abortion generally, only abortion in such cases of fetal deformity — but that was enough to give the word "abortion" a positive meaning in some press accounts. For example, an Associated Press story early in 1964 acknowledged that "Abortion is an ugly word to most people, conjuring up pictures of an illegal operation performed by an incompetent in a back room." The reporter went on, however, to invest in the word a new meaning: "Hope for women doomed by disease or drugs to bear deformed children."[47] That abortion could now be equated with hope was a stunning reversal.

JUSTIFYING LIMITED ABORTION

Press articles on abortion during 1963 and 1964 suggested that abortion was justifiable in many instances. Magazine coverage of infant deformities resulting from the German measles epidemic of 1963 through 1965, which left many women in the position of Sherri Finkbine, was highly favorable toward abortion in such cases.[48] Essentially, the Taylor position at the 1955 gathering—legalized abortion under extenuating circumstances—was gaining support. A survey conducted by the National Opinion Research Center in December, 1965, asked six questions of a representative sample of 1,484 adult Americans. Some 71% of those questioned thought abortion should be legal if a woman's own health was seriously endangered by the pregnancy, 56% said abortion should be legal if a woman became pregnant as a result of rape, and 55% approved of legal abortion if there was a strong chance of serious defect in the baby.[49]

The survey also showed, however, that 77% thought abortion should not be legal "if the family has a very low income and cannot afford any more children," 80% disapproved of legal abortion for a woman who "is not married and does not want to marry the man," and 83% did not want legal abortion for a woman who "is married and does not want any more children."[50] Because those situations resulted in the vast majority of illegal abortions, the American public was still expressing opposition to abortion except under special circumstances.

In short, pro-abortion forces pushing for more than "half-way measures" still had a long way to go. They would have to convince the American public that partial legalization would not work. One way of doing that was to portray the abortion problem as so huge that only extreme steps would suffice. *Time*, on Christmas Day, 1964, specified that each year "a million abortions are performed in the U.S., and 99% of them are illegal."[51] Nine months later *Time*'s guess was up to 1.5 million.[52] *Newsweek*, using the figure of 1 million, presented "the shocking fact that an 'abortion epidemic' now grips the United States."[53] Other magazine estimates went as high as 3 million.[54]

Acceptance of the numbers led to a sense of crisis and played into the pro-abortion goal of moving from legalization for "hard cases" to acceptance of abortion in all kinds of cases, in order to eliminate illegal abortion. And yet, no evidence to support such numbers existed. Christopher Tietze, who in 1955 proposed the range of 200,000 to 1.2 million abortions annually, acknowledged a decade later that the range still could not be narrowed: "No new data have become available since 1955 on which a more reliable estimate could be based."[55] That did not keep reporters from estimating at the top of the range, or even beyond it.

The number of abortion-related maternal deaths was also exaggerated by many publications. The decline of maternal deaths from over 5,000 during the 1930s to perhaps 300 (officially, 160) in 1967 was striking.[56] Yet, pro-abortion leaders of the 1960s such as Dr. Bernard Nathanson gave "5,000 to 10,000 deaths a year" as the current figure; Nathanson, after becoming opposed to abortion, acknowledged that "I knew the figures were totally false, but they were 'useful'. . . . The overriding concern was to get the laws eliminated, and anything within reason that had to be done was permissible."[57]

Such false figures were accepted by the press in a clear case of agenda setting. By 1965, the uneasy abortion armistice of the previous half-century was ending, and pro-abortion forces were obviously on their way to victory in what are called the "hard cases": fetal deformity, rape, and incest. Yet, because those cases represented a very small percentage of all American abortions, the question Dr. Harold Taylor had asked a decade before was still unanswered: Would Americans accept limited legal abortion as "compassion" for women in difficult circumstances, or would they go all the way to widespread legal abortion as a way to "put the illegal abortionist out of business"?

In 1965, when the U.S. Supreme Court in *Griswold v. Connecticut* struck down the last state prohibitions of contraception, public relations experts (such as Lawrence Lader) were now free to move on to other tasks. As the next section shows, some saw unlimited abortion as the new frontier. Abortion War II was about to begin. But in one sense, it was almost over before it started. Taussig's work in the 1930s, the pro-abortionist conferences and Guttmacher public statements of the 1940s and 1950s, and the books of Rosen, Fletcher, Williams, and others had softened up doctors, lawyers, theologians, and others among the elite. Coverage of the Finkbine incident had done the same for a wider population. Everything was ready for an abortion blitzkrieg.

PART III

ABORTION WAR TWO, 1965–

The Omaha *World-Herald's* portrayal of one women's post-abortion experience: "When I got up, I felt like a brand-new woman. I felt so happy."

Long Island *Press* portrayal: "Oh, thank you, thank you," she told the abortionist. "Within the next half hour she will have some cookies and a soft drink . . . and be on her way back home."

San Francisco *Chronicle* portrayal: She "came back from her abortion smiling and saying, 'I feel fine. . . . Let's go to lunch.' "

Chicago *Sun-Times*: "Women who elect abortion show love . . . the current movement is to regard abortion as a positive experience."

Chapter 11

The Triumph of Public Relations

The mid- and late-1960s was the ideal period for pro-abortionists to attempt to fulfill their dreams of many years. The new technology of birth control pills combined with the renewed popularity of an old philosophy, hedonism, to bring on the sexual revolution; like other revolutions, it was greeted with enthusiasm at first, and it would take a decade or two before obviously unpleasant consequences emerged. A 1962 Supreme Court decision forbidding prayer in public shools symbolized the final removal of biblical Christianity from any semblance of official authority. The Johnson administration's "War on Poverty" indicated a governmental desire to expand its power to act on inequities real or perceived, and the military draft designed to supply soldiers for an increasingly unpopular Vietnam War set off a male chorus of "Our bodies, our selves."

All of this turmoil would soon have direct consequences for Abortion War II. The radical spirit encouraged by anti-war demonstrations led to the female version of "our bodies, our selves" that became known as "women's liberation." Many journalists minimized commitment to family and glorified "self-fulfillment" in a way that did not allow much room for "unplanned" children. Concern about "over-population" coupled with growing environmentalism led to glowing stories about "population control" programs that were introduced and given heavy funding by major foundations and governmental agencies.[1]

Furthermore, from 1965 through 1969 the long press tendency to ignore the existence of the unborn child (or to describe him or her as a "fetus") reached its climax. For example, an editorial in the New York *World-Telegram* and *Sun* during March, 1965, claimed that "liberalization" of abortion laws would stop "hypocrisy, pretense and evasion. And the lethal abortionist."[2] Leaving aside the 1960s philosophy that pretense is the worst of all sins, the logic was clear: Because any abortion is lethal, but because allowing more abortions will stop the lethal abortionist, the unborn child did not really exist.

Madame Restell had accurately perceived the environment of the 1830s and 1840s and found imaginative ways to promote her pro-abortion agenda within it. Dr. Holmes did the same early in the 20th century for his anti-abortion agenda in Chicago. In the mid- and late-1960s, four social entrepreneurs joined sympathetic journalists in going further in a short period of time than even pro-abortion partisans at the conferences of the 1940s and 1950s thought was possible.

ABORTION PUBLIC RELATIONS
IN THE 1960S

Lawrence Lader, a free-lance journalist and publicist, was a friend and biographer of Margaret Sanger. His book *Abortion*, published in 1966, was a smooth, popularized synthesis of the concepts developed in the conferences and publications of the 1940s and 1950s.[3] With statistics comparing the frequency of abortion for affluent patients who could pay doctors to provide legal reasons for abortion, compared with the relative infrequency of legal abortion among poorer "ward patients," Lader played heavily on the theme of "inequality" that Williams predicted would arise as abortion restrictions decreased.[4] Lader also succeeded in giving abortion a millenialist focus by calling it "The Final Freedom": If only each woman has the right to abort, the final victory of the birth control movement and female autonomy will be assured.[5]

Along with providing the synthesis, Lader also developed the tactics that would enable pro-abortionists to overwhelm their opposition during the late 1960s. "The best chance to build a movement," Lader argued, "was through public relations,"[6] and specifically through appealing to religious prejudice by making the abortion fight a battle against Catholic leaders. The selection of anti-Catholicism as theme was due partly to Lader's own prejudice and partly to careful calculation; he told colleagues that "every revolution has to have its villain . . . it really doesn't matter whether it's a king, a dictator, or a tsar, but it has to be *someone*, a person, to rebel against. It's easier for the people we want to persuade to perceive it this way."[7] As to the choice of which particular villain for the abortion revolution:

> A single person isn't quite what we want, since that might excite sympathy for him. Rather, a small group of shadowy, powerful people . . . the Cathol-

ic hierarchy. That's a small enough group to come down on, and anonymous enough so that no names ever have to be mentioned, but everybody will have a fairly good idea whom we are talking about.[8]

Lader saw news media as crucial for presenting his attacks on the Catholic leadership; he decided to escalate his campaign for repeal of all anti-abortion laws only after he found reporters sympathetic and developed the "reasonable assurance that repeal could stir some excitement in the press."[9] When Lader founded the National Association for the Repeal of Abortion Laws (NARAL)[10] and saw the support he was receiving from journalists, he "was sure we could ignite the country."[11] The press, he found, was on his side and eager to cover NARAL demonstrations: "The press turned out strongly in every city (three TV cameras in New York alone)," he wrote, "and NARAL had suddenly become a national force." [12] Lader was accurate in reporting that NARAL was not a major force until news media made it one.

The seond public relations strategist, Howard Moody, was a liberal Protestant clergyman who followed Joseph Fletcher's style of situation ethics. Just as Lader worked hard to have Catholic leaders become the bad guys for the press, so Moody worked hard to have "good" abortionists and their allies portrayed favorably.

When Moody and his allies formed a "Clergy Consultation Service" designed to refer women for illegal abortions, he puzzled over "how to announce what the clergy were about to do, publicly and officially."[13] He knew most reporters were with him, but "the media, even if sympathetic, could, by incorrectly stating our purpose or using the wrong language, state our case in an unhelpful way."[14] Besides, if Moody held a press conference, it was possible that an anti-abortion reporter might show up: "One determined, antagonistic reporter can make any group look very bad if he wants to . . . we were unwilling to be questioned by one who was anti-abortion."[15]

Moody decided to give the sympathetic "religion editor" of the New York Times a scoop. His strategy worked perfectly: The Times article, in Moody's words, was "a superb media interpretation of our aims and goals. . . . It made our actions acceptable to many people who otherwise might have thought this to be the work of wild-eyed radicals breaking the law."[16] Moody went on from there to kill a New York Post article that would have appeared several weeks later without the right slant:

We asked a friend to intercede with the publisher of the Post. The inner counsels of that newspaper finally decided that the story would be detrimental to what the clergy were trying to do and so it was killed. We were very grateful to the New York Post and hoped that it viewed the situation as the working of a responsible newspaper rather than the suppression of freedom of the press.[17]

The third masterful public relations leader of the pro-abortion movement was Dr. Robert Hall, a professor of obstetrics at Columbia-Presbyterian Medical Center in New York, and president of a group he helped to found in 1964, the Association for the Study of Abortion. Lader in 1966 praised the multi-orbed public relations outreach of Hall and his associates:

> The Association uses the influence of its many medical experts to educate the public toward reform with speakers appearing regularly at civic meetings and on radio and television. It concentrates particularly on professions related to the abortion problem. Its committees on religion and social work already include hundreds of clergymen, sociologists, and social-welfare aides. Its medical committee carries its reform program to hospitals.[18]

Officially, the Association was a non-ideological organization solely interested in impartial study. In practice, the Association published and republished only materials favorable to abortion; supplied pressure groups, legislative committees, and journalists with pro-abortion speakers and interview subjects; and assisted a variety of groups working directly for abortion law change and eventual abolition. Hall himself made it onto "call lists" of reporters at major newspapers so that when a new front in the abortion war opened up, Hall would be called for expert analysis of the issue.

Hall, in a *Playboy* article entitled "The Abortion Revolution," displayed what he told reporters during such interviews. He stated emphatically that what prompted 19th century anti-abortionism was "medical hazard, not moral compunction."[19] (Leaders of the American Medical Association, editors of the New York *Times* and the *National Police Gazette*, and various judges, prosecutors and authors quoted in part one of this book would have been surprised to hear that.) He said that the abortion controversy developed out of "theological metaphysics" rather than medical science.[20] (Nineteenth century anti-abortionists who emphasized medical advances showing the humanity of the unborn child would have been surprised to see themselves regarded as anti-scientific.) Hall declared that women were faced with the choice of either childbirth or back-alley abortion.[21] (*That* would surprise even Mary Calderone, president of Planned Parenthood, who said in 1960 that "90% of all illegal abortions are presently done by physicians."[22])

Nevertheless, Hall's inaccurate statements, along with Lader's attacks on Catholic leaders and Moody's heroic poses, were disseminated widely.[23] A pro-abortion stance in the mid-1960s was eminently respectable, and becoming almost obligatory, in "establishment" publishing, legal, and philanthropic circles; officials of the Association for the Study of Abortion included Cass Canfield, chairman of the executive committee of Harper and Row, and noted lawyers Theodore Kheel and Harriet Pilpel.[24] John D. Rockefeller III, keynote speaker at an Association conference in 1968, urged repeal of all abortion laws and backed up words with his dollars and organizational influence.[25]

Lader, Moody, and Hall handed the press smooth statements apparently based on ample evidence, but pro-abortion shock troops also had an influence. Reporters wanting a walk on the wild side interviewed Pat Maginnis, founder and head of the San Francisco-based Society for Humane Abortion; Maginnis, who appeared on radio or television talk shows and interview programs across the country, talked about how she had twice administered abortions to herself by digitally irritating her own uterus to bring on contractions and eventual miscarriage.[26] Maginnis, in Lader's words, never "built a broad base of support among California women,"[27] but she did receive respectful coverage from the Washington *Post*[28] — and she made Lader seem moderate in comparison.

Also influential, although abortion was only one of her concerns, was Betty Friedan, originator in 1966 and president of the National Organization for Women (NOW). She and a group of younger women pushed for a pro-abortion plank at the NOW convention in 1967 and won, with some original NOW delegates who were anti-abortion (like 19th century feminists) resigning in protest. Friedan became a media celebrity and was criticized for that by some of her colleagues, but in Lader's words, "she simply gave what the broadcasting and press media demand — the focus on an individual, like Ralph Nader in consumer protection, who can project the aims of a whole movement."[29]

Friedan and Maginnis represented somewhat different elements in the feminist constituency, as did Lader, Moody, and Hall among the journalistic, theological, and medical professionals, but "moderate" pro-abortionists combined with "radicals" to make much discussion of abortion seem like a question of whether to repeal *some* restrictions on abortion or *all*; as the nursery rhyme goes, "Jack Sprat could eat no fat, his wife could eat no lean; between the two of them, they licked the platter clean." Pro-abortionism in the era of "radical chic," to use Tom Wolfe's expression,[30] could be both "radical" and "establishment"; as such, it was ideal fodder for newspapers that catered to power but wanted to appear as tribunes of the people.

Given societal conditions, effective pro-abortion public relations, and the absence of much organized opposition (except for the limited involvement of the Catholic Church, which in itself played into the hands of Lader's partisans), the press swing is not surprising. So many newspapers became carriers of the pro-abortion mail that one chapter cannot give all the details, but description of stories in key newspapers from New York, Chicago, and San Diego will show the trend.

The New York Times' Pro-Abortionism

In describing the position of the New York *Times* during the late 1960s we have the advantage of a doctoral dissertation written with a quantitative bent. Nguyenphuc Buutap found that 90% of New York *Times* articles and editorials from 1965 through 1972 that expressed a position on abortion clearly favored it.[31] He noted that the 10% of *Times* articles in his study that were not pro-abortion expressed not anti-abortion views but a bit of ambivalence.[32]

Going beyond Buutap's useful work, a qualitative examination of *Times* editorials and news articles during the 1965–1969 period shows how the newspaper became a pro-abortion leader. In February, 1965, an editorial entitled "A New Abortion Law" proposed that abortion be legal whenever a doctor said that "continuance of the pregnancy would gravely impair the physical or mental health of the mother."[33] Mental health was the magic door opener desired at the abortion conferences of the 1940s and 1950s, because the analysis of grave impairment could be deeply subjective. In April, 1965, a *Times* editorial entitled "The Cruel Abortion Law" ignored studies showing the predominance of abortion by skilled physicians and argued that New York's "overly restrictive" law sentenced women "to a barbaric, primitive underworld of crude clandestine surgery, where their lives are in danger."[34] The *Times*, developing a new euphemism, claimed that "civilized compassion demands a liberalization of abortion law."[35]

Soon after publication of that editorial, the *Times* turned over several pages of its Sunday magazine to Lader, who argued that legalization of abortion on demand would be a sign of American social maturity.[36] The drumbeat continued into December, 1965, with an editorial entitled "A Sensible Abortion Law."[37] In 1966 and early 1967 six editorials called New York anti-abortion law "cruel and unrealistic," full of "harsh rigidities,"[38] "savage,"[39] and "oppressive."[40] With enormous exaggeration the *Times* contended that anti-abortion laws led to "2,000 abortion deaths every year in New York alone,"[41] and caused "the needless death of four thousand mothers each year."[42]

News pages of the *Times* did their part by giving great attention to pro-abortion demonstrations even when they fizzled before the public. In 1967, for example, the *Times* ran an article and picture about a New York pro-abortion demonstration that, as even the reporter acknowledged, "attracted little attention."[43] Nevertheless, the *Times* gave it attention, and quoted at length from Dr. Nathan H. Rappaport, a 66-year-old abortionist who spoke at the rally and admitted to having performed 25,000 abortions and spending 9 years in prison because of one of them. "I violated the law," Rappaport was quoted as saying, "as a matter of civil disobedience. I practiced medicine for the benefit of my patients."[44] Thus, an abortionist shared in the halo of Thoreau, Gandhi, and others.

An exceptionally large abortion-legitimating story — half of a full page — appeared in the *Times* early in 1968 under the headline, "Abortion: Once a Whispered Problem, Now a Public Debate."[45] The article abundantly quoted Lader and other pro-abortion publicists but included not a single word from opponents of abortion; the "public debate" apparently was between those favoring the American Law Institute's model abortion law, which "would barely touch the huge iceberg of criminal abortions," and those favoring removal of all abortion laws.[46] The *Times* also ignored the unborn child, suggesting that the development of "morning after" pills or "menstrual flow initiators"[47] would solve the abortion problem anyway: "In both cases, the woman never knows if she really was pregnant. If not, well and good. If so, she has an instant, safe and sure abortion in the privacy of her personal life."[48]

News pages of the *Times* adopted Lader's version of abortion holy wars. American Protestantism during the 1960s was divided into liberal and conservative wings, but unless a reader read *Times* coverage very carefully he or she would think that all Protestants favored abortion; that message was transmitted clearly by a 1969 article describing "the Protestant position" as one tending toward "total repeal of abortion laws."[49] *Times* articles also showed the astuteness of Glanville Williams' prediction a decade earlier that the allowance of abortions for reasons of "mental health" would lead rapidly to legalization of abortion for all reasons, because the authorization would be so subjective. One article, for example, pointed out that in California, where abortion law was liberalized in 1967, psychiatrists were diagnosing many more women as mentally ill in order to satisfy legal requirements; the *Times* did not criticize the psychiatrists, but called the law an unfair and burdensome creator of hypocrisy.[50]

Overall, the *Times* reported that liberalized laws passed in Colorado, California, and North Carolina during 1967 were a failure because they "simply don't work" to wipe out illegal abortion; the *Times* did not point out that the reason for passage of the laws was to provide alternatives for women in cases of rape, incest, or fetal deformity, and that the issue of eliminating illegal abortion, as Taylor had pointed out at the 1950s conference, was an entirely different one.[51] *Times* news pages regularly used loaded language such as "rigid" in describing New York's abortion law;[52] *rigid* may be an objective term in describing a guy wire, but it hardly is neutral in discussing anything human or sociological short of rigor mortis.

By the end of the 1960s, *Times* news stories and editorials were working in close conjunction with articles on abortion arrests followed by pro-abortion editorials.[53] For example, when a news story reported police breaking up an abortion ring operating out of a suite at the New York Hilton, the editorial page quickly followed with its position that the only way to stop illegal abortion was to legalize it, and that the police success "ex-

poses once more the need for abortion law reform."⁵⁴ Other arrests led to
a repetitive editorial: "The need for reform of this state's abortion law was
again strikingly illustrated a few days ago when four persons were arrested
in the Bronx."⁵⁵

As the *Times* editorial page became more and more vehement,⁵⁶ the
news pages not only played up stories that could be supported in support
of the newspaper's position, but downplayed stories that could hurt the pro-
abortion movement. Lader was very worried when an abortionist ally was
arrested; the arrest, he wrote, "threatened the whole [illegal abortion] referral system, and numerous NARAL members, myself included."⁵⁷ Members
of NARAL's board of directors were deeply divided on whether to continue
breaking the law, according to Lader, until they saw the *Times* reaction:
The *Times* quoted an anonymous woman saying "the conditions were antiseptic and sanitary," and for the *Times* in 1969, that about ended the dis-
cussion.⁵⁹

Abortion coverage in the New York *Times*, which prided itself on "objectivity," can be compared with coverage in two Chicago newspapers with
a heritage of outspoken liberalism and two San Diego newspapers with a
conservative tradition.

Chicago and San Diego Cheerleading

The Chicago *Sun-Times* and *Daily News*, morning and afternoon
newspapers owned during the 1960s by Marshall Field IV, regularly followed the pro-abortion formula. For example, a series of articles in the
Chicago *Daily News* during 1967 began with stories of a 48-year-old woman discovering she is pregnant, an 18-year-old who dies while undergoing
an abortion, and a woman who has been raped. These were hardly typical
situations that could provide an accurate picture of abortion incidence, and
the statistics that followed were the usual propaganda: "Some 5,000 to
10,000 women die each year as a result of illegal abortions."⁵⁹ The article
also rounded up the usual suspects: "A number of groups are studying ways
to change existing abortion laws, but opposition to change is strong. The
Roman Catholic Church."⁶⁰

A Chicago *Sun-Times* series in 1968 followed a similar pattern. The *Sun-
Times* reporter called a "good" abortionist "something of a hero."⁶¹ The articles saw anti-abortion laws as having no effect at all on reducing the number of abortions; under one headline, "PENALTIES NO PREVENTIVE," the
Sun-Times claimed that the law merely drove abortionists underground.⁶²
The *Sun-Times*, ignoring the unborn child, called legal abortion a "procedure no more dangerous than a tonsillectomy."⁶³ The *Sun-Times* itself
would discover 10 years later that legal abortion is not necessarily safe even
for the mother,⁶⁴ but at this time it merely recited the incorrect statistics:
"Some 5,000 women die" annually because of abortions.⁶⁵

The *Sun-Times'* cheerleading was obvious on not only the editorial page but the news pages as well. Newspaper editorials demanded pro-abortion legislation in Illinois, and news pages heaped praise on a member of the Illinois legislature, Leland H. Rayson, who sponsored pro-abortion legislation.[66] An article in February, 1969, "No Help Here for Woman in Trouble," lovingly quoted abortion public relations leaders such as Howard Moody and complained that Chicago "has nothing like" Moody's abortion referral group.[67] Later that year a similar organization started up in Chicago, and the *Sun-Times* was back to puff the result of its pushing.[68] The *Sun-Times* ran a glowing profile of Dr. Lonny Myers, "a woman, a mother and a physician . . . these qualities combined uniquely suit her to lead the fight in Illinois for abortion law repeal."[69] The *Sun Times* did not mention her other interests that were later chronicled in the pages of *Playboy*: There, she was admiringly portrayed as the owner of a "sex therapy" business who played clients a song to the tune of *Jimmy Crack Corn* that was filled with four-letter words for intercourse.[70]

Turning to the San Diego *Union* and *Tribune*,[71] it might be suspected that abortion coverage in those newspapers with conservative reputations would differ substantially from coverage in the liberal Chicago *Sun-Times* and *Daily News*. The San Diego editorial pages were different: They preferred "moderate" liberalization to the full-scale legalization demanded in other newspapers examined. Abortion news coverage, however, was similar. Headlines such as "More Liberal, Realistic Laws Urged on Legal Abortions" showed bias by equating a pro-abortion position with realism.[72] Articles such as "N.Y. Women Dial To Solve Problems" — a story about an abortion referral group that "starts [women] on the road to help" — assumed that abortion solves problems and helps women.[73]

In San Diego, as in New York and Chicago, figures of "one million criminal abortions and resulting 5,000 deaths" were used without correction. One small article noted that even the pro-abortionist Tietze had called the estimates of 5,000 to 10,000 "unmitigated nonsense,"[74] but other articles continued to cite those figures. Pro-abortion "experts" were quoted without even critical balancing. For example, one "expert" combined three errors in one sentence by asking rhetorically, "Since it is an obvious fact that the primary goal of the law [passed in the 19th century] is to prevent death or injury to the mother, is society indeed protecting the mother's welfare by maintaining harsh and unyielding laws which drive her to the unskilled criminal abortionist?[75] As we have seen, the goal was to protect both unborn child and mother, interpretations of the law were not unyielding, and the criminal abortionist usually was not unskilled, but the "obvious fact" went unquestioned.

All of the newspapers studied for this chapter emphasized unusual abortion cases and exaggerated numbers. National magazine coverage of abortion during this period was similar, according to a study by Tatalovich and his associates.[76] All of the newspapers excoriated "back alley butcher quacks," praised some regular abortionists, ignored the existence of unborn children, and attacked Catholic leaders. All, in short, embraced the positions put out by pro-abortion public relations — and those positions became standard not only in media but in the legislatures that passed liberalized abortion laws.

This is not to say that news media were necessarily setting the agenda for politicians and other leaders. Pro-abortion forces were lobbying not only journalists, but lawyers and judges, as well as doctors and medical groups such as the American Medical Association and the American College of Obstetricians and Gynecologists. The triumph of pro-abortionism in such vital groups has been told in many books, including one by Grisez (from an anti-abortion viewpoint) and Lader (from a pro-abortion view).[77] But use of news media was a crucial component of all those drives with legislative and professional groups. Use of news media was essential for influencing members of the general public who in turn would influence those groups. As Tatalovich notes, "During the 1960s public opinion had to be molded and cultivated by those activists who championed the cause of abortion liberalization."[78] Journalists helped the activists to succeed.

Chapter 12

Pulpits for Abortion, 1970–1974

Writing in *Playboy* in 1970, Dr. Robert Hall, president of the Association for the Study of Abortion, complained that the anti-abortion side had an unfair communication advantage. "On several occasions during the legislative battle to repeal New York's abortion law," Hall protested, "the state's eight Catholic bishops issued a joint pastoral letter that was read from the pulpit of 1700 churches."[1] Hall stated that "The advocates of abortion reform had no such power. Two national groups were organized, but they had little money and no pulpits."[2]

Hall was wrong. In 1970, pro-abortion thought controlled the most powerful pulpits in the land — the front pages and editorial pages of leading newspapers. Overall, in 1970 newspapers gave so many sermons favoring abortion that, in a narrative history of this sort, there is room enough only to point out typical coverage and highlights. On editorial pages, for example, the Cleveland *Plain Dealer* proclaimed that "Ohio's present abortion law is inadequate, unfair and inhumane."[3] The Detroit *Free Press* opined, "Repeal of Michigan's abortion law is an idea whose time has come."[4] The New York *Times* and the St. Louis *Post-Dispatch* ran repeated pro-abortion editorials.[5] The Chicago *Sun-Times* ran at least five between April and August, 1970, and claimed that man, like animal, must abide by "the fundamental instinct for survival of the species. Today it is overpopulation, not underpopulation, that threatens the species and the public weal."[6]

Turning to the more crucial news pages, an examination of hundreds of stories shows a treacly tendency to make abortion seem easy. The Omaha *World-Herald* quoted "Betty" describing her abortion experience: "I had to stay quiet for 15 minutes. When I got up, I felt like a brand-new woman. I felt so happy."[7] The *Long Island Press* quotes "Susan" telling the abortionist when the operation was over, "Oh, thank you, thank you."[8] The reporter added, "Within the next half hour she will have some cookies and a soft drink in the recovery lounge, fill out a few forms, pay a fee of $200 and be on her way back home"—probably skipping, the article seemed to suggest.[9] The Hartford *Courant* reported that abortion "is safe and usually without complications,"[10] and the *Oregonian* called abortion in Portland "a simple operation" that symbolizes "society's concern about overpopulation, pollution and survival."[11]

Similarly, the San Francisco *Chronicle* discussed "products of conception"[12] and—having dismissed the second patient in an abortion—proclaimed that "abortions can now be performed safely, efficiently and economically."[13] The *Chronicle* told how a typical young woman "came back from the abortion smiling and saying, 'I feel fine.' "[14] The reporter portrayed the woman putting on a "a bright scarf over her hair" and telling her patiently waiting mother, "I'm starved. Let's go to lunch."[15] The reporter added that the abortion "procedure is so simple and over so quickly that they [women undergoing abortions] have no feelings of guilt."[16]

Stories on abortion typically portrayed pro-abortionists as merciful and anti-abortionists as closed-minded. The Memphis *Commercial Appeal*, under a headline "Hand of Mercy Extends in Abortions," indicated that pro-abortionists counseling pregnant women "are answering these women's needs."[17] A Newark *Evening News* headline concerning the governor of New Jersey read, "Cahill Vows to Keep Open Mind on Abortion Law Liberalization," with the implication that those opposed to abortion have closed minds.[18] Anti-abortionists who wanted to reopen the debate in states that had liberalized abortion rules were not considered to be promoting open-mindedness, however; a Washington *Post* story, "K of C Injects Abortion Issue Into Md. Races," insinuated that the Knights of Columbus were ruining democracy by forcing candidates to deal with something already decided.[19]

Some news stories that might seem "balanced" showed subtle tilting in two ways. One could be called "differential vividness": When the Baltimore *Sun* ran back-to-back paragraphs presenting opposed positions on abortion, one paragraph vividly emphasized the "agony" of pregnant women and "unwanted" children, and the other noted in abstract terms the position that there is "a human being from the moment of conception."[20] The two paragraphs were hardly balanced. A second quiet biasing came through the "ABABCCC" method of structuring a news story: Quotations from the warring parties (ABAB) followed by quotation from "experts" who could tell the confused reader which side was right (CCC). The "experts" always seemed to be pro-abortion.

Some newspapers dispensed with the ritual of objectivity on their news pages and journeyed straight to advocacy. When pro-abortionists circulated petitions for a referendum on unrestricted abortion, the San Francisco *Chronicle* led the cheers and notified readers that "information and petitions may be obtained by writing the Abortion Initiative Project, Box 734, Sunnyvale or calling 241-7990."[21] The *Chronicle* news pages also presented a how-to guide to an abortion, complete with free advertising for Planned Parenthood, which had taken an ardently pro-abortion position, and telephone numbers for abortion referral services.[22] Even the few large city newspapers with anti-abortion editorial pages, such as the San Diego *Union*, seemed swept along by the front-page onslaught.[23]

To Lader's delight, newspaper articles frequently suggested that only Catholics opposed abortion. The New York *Times*, for example, covered the New York legislature's tumultuous abortion debate in 1970 by noting frequently which assemblymen were Catholics, what comments had been made in which Catholic churches, and so on. The *Times* did not provide this service concerning legislators of other religious persuasions, and did not note that pro-abortion leaders also were proceeding out of their own worldviews. For example, the *Times* contended that the pro-abortion bill's sponsor, Constance Cook, became involved in the abortion question not because of her philosophy but because she has "a talent for grasping complex issues."[24]

The touch of pro-abortion public relations skill was evident in other parts of the country as well. Many newspapers, including two of the Texas leaders — the Houston *Post* and the Dallas *Morning News* — ran series of articles that amounted to little more than pro-abortion propaganda. A six-part series in the *Post* began, "Though even legal abortion is not without a small risk, the illegal ones are the real medical problems."[25] The third article in the series began with a quotation from a pro-abortionist: "People say an aborted child might have grown up to be President. There's a better chance he would have grown up to be the one who shot the President."[26] The article attacked anti-abortion laws that were "passed before women could vote, based on ideologies conceived by men."[27]

The Dallas *Morning News* series in November, 1970, began with the contention that "abortion has become a simple procedure when performed in early pregnancy by a physician in proper surroundings."[28] The first article of the series assumed that abortion should be legal and then went on about "untold mental anguish borne by the women who must sneak around, undergo humiliation at the hands of the abortionists and break the law in the process."[29] The second article in the series criticized the "inept blundering" of officials in a California hospital who asked a woman to "sign a fetal death certificate as 'maternal parent of the deceased.' "[30] The final article in the series followed the Lader line in blaming Catholics for getting in the way of progress: "Does the Catholic Church, a powerful political as well as religious force, have the right to impose its beliefs on the rest of society?"[31]

Newspapers that did not want to propagandize for abortion had many options available to them. The realism of these options is shown by the handful of newspapers that did not fall in line. The Indianapolis *Star* provided useful information by publishing a diagram showing the growth of unborn children within the womb.[32] The Buffalo *Evening News* used public documents to tally death totals that included unborn children as well as maternal fatalities: One of its stories began, "A total of 877 fetal deaths, the majority due to abortions induced by physicians under the new liberal state law, were reported by Erie County hospitals to the County Health Department in July and August. There were no maternal deaths."[33] The Cincinnati *Enquirer* interviewed doctors troubled by abortion: "I thought that I'd react differently — that I'd think it was better for the mother," the *Enquirer* quoted one doctor as saying. "That's the way I feel when I sit around and chat. But no, when you're in the operating room and look down in to the gauze and see the little hands there, you think, 'I've just killed something.' It's awful."[34]

Those were rare exceptions. An examination of hundreds of articles shows the accuracy of Judge John Noonan's appraisal:

> The press was for the abortion liberty. Virtually every major newspaper in the country was on its side, as were the radio stations, the news commentators, the disc jockeys, the pollsters, the syndicated columnists, the editorial writers, the reporters, the news services, the journals of information and the journals of opinion. With the notable exception of three or four syndicated writers . . . every major molder of public opinion in the press was pro-abortion or indifferent to the issue.
>
> There was a massive barrier through which any news or opinion contrary to the liberty had to travel. There was not a single large urban newspaper regularly carrying the anti-abortion viewpoint the way Horace Greeley's *Tribune* had carried the anti-slavery viewpoint.[35]

Why was there such journalistic unanimity? To judge from the stories, reporters accepted the ideology of both Madame Restell and late 20th century radical feminism. Their stories portrayed abortion as freedom from exploitation, and saw any restrictions on abortion as discrimination against those economically poor.

Reporters also responded to power. Upper middle class lawyers who formed the leadership of the American Civil Liberties Union, politically conservative doctors who wanted autonomy in their practice, and welfare administrators who needed to make their budgets politically acceptable, all were pro-abortion. So were many wealthy philanthropists, tithing with religious fervor (after the image of John D. Rockefeller III) to dismantle what they saw as a population bomb. Together, these groups of individuals formed a powerful alliance that dominated abortion policy in both political parties until 1972, when Republicans began to move toward their present anti-abortion stance.

Within the executive branch, for example, Richard Nixon in 1969 and 1970 made four critical appointments that affected abortion policy. John Ehrlichman, who was pro-abortion, became domestic chief of staff; Louis Hellman, a director of the Association for the Study of Abortion, took the key spot for abortion policy in the Department of Health, Education, and Welfare; John D. Rockefeller III, who spoke for and heavily funded the pro-abortion forces, became chairman of a "Commission on Population Growth and the American Future"; and Harry Blackmun became a Supreme Court justice.[36] Although Nixon himself made a few politically useful anti-abortion comments, his administration included ardent pro-abortionists such as Reimer Ravenholt[37] who helped to fund many pro-abortion conferences. Of Nixon's 20 appointees to the commission chaired by Rockefeller, 16 were pro-abortion, and it predictably recommended abolition of all abortion laws.[38]

Arrayed against all this were the poorest of the poor: unborn children. But the 20th century journalistic tradition of not paying attention to such invisible creatures made it easy for reporters to ignore them; reporters could win plaudits from the powerful and feel like crusaders for justice at the same time. Without danger of significant social rebuke, leading journalists could be part of a larger trend in world views summarized well by *California Medicine* in 1970: The ethic of "reverence for each and every human life . . . is being eroded at the core and may eventually be abandoned."[39]

The change in ethics evidently came faster in media, medical, legal, and other leadership circles than in the populace generally. In 1972, although Detroit newspapers heavily supported a Michigan referendum to legalize abortion on demand through the first 5 months, 61% of Michigan voters said no. In North Dakota, 77% of voters turned down a similar referendum. Overall, despite clever tactics, overwhelming press sentiment, and the support of powerful interests, pro-abortion forces by the end of 1972 had been able to win unrestricted abortion in only 4 states, and various stipulations concerning mother's health, fetal deformity, and rape or incest cases, in 15 other states. Thirty-one states resisted any liberalization. The press had contributed to setting the agenda, but a Gallup Poll in 1972 showed 66% of all Americans opposing elective abortion.[40] Other public opinion surveys, as well as the limited amount of legislative action, indicated that newspaper readers could be led to abortion but would not drink it in.[41]

ROE V. WADE

Journalistic agitation to change abortion laws continued to be furious until
January, 1973. In that month the abortion world turned upside down as
the U.S. Supreme Court in *Roe v. Wade* mandated abortion anywhere
without restriction during the first 3 months, abortion in hospitals without
restriction during the next 3 months, and abortion in hospitals following
paperwork during the final 3 months. Justice Blackmun's decision ostensibly refused to declare when human life began, but in practice it did exactly that, because hunters do not shoot at an object in the forest if it *may*
be a human being.

The most influential U.S. newspapers all cheered. The New York *Times*
called the decision "a major contribution to the preservation of individual
liberties . . . it wisely avoids the quicksand of attempting a judicial
pronouncement on when life begins."[42] The St. Louis *Post-Dispatch* called
the decision "remarkable for its common sense" and "its humaneness."[43]
The *Christian Science Monitor* applauded the Court for its willingness to
"stretch the application of the 14th Amendment," and ended its editorial
with a sentence, "The Court continued to be unpredictable, and in this delicate case, we think it was right."[44]

The press verdict was not unanimous. The Indianapolis *News* called the
decision "a shocking inversion of fact" and a "grim Orwellian reversal of
the simplest ethical values."[45] Some smaller city newspapers, such as the
Orlando *Sentinel*, were prophetic:

> The devaluation of morality induced by abortion on demand could, and in
> all likelihood will, have far reaching effects. Among them are the promotion
> of promiscuity, depersonalization of the concept of life and activating the de-
> struct button on the family unit as we know it. . . . And what of the woman
> herself? Abortion by whim could have grave future consequences to her. There
> is enough unavoidable pain in living without inflicting on oneself, in a peri-
> od of extremity, the haunting memory of a child that might have been.[46]

A few newspapers raised constitutional questions: The Omaha *World-
Herald* argued that abortion was a concern for "legislators, not of would-
be legislators and sociologists on the nation's highest court,"[47] the Norfolk
Ledger-Star proposed that it would have been "much wiser and safer for
the court to have let the states continue to handle the problem,"[48] and the
Birmingham *News* complained of "raw judicial power."[49] But most editorials examined for this chapter, and particularly those from nationally influential newspapers, were jubilant.

Many editorial writers wiped off their crystal balls and predicted an end
to the abortion debate. The Des Moines *Register* said goodbye to "emotion-
charged hearings" on abortion,[50] and the Louisville *Courier-Journal*

praised the Court's "bold and unequivocal decision" for virtually ending the war.[51] The Milwaukee *Journal* declared that "politicians and policemen and judges" would no longer have to be concerned with the "distractive" issue.[52] The New York *Times* was less positive, but hoped that the "emotional and divisive public argument" concerning abortion would be over now that there was "a sound foundation for final and reasonable resolution" of the debate.[53]

THE BREZHNEV DOCTRINE OF ABORTION POLITICS

News pages followed the slant of the editorial column: Abortion was part of the 1960s and early 1970s agenda and was now a dead issue. Just as Soviet leader Brezhnev proclaimed at this time that a nation brought under Communist control would never be allowed to leave it, so newspapers stated or implied that there was no turning back on abortion. For example, the Dallas *Morning News*, under a headline "Mechanics More Than Morality Main Concern," suggested that ethical issues would now be put to rest as questions of efficient provision of abortion came forward.[54] The Milwaukee *Journal* reported that the abortion issue was "resolved."[55] The Fort Worth *Star-Telegram* hailed abortion as a growth industry, "a booming reality at Fort Worth hospitals."[56] A Cleveland *Press* headline read, "Everyone seems calm about abortions here."[57]

And yet, opposition to abortion continued, and began to increase. In Cleveland, for example, anti-abortion partisans were staging protests a few days after the headline proclaimed calm. The story did not die, and news pages continued to run pro-abortion stories. Reporters typically described abortion as easy for women; the Oakland *Tribune* told of how women "can stay for a while if they like after the operation, but they can leave almost immediately if they want, as the procedure is very easy."[58] Newspapers cheered anticipated price reductions for abortion and complained when the prices did not come down as fast as expected.[59] The San Antonio *Light* provided free publicity for a Planned Parenthood Wine and Cheese Fest designed to raise funds for a lower cost abortion center,[60] and the Atlanta *Journal* publicized a "pregnancy termination clinic" described as "a clean modern facility": The last paragraph of that story read, "The pregancy termination clinic is located at 81 Peachtree Place NW and the telephone number is 892-1553."[61]

THE NEW GOOD GUYS

Madame Restell had to pay for her advertising, but newspapers helped abortionists for free and refurbished their images, as Madame Restell had tried to refurbish her own by claiming experience in the great hospitals of Europe. A Chicago *Sun-Times* profile of abortionist T. M. Howard called him "a long-time civil rights advocate" and noted that he was director of the finance committee for Operation PUSH and Tabernacle Community Hospital. His clinic, soon to open a "division of pregnancy termination," was "as equipped as most hospitals — but its decor looks more like a Loop dress shop than a hospital. The entire place is carpeted."[62] The Cleveland *Press* quoted local abortionist Robert H. Schwartz as saying, "I enjoy helping people and therefore I enjoy doing abortions."[63] Anti-abortionists were not quoted.

The Detroit *Free Press*, under a headline "Abortion Pioneer Reflects On Years of Abuse, Shame," told of how one man "has been called killer, money-driven, cold, he has been jailed and beaten. But at 60, Dr. Edgar Keemer still does what has been his life's work — he performs abortions."[64] The article described him as a saint who had undergone persecution but had persevered for humanitarian reasons. Now that many newspapers were trying to push the abortion issue off the agenda, reporters glamorized such "pioneers" and did not challenge assumptions that legal abortion meant safe abortion. When the Detroit chapter of the National Organization for Women gave a "good" rating to the "quality of abortion procedures in Detroit," the Detroit *Free Press* accepted that evaluation and did not bother to send out its own reporters to investigate.[65]

Abortion coverage immediately following the *Rose v. Wade* decision could have been handled very differently, and in a few cases was. One Milwaukee *Journal* article, "Abortion Business Here is Brisk and Efficient," described first the women in crowded abortion business waiting areas, and then the men: "About 30 men stood or sat against the walls, looking worried, guilty, or just stony eyed. 'The casket faced brigade,' an assistant at the clinic called them. The air was hot and thick with smoke. 'It's like cattle,' one girl said as she left after her abortion."[66] A second atypical article, published in the Dallas *Morning News*, noted that "Some psychiatric consequences ranging from mild regret to deep depression can be expected in the next few years as the Supreme Court's decision on legal abortion is implemented."[67] But such articles were rare, and were overwhelmed even in their own newspapers by pro-abortion coverage, and by attacks on "naively simplistic" anti-abortionists who "post the gory pictures on the wall."[68] Major newspapers declared on both their news and editorial pages that the abortion war was over.

Throughout 1974 and 1975, news pages continued to present abortion as a practice disliked largely by Catholic leaders and embraced by others; journalists distorted public opinion findings to the contrary.[69] Reporters assumed that legalizing abortion made it safe for women, even though abortion practices were not very different from when they were illegal.[70] They also continued to report, frequently, that the Supreme Court legalized abortion only in the first trimester, instead of noting that, according to *Roe v. Wade*, abortion could not be prohibited at any stage of pregnancy. As other Supreme Court decisions extending *Roe v. Wade* emerged during the mid-1970s, most major newspapers stayed firmly in the pro-abortion camp. And yet, anti-abortion forces grew as more evangelicals entered Abortion War II.

In 1976, the Supreme Court voted 6–3 that states could not require a woman to obtain her husband's consent to an abortion, and 5–4 that states could not require all women under age 18 to obtain parental consent. Editorials in newspapers such as the Los Angeles *Times*, the St. Louis *Post Dispatch*, the Cleveland *Press*, and the Chicago *Daily News* praised the Court.[71] The *Arizona Republic* criticized the decisions as extreme,[72] but the Providence *Journal* took the typical press position of arguing that "The Supreme Court has taken a reasoned and moderate view."[73] A New York *Times* editorial provided a public tribute to pro-abortion public relations by proclaiming, "One would hope, with Ilse Darling of the Religious Coalition for Abortion Rights [a leading pro-abortion group], that the Court's reaffirmation of this most intimate of privacy rights might ultimately drain some of the heat from the abortion issue."[74]

During the 1976 election campaign, many reporters again tried to declare abortion off the agenda. The Washington *Post* stated that the abortion issue "has in fact got somewhat overblown and out of hand."[75] The Los Angeles *Times* urged "proper perspective"[76] and the Boston *Globe* wanted to place "the abortion question in perspective," which meant off page 1. Editors at the Cincinnati *Post* also wanted to sideline the abortion issue and replace it with "plenty of issues begging for definition and debate."[78] The New Orleans *States Item* complained that abortion is "one of those emotional, divisive issues."[79] The Milwaukee *Journal* editorialized that all should accept the Supreme Court's decisions and not urge Constitutional amendment: "Certainly the wisdom of changing the nation's organic law to reflect one side of a closely divided moral controversy is questionable."[80]

Sometimes the same pro-abortion lines were visible in editorials from newspapers in different parts of the country. In 1977 a Rochester *Democrat Chronicle* editorial calling for federal payment for abortions quoted a Planned Parenthood director as saying that a woman "asked us which was the better method [for abortion], turpentine or a coat hanger."[81] The Memphis *Commercial Appeal* used the same line: "What do you do when a women wants to know if it's safer to use a coat hanger or turpentine?"[82] When journalists were not pulling lines from Planned Parenthood press releases, it seemed they were asking readers to send in money to pay for additional releases. For example, in Kansas City the *Times* suggested that readers contribute to "Planned Parenthood of Western Missouri and Kansas," because "the choice [is] between Planned Parenthood and the back-alley quacks of old."[83] The Kansas City *Star* similarly praised "the good work of Planned Parenthood."[84]

The press sermonizing, on both editorial and news pages, was virtually a constant. The Chicago *Sun-Times* even ended one news story with the reporter's homily about how "women who elect abortion show love. . . . Abortion as love may be a bit much for antiabortionists to understand, but the current movement is to regard abortion as a positive experience."[85] In retrospect, it seems remarkable that anyone stood up to the massive media barrage; but anti-abortionists did, as succeeding chapters in this volume show.

Chapter 13

"That No Fetus Will Be Born Alive"

After 1973 the issue seemed settled: Madame Restell had won. Husbands and boyfriends could push women to abort unborn children so that the men would no longer be "tugging at the oar of incessant labor."[1] Women would no longer have to battle their way out of "that melancholy of mind and depression of Spirits" that unexpected pregnancy could bring.[2] Women and men planning abortion could answer ads offering removal of the "products of conception," the modern equivalent of Madame Restell's willingness to "remove female blockages." And everything was legal.

But "dreaded complications" could not be forgotten so easily.

The "dreaded complication," to an abortionist, is the survival of an unborn child scheduled for death. For example, in 1973 a 4½ pound child emerged alive following a saline abortion in Bakersfield, California. The abortionist, informed by phone, ordered two nurses not to give oxygen to the baby; another doctor overrode those instructions. The baby survived and later was adopted. The abortionist was indicted for solicitation to commit murder, but the case was dismissed and the incident received little publicity.[3] The press was not interested.

Another case arose in 1974, when Pittsburgh physician Leonard Laufe induced an abortion by injecting prostaglandin, a substance that stimulates muscle contraction and delivery. The operation, filmed for later instructional use, attracted attention outside the classroom when the film showed a newly delivered, 3-pound baby moving and gasping. The film record was supplemented by testimony from a nurse and medical student who said they had seen signs of life, but Laufe stated that the baby sustained fatal damage during delivery. No charges were filed, and the incident did not receive much publicity at the time.[4] The press was not interested.

Many such cases were brought during the mid-1970s, as anti-abortionists staged a rear-guard action against *Roe v. Wade* and attempted to erect a wall between abortion and infanticide. For the most part, however, the cases were like trees falling in the forest, with little news coverage and typical highway travelers unaware.

The Edelin case — Boston, 1975 — was different, for two reasons. First, the competitive Boston press was not like that of Bakersfield or even Pittsburgh. The pro-abortion Boston *Globe* dominated Massachusetts journalism, but the abortion-ambivalent Boston *Herald* and the city's other media would not let the Globe get away with covering up a gripping story. Second, the *Globe* had reasons to play the story big: Kenneth Edelin, the abortionist involved in the trial was Black, and prosecution of him, to the liberal *Globe*, smacked of racism — an aspect the Globe wanted to cover.[5] As William F. Buckley, Jr., noted about the attention given the case,

> One must ask, why Edelin? On the face of it, he is a dubious hero for the Champions of permissive abortion. He killed a well-formed child, whether with technical legality being a secondary point. Prudence would seem to recommend that pro-abortionists keep a discreet distance from such a case. . . . But Edelin [is black]. The case can be presented as the lynching of a black Marcus Welby by a bigoted community.[6]

Ironically, it seems likely that Boston prosecutors might have tried to dodge the case had they known the potential racial issues involved. One author described Edelin as having "a complexion I would call lighter than Mediterranean. He is, in fact, a white black man."[7] Newman Flanagan, assistant district attorney for Suffolk County, later said,

> I was shocked when I learned, long after I'd first seen him, that he was black. I don't remember exactly how I found out — I think it was from a newspaper story — but I do remember going to [District Attorney] Garrett and saying, "Damn it, Garrett, Edelin is black." He wasn't any happier than I was. We knew that, with the busing issues still hot here in Boston, we'd run into cries of "racism" before the trial was over.[8]

Edelin's defense attorney also noted, "It wasn't until after I'd met with Ken two or three times that I learned he was black."[9]

The story itself began in September, 1973, when a 17-year-old Black girl went to Boston City Hospital for an abortion. Doctors estimated that she was 20 to 24 weeks pregnant. On October 2 and 3, they tried three times to kill the unborn child by salt poisoning. Their attempts were unsuccessful. After the third miss, they decided to perform a hysterotomy by making an incision on the abdomen and uterus. (The procedure is similar to a Caesarian section, except for the intention that the unborn child, too small to survive the operation, will die.)

Dr. Kenneth Edelin cut into the womb of the girl and detached the placenta and child from the uterine wall. What happened then became a focus of judicial controversy. Some said the just-born child already was dead and Edelin simply sent the corpse to the pathology department. Others said the unborn had been born and Edelin, upset at falling victim to the "dreaded complication," kept his hands over the child for 3 minutes until he was sure breathing had stopped.

Whatever the action, no one signed a death certificate. The well-developed corpse, stored in a bottle in the pathology department, came to the attention of District Attorney Garrett, who ordered an investigation. On April 11, 1974, a grand jury handed down an indictment charging Edelin with manslaughter. The indictment said Edelin "did assault and beat a certain person, to wit a male child described to said jurors as Baby Boy, and by such assault and beating did kill the said person."

The wording of the indictment was careful. Edelin was not charged with abortion, which was clearly legal under *Roe v. Wade*. Edelin was charged with suffocating a child. The prosecution's goal, therefore, was to show that the child removed from his mother by Edelin breathed on his own, and was sufficiently well developed to have the possibility of survival. The defense would argue that a child never had been born, and that Edelin was just doing his *Roe v. Wade* duties in ending the life of a creature who never breathed on his own and was thus still a "fetus." Many technicalities of the case would require several chapters to explain,[10] but, as in the Finkbine incident, terminology was crucial. *Globe* journalists from the start recognized the importance of words: "Edelin trial semantics crucial," the *Globe* proclaimed when the trial began in January, 1975: "Words may play crucial role."[11] Reporter Nils J. Bruzelius wrote, "Major issues in the case will revolve not so much around what was done, as what to call it."[12]

Bruzelius was careful to quote chief defense attorney William Homans as saying, in his opening statement, 'You will hear evidence as to the meaning of words." Homans wanted the word "fetus," rather than the "baby boy" of the indictment, used throughout the trial. Prosecutor Newman Flanagan, however, stressed use of words such as "baby boy, male child, suffocate, smother, murder."[13] In the courtroom, Judge James P. McGuire ordered a compromise: "Baby boy" could not be used in court, but "male child" or "male human being" could be used; the words "smother" or "murder" were banned, but "suffocate" was permissible.[14] In the court of public opinion, reporter Bruzelius also tried to find a middle ground: When citing prosecution evidence he referred to "the male child,"[15] and when citing defense evidence he referred to the "fetus."[16]

However, the *Globe* reporter who regularly covered the Edelin case, Diane White,[17] wrote sentences such as this one: "The prosecution contends that the fetus . . . would have lived outside its mother but for the defendant's deliberate delay in removing it from the uterus."[18] The prosecution, of course, said no such thing: Crucial to its case was the point that the unborn child, when detached from the uterine wall, was no longer a "fetus" but a boy.[19] Occasionally the *Globe* reporting was fair: "The prosecution claims the *child* was born. . . . The defense argues that the *fetus* never lived." But, more frequently, coverage was "The prosecution claims the *fetus* was born as soon as the placenta was detached from the uterine wall. The defense argues that the *fetus* never lived outside the uterus"[20] (italics added).

Typical *Globe* reporting even misstated the charge: "Edelin is charged with manslaughter in the death of a fetus."[21] That was clearly not a crime under *Roe v. Wade*, but killing a "baby boy," as the indictment actually read, was."[22] Even on February 14, as trial arguments concluded, the *Globe* was still inaccurately summarizing the prosecution's contention: "Edelin deliberately killed a viable fetus while performing an abortion."[23] Overall during this trial in which nomenclature was crucial, the *Globe* misstated the indictment and the prosecution contention over 100 times.

Globe coverage of testimony by expert witnesses also was revealing. When witnesses favoring the accused abortionist took the stand, the front-page lead was "Two expert witnesses for the defense testified yesterday."[24] The position on abortion of those witnesses was not identified. A story the next day, under the headline, "Edelin delay in taking fetus proper practice, expert says," did not identify the position on abortion of two more experts.[25] Another story, "Edelin's judgment sound, say experts," again did not identify the position on abortion of the experts, even though one spoke of "products of conception"; that terminology is usually an indication of pro-abortion sentiment.[26] The *Globe*, in summarizing testimony, termed the defense witnesses "medical experts . . . experienced obstetricians . . . expert witnesses," but termed expert witnesses called by the other side merely "prosecution witnesses" representing the "anti-abortion" position.[27]

Overall, the prosecution presented 15 witnesses and the defense 16; most witnesses from both sides were medical experts. For example, the prosecution called Dr. John Ward, associate pathologist at Mercy Hospital in Pittsburgh, who testified that his examination of fetal lung tissue indicated the fetus breathed in air; Dr. Mildred Jefferson, a surgeon at Boston University's School of Medicine; and Minneapolis obstetrician Dr. Fred Mecklenburg, who testified that steps taken by Edelin were "not consistent with good medical practice." The judge ruled that the main prosecution witnesses should be considered "experts." But the Boston *Globe* ruled otherwise.[28]

The *Globe* also joined the defense team by running glowing descriptions of the accused doctor, Kenneth Edelin. The prosecution depicted him as a man not above killing a newborn child, but the *Globe* called Edelin "an unusually dedicated doctor" who combines "energy, concentration and dedication" and "has spent much of his skill and time trying to improve care for poor and minority women."[29] The *Globe* kept referring to Edelin as "the 26-year-old black doctor who sits with his back straight at the defense table each day.[30] The sequestered jury apparently was unaware that racism was becoming an issue in the trial; the jury knew, because it was in the indictment, that the abortion victim was Black, but Edelin's race was never mentioned in the courtroom, and one juror said "I never realized that Edelin was black until after the trial."[31]

Although jurors lacked the one piece of information that the *Globe* suggested would figure in the decision, Edelin's race, they did have access to another piece of information that *Globe* readers were without: A photograph of the abortion victim. Edelin's lawyer protested the admission of "a photograph of the dead fetus . . . lying as if discarded on a metal work bench or photographic stand," and charged that the picture "was (and is) utterly shocking and inflammatory to the mind of lay person."[32] The prosecutor referred to the photo in his closing argument to the jury:

Take a look at the picture of the subject. Is this just a specimen? You tell us what it is. Look at the picture. Show it to anybody. What would they tell you it was? Use your common sense when you go to your jury deliberation room and humanize that. Are you speaking about a blob, a big bunch of mucus, or what are we talking about here? Subjects? I respectfully submit we're talking about an independent human being that the Commonwealth of Massachusetts must protect as well as anybody else in this courtroom.[33]

The *Globe* never published that picture. The pro-abortion author of a book on the Edelin case, Dr. William Nolen, noted that the photograph "was undoubtedly inflammatory," but "inflammatory for a good reason: this was and should have been an inflammatory case."[34] He pointed out that the victim "looked like a baby because it was, in fact, a baby. Not legally — as long as it was in its mother's uterus — but in every other way. It had a head, legs, arms, genitalia."[35] Nolen looked at the photograph and still favored abortion; *Globe* readers did not have that opportunity to make an informed choice. Instead, the *Globe* inflamed the situation in another way, by emphasizing the color of Edelin's skin, without noting once the trial began that the dead abortion victim was Black also. The *Globe*, in short, not only used one-sided nomenclature, but also prepared for a possible verdict against Edelin by setting up the story as one not of oppression against a child, but racial oppression.

Boston *Herald* reporting, as it turned out, was similar to the *Globe*'s; like the San Diego *Union*, the *Herald* was conservative on the editorial page but mainline liberal on the front page. The *Herald* also adopted the defense position by referring to the victim as a "fetus," even when summarizing the prosecution's case.[36] It too called pro-abortion doctors disinterested "experts"[37] and emphasized the interests of anti-abortion doctors: "Dr.

Mecklenburg, who has acknowledged his interest in trying to preserve the life of a fetus."[38]

According to both pro- and anti-abortion Massachusetts residents, other news media also were pro-Edelin. "He deserved support and he got it," one pro-abortion partisan said of Edelin.[39] Another said, "There's no question in my mind; the media went all out for Ken."[40] An anti-abortionist said,

> I went to the trial a few times and then at night I'd watch the television reports and the next day I'd read the papers. I could hardly believe the reporters were at the same trial I attended. They'd leave out anything that tended to discredit the defense and emphasize every minor slip the prosecution might make. It's a good thing the jurors weren't allowed to listen to television or radio reports or read the papers. If they had, I think they'd have been scared to vote for conviction even if they felt Edelin was guilty. They'd have been afraid their neighbors would be ready to lynch them when the trial was over."[41]

The jury, without the benefit of media reports on the trial, found Edelin guilty. The *Globe* exploded: An editorial stated that Edelin was "a victim of legislative and judicial inadequacy which no just society should tolerate."[42] Along with an editorial and news stories suggesting juror and prosecution racism, the *Globe* ran an accusatory story under the headline "Edelin's wife blames bias, religion for conviction." According to Professor Ramona Hoage Edelin, the case was not one of "abortion or manslaughter but a case whose major issue was racism, and a judgment from the perspective of the Catholic Church."[43]

The *Globe* hammered away at that theme, frequently implying that a White, predominately Catholic jury could not be fair to a Black doctor. (The *Globe* never showed pleasure at a White jury taking seriously the death of a Black child.) The *Globe* did state that lawyers believed the trial judge to have been fair, "even though he is a church-going Catholic."[44] Under pressure, the *Globe* later apologized for suggesting that Catholicism and fairness were unlikely bedfellows, but Russell Shaw (representing the National Conference of Catholic Bishops) suggested that some journalists were "unable to restrain their fury at those who they hold responsible for his [Edelin's] conviction."[45]

Until the conviction, newspapers around the country had been giving the Edelin trial only cursory coverage. Charges by Edelin "that racial and religious prejudice made a fair trial in Boston impossible," however, hit the front page of the New York *Times*,[46] and other newspapers soon saw the story as an important one. The *Times* echoed the terminology of the Edelin defense and the *Globe* by headlining its story, "Doctor Guilty in Death of a Fetus in Abortion."[47] The *Times*, like the *Globe*, showed shock at the verdict: "Exclamations of displeasure . . . sounded through the courtroom . . . some spectators asked each other, 'How could they do that?' "[48]

The *Times* proceeded to answer its own question: The jury acted out of racism, bias, and emotional pressure due to poor choice of words by the prosecution, which was able to "confuse the jury by using interchangeably the terms 'fetus' and 'baby.' "[49]

During the ensuing coverage it did not seem to matter that jurors evidently had not been confused. One juror explained that he and others found Edelin guilty because they believed the child to have been born:

> From the time we started deliberating I don't think the word "abortion" came up twice. When it did, we all agreed that yes, there had been a legal abortion and that once the baby was detached from the mother the doctor's obligation to the mother was completed. But then we asked ourselves: did the doctor owe this baby an obligation . . .?[50]

Another juror responded similarly: The evidence indicated the child had taken a breath and was therefore no longer a "fetus," but a baby; the issue was not abortion but infanticide.[51] The press around the country, though, followed the *Globe* and the *Times* in reporting that Edelin "was convicted of manslaughter for killing the fetus."[52]

Newspaper editorial writers, following the *Globe* and the *Times*, saw racial and religious prejudice behind the verdict, and did not deal with the question of infanticide. The Washington *Post* charged that "by convicting Dr. Kenneth Edelin for manslaughter, the State of Massachusetts has brought disgrace to itself and to the whole judicial system."[53] The St. Louis *Post-Dispatch* called the trial result "the most reckless and wanton kind of abuse of the judicial process."[54] The Los Angeles *Times* argued that "an injustice has been done."[55] The Richmond *Times-Dispatch* called the decision "unfair, even incredible."[56] News magazines also loaded on the scorn, with *Time* citing comparisons to the 1925 Scopes "monkey trial" concerning the teaching of evolution: "Although Scopes was found guilty, the resulting public outcry led to a national debate that in turn eventually produced an enlightened consensus on evolution."[57]

Newspapers around the country urged a higher court reversal of the verdict, both on grounds of alleged racial and religious prejudice, and because the verdict could challenge the abortion status quo. The Chattanooga *Times* called the entire trial "a gross miscarriage of justice in that it thrust upon the jurors a question that never should have raised in a criminal courtroom."[58] An Oregon *Journal* editorial contended that "the unfortunate aspect of the conviction in Boston . . . is that it settles nothing and adds more fuel to an already raging controversy."[59] The Des Moines *Register* also wanted a ceasefire that would preserve *Roe v. Wade*: "The conviction of the Boston doctor accused of killing a fetus has increased tensions over legalized abortion."[60] The Philadelphia *Inquirer* worried about a "chilling effect" on abortions over 20 weeks, with physicians hesitating lest the unborn child emerge alive and born.[61] The Los Angeles *Herald-Examiner*, following through on the new abortion conservatism, did not want the verdict to "scare physicians away from performing" abortions.[62]

Immediately after the verdict the New York *Times* predicted that the Edelin case "would leave an indelible imprint on American medicine."[63] Media coverage, however, helped to create a different imprint than originally anticipated. The Massachusetts Supreme Judicial Court, a body known for having its collective ear attuned to media tremors, reversed Edelin's conviction, in part because of a new U.S. Supreme Court decision, *Danforth v. Planned Parenthood of Central Missouri*, that gave doctors additional power to make determinations of fetal viability. Edelin emerged a hero, with a booming private practice. Prosecutors who had faced enormous press attacks, including charges of racism and religious prejudice, ended up with a dead case. Jurors who found Edelin guilty had suffered much abuse, with one acknowledging that he "received vicious phone calls, some from people who threatened to kill his wife and children."[64]

Understandably, few on the anti-abortion side were eager to become involved in another Edelin-type case. Yet, the "dreaded complications" continued to appear. None received much media attention during the next 2 years, but on March 2, 1977, the wish of the Los Angeles *Herald-Examiner* that the Edelin jury verdict would not "scare physicians away from performing" abortions came true dramatically in its own metropolitan area.

That story began after Dr. William Waddill performed an abortion by salt poisoning at Westminster Community Hospital, south of Los Angeles. Waddill left the hospital, only to receive a frenzied call from nurses: A live baby rather than a corpse had emerged from the woman—and the baby was crying out and breathing, with a beating heart.

Waddill headed for the hospital, and nurses administered life-preserving techniques as they waited for him to arrive. When he did he was visibly angry, according to trial testimony. He told all staff members to leave the nursery; Registered Nurse JoAnn Griffith did not want to leave, because "there was life in that body,": but she said Waddill pushed her out of the room. Only Dr. Ronald Cornelsen, chief of pediatrics at the hospital, was in the nursery when Waddill clutched the baby's throat and commented that if the child were allowed to live she would have massive brain damage and be the evidence in a lawsuit totalling millions of dollars in damages.[65]

The Los Angeles *Times* also reported Cornelsen's testimony that Waddill suggested other methods of "disposing of" Baby Girl Weaver, including "holding the baby's head under water or injecting it [sic] with potassium chloride." But Waddill decided to strangle the child, according to Cornelsen's later testimony: "I saw him put his hand on this baby's neck and push down. He said, 'I can't find the trachea' and 'This baby won't stop breathing.' Cornelsen made no physical attempt to stop what he thought was murder: "I was frightened. I was scared. I couldn't believe that this was happening."[66]

Five days later Cornelsen went to the police. He told the jury during the trial that his conscience was troubling him, and that he could not sleep at night. Police had Cornelsen telephone Waddill while investigators taped the call. According to trial records, Waddill told Cornelsen, "I think I did a very bad thing," but "If you and I tell the same story everything will be OK. . . . You and I must stand together in this thing because if the truth gets out, they'll kick my ass."[67]

The Orange County coroner's office carried out an autopsy on the dead child and returned a finding of manual strangulation. Cornelsen went on to testify that he saw Waddill choke the baby girl at least four times. Waddill himself said at the trial that "he never heard a heartbeat and never considered the baby to be alive."[68] In the Edelin case lawyers and witnesses argued about whether an unborn child had been born alive; here there was no argument, because Waddill's lawyers, after some initial hesitation, accepted the infant as a live birth, and even referred to her as a baby or infant. They argued, however, that there was no proof that strangulation caused the death of the unwanted survivor of abortion; she would have died anyway, they said, and there was no reason to work hard to prevent that, because the child was unwanted. The Los Angeles *Times* quoted Waddill defense attorney Malbour Watson as saying that Waddill was innocent because *Roe v. Wade* allows "legalized murder."[69]

Evidently, some jurors agreed with the defense, for the Waddill case ended up with a hung jury. Confusion about what constituted "brain death" may also have contributed to the jury non-decision, and Los Angeles prosecutors gave up."[70] They could do so because the case received very little press coverage; the 1978 Los Angeles *Times* index, for example, lists only one story on the trial.

The cases kept coming after that, but once again, the press seemed uninterested. Los Angeles newspapers were uninterested in 1979 when Dr. Boyd Cooper delivered a baby after an abortion at Cedars-Sinai Medical Center in Los Angeles. The baby made gasping attempts to breathe but no efforts were made to help him, and he was taken to a small utility room. Told of the continued gasping, Cooper told a nurse, "Leave the baby there—it will die." Twelve hours later, according to the testimony of nurse Laura VanArsdale, she found the baby still gasping in the closet. Cooper reluctantly agreed to have the baby boy transferred to an intensive care unit, where he died 4 days later. A coroner's jury ruled the death "accidental" rather than natural but did not propose criminal charges against Cooper, and the case died.[71]

Coverage of the "dreaded complication" dwindled early in the early 1980s, even though by then some 500 to 1,000 aborted unborn children each year were having live births (1% or 2% of those survive into a normal infancy).[72] Even the small coverage such births received tended to end with a pro-abortion spin. For example, the Detroit *Free Press* ended its story on the issue with accusations that the live-birth "problem" is "an emotionally-charged distraction from the real business of protecting women's right to control their lives."[73] The Cleveland *Plain Dealer* announced in its story that the problem of live births following abortion was just a temporary one, because medical technology was improving to the point where doctors could some day "guarantee that no fetus is born alive."[74]

Chapter 14

Ideology Versus Investigation, 1978–1985

The Edelin aftermath and Waddill trial turned unborn children, even when born, into invisible creatures. But what about the safety of their mothers? Many journalists, embracing the view that illegal abortion was unsafe, assumed that legal abortion would be safe. Most newspapers seemed content not to disturb that understanding.

Occasionally, press reports of curious occurrences surfaced. In 1974 women reporters at the New York *Post* visited two abortion businesses, submitted male urine specimens for testing, and were told they were pregnant. The abortionists denied there was a problem and said that human error was the cause of it. The New York *Post* reporters did not indicate blame or shock, but just stated that tests are not dependable.[1] In 1975, similarly, the New York *Daily News* reported that many women given "abortions" were not even pregnant. The *Daily News*, noting that "Abortion today has become as versatile as Burger King," mentioned "desperate measures to cut costs and attract business,"[2] but argued against restrictions on abortion and in favor of governmental supervision to ensure efficient abortion.[3]

Journalistic efforts in most other cities were like those in New York: If there was any mention of problems in abortion businesses, they were usually described in general terms and said to be easily reparable by pro-abortion governmental control. But in 1978 the Chicago *Sun-Times*, a newspaper serious about investigative work — it would purchase and run a tavern, the Mirage, in order to expose bribe-taking building inspectors — looked deeper. On November 12, in a front-page story headlined "The Abortion Profiteers," reporters Pamela Zekman and Pamela Warrick described how "desperate women make their way to appointments at Michigan Av. abortion mills." They reported that the women, whether pregnant or not, "will be sold abortions. For the abortion profiteers, there is money to be made and no time to waste."[4]

The story was the first in a 2-week-long series that represented the fruits of 5 months of research and undercover reporting. No major metropolitan newspaper had spent such resources on an abortion expose since the New York *Times* put out its memorable "Evil of the Age" article in 1871. For the *Sun-Times*, as for the New York *Times* a century earlier, the effort paid off. Zekman and Warrick were able to give specific detail concerning sensational findings: "Dozens of abortion procedures performed on women who were not pregnant," and "an abortionist whose dog, to one couple's horror, accompanied the nurse into the operating room and lapped blood from the floor." They described "counselors who are paid not to counsel but to sell abortion with sophisticated pitches and deceptive promises."[5]

Zekman and Warrick looked at abortion advertisements, including those in the *Sun-Times* itself, and noted that "In this newspaper alone, the Water Tower clinic ran nine different ads a day, with nine different numbers and nine different names."[6] The reporters gave specific detail of attempts to sell more abortions: "An administrator told women answering phones 'We have to corral the patients'. . . . Clinic workers get $5 cash bonuses for each abortion they sell over the phone."[7] The reporters told how one of their undercover investigators "was admonished for not selling hard enough," and quoted a clinic operator saying, "no matter how you put it, we're in the business of selling abortions. Use a positive approach. It's not, '*Do* you want a termination, but *when*?' "[8] According to Zekman and Warrick, abortion business owners were selling "abortions like other hucksters sell food freezer plans or slick magazines."[9]

The article also lambasted faulty counseling procedures, noting that abortion business employees rarely provided counseling and were "under orders not to say anything to scare the women away." Reporters quoted abortionists telling employees, "Don't say that it hurts. Don't answer too many questions because the patient gets too nervous, and the next thing you know they'll be out the door.' "[10] The article described how some non-pregnant women were given abortions, and how an abortionist measured neither pulse rate nor blood pressure as he raced from one abortion to the next "without washing his hands or donning sterile gloves."[11] Overall, the November 12 article was reminiscent of 1950s-style reports of back-alley quacks involved in illegal abortion — except now, the butchery was legal.

The next day's article was hard-hitting as well. Five photos of tough-looking men paraded under a headline, "Meet the Profiteers." Three of the pictures were headshots, one was of an angry-looking man with finger pointed at the camera, and the fifth was of a man behind a half-closed door. One photo was captioned, "He sells trucks, condos, land — and abortions."

Another caption included a quotation: "I'm the most notorious physician in this city."[12]

The story itself dramatically described "the men who run the four Michigan Av. abortion mills" and "pay high rents for fancy addresses, but cut corners on patient care." Reporters told of how one abortionist was indicted for "theft by deception, for telling women they were pregnant when they weren't." The abortionist was quoted as ordering an undercover investigator to cut down on the number of cookies given weak and hungry women in the recovery room after abortions: "Cookies cost money, no more than three cookies each."[13] Detail of that sort filled four full pages of the tabloid-sized *Sun-Times* on November 13, three more on November 14, and two or more pages over the next 2 weeks. The news stories and features were backed up by an initial editorial attacking "men and women for whom the dollar is more important than medical ethics, medical knowledge or even normal human respect for other people."[14]

The series dramatically attacked deceptive practices in abortion counseling and soliciting. Zekman and Warrick described how abortionists "use every trick in the book to peddle abortions to confused and frightened women," and noted that telephone "counselors" were told not to use the word "baby" but to talk about removing "all the liquid."[15] A story beneath one front-page headline, "12 Dead after Abortions in State's Walk-in Clinics," revealed that the official information on abortion safety following legalization was inaccurate: "Although state health officials knew of not a single clinic death just a week ago, [we] have learned of a dozen women who suffered fatal infections or bled to death after undergoing abortion procedures in state-regulated clinics."[16]

The series substantiated what anti-abortionists had said for years. It was an "enormous boost" for Chicago anti-abortion forces, according to Joseph Scheidler, head of the Pro-Life Action League.[17] Leaders of two Illinois anti-abortion groups were quoted as saying, "We think the stories will help our cause."[18] Pro-abortionists, who had long considered the *Sun-Times* part of their team, were furious. A coalition of pro-abortion groups charged that the *Sun-Times* was acting irresponsibly. "We feel that the recent articles have contributed to the pre-existing climate of fear around abortion," a Chicago Women's Health Center spokeswoman said.[19] The anger increased: As soon as the first article appeared, Scheidler recalls, "the pressure on the *Sun-Times* became enormous."[20]

Sun-Times editors tried to make it clear from the start of the series that they did not share anti-abortion views, but were just reporting a story too hot to overlook. They inserted a box near the front page every day suggesting that abortion seekers should not be dissuaded, but should merely seek information from two pro-abortion groups, Planned Parenthood and the Health Evaluations Referral Service (HERS).[21] A *Sun-Times* editorial warned against "traps being set by abortion foes" who would "deny a choice on abortion" and "revive back-room abortion butcher shops."[22] The editorial warned of attempts "to frighten women out of having abortions through excessive, highly emotional and misleading warnings."[24]

That was not enough, however. As pressure increased, the *Sun-Times* editorial page began acting as the explicit public relations agent of "reputable" abortionists. A November 20 editorial argued that "Legislation being revived in the General Assembly . . . worries reliable groups like Planned Parenthood," and should be killed.[24] The *Sun-Times* continued to provide addresses, phone numbers, and other free advertising for Planned Parenthood and HERS. Ironically, abortion businesses recommended by those agencies as "safe" were also guilty of serious abuses, according to anti-abortion forces — but evidence of such abuses, given to the *Sun-Times*, was not reported.[25]

During the last week of the series, schizophrenia reigned on the news pages of the *Sun-Times*. Typically, a story in one column would be filled with evocative detail: For example, an abortion operation is stopped when the woman begins hemorrhaging, and afterwards she gives birth "to a baby girl — apparently normal except the infant is missing a piece of scalp about the size of a 50-cent piece."[26] A story in the next column would attempt to remind readers that abortion in general is a boon to humankind, and that abortion merely involves the removal of "tissue."[27] One article would show massive falsification of records at abortion businesses so that deaths and "accidents" were not reported to government agencies; the next article would state that government statistics proved legal abortion safer than pre-legalization butchery.[28] The series was a jet plane hurtling toward the runway and pulling up at the last moment.

The last few days of the series juxtaposed stories obviously produced by months of investigative journalism with puff pieces seemingly thrown together in haste. A story on November 24 was *film noir*, with a lead paragraph noting that "Not all women who go to abortion clinics are sure they want abortions. Some arrive confused and frightened, not at all sure they want to be there. Some have been dragged into clinics by relatives, others pressured into abortion by husbands or boy friends."[29] A story on November 26, however, featured a Doris Day-style portrayal of young women after the "relatively painless procedure" of abortion at a "good clinic" found in Chicago: "The patients weren't screaming. . . . Smiling nurses measured their blood pressure and fetched them punch and cookies. The recovery room looked like a slumber party."[30]

Customarily, investigative series that require months of staff time and newspaper expense build to a bang and propose specific changes. This *Sun-Times* series, however, ended with a whimper; its last two articles appeased pro-abortion forces by attacking anti-abortionists as loudmouths (for saying virtually what the *Sun-Times* itself had begun to state). The *Sun-Times* series also shied away from an examination of whether *any* abortion counseling in Chicago provided full information concerning stages of fetal development. Did the "good guy" business that provided tasty cookies show what unborn children look like at particular ages, or what they can feel and do? Women thus informed would be able to know what was being killed, should they decide to go ahead with an abortion, but the *Sun-Times* never indicated whether that type of information was available anywhere.

The *Sun-Time* series, cut off at the knees, seemed to have little long-term impact on abortion in Chicago. Even in the short run, a story on the last day of November reported that nothing much seemed to have changed: "It was business as usual at two clinics" that had been investigated.[31] Nor did the series seem to have much impact outside of Chicago. Often, when a newspaper investigation in one city finds dynamite, Pulitzer prizes result and newspapers in other cities pursue parallel stories in their own areas. Not this time, however. Other newspapers did not imitate the *Sun-Times* success even though evidence was building that abortion dangers were great not only in Chicago but throughout the country. Ideology won out over the pursuit of dramatic stories.

For the most part, following the *Sun-Times* series, other newspapers avoided hard investigative digging on abortion and instead remained pro-abortion lap dogs. Puff pieces for Planned Parenthood were common: The Cincinnati *Post*, under a headline "They work to preserve abortion rights," praised the "keen-eyed woman" who runs Planned Parenthood in Cincinnati and attacked "terribly vengeful" anti-abortionists who had "reduced their cause to a mob mentality."[32] The Philadelphia *Inquirer*, boosting Planned Parenthood spokeswoman Faye Wattleton, called her "an urbane woman" and "a woman of intellect" whose speaking abilities rivalled those of Demosthenes.[33] The Cleveland *Plain Dealer* and the (Portland) *Oregonian* were among the many newspapers to puff Nanette Falkenberg, executive direction of the National Abortion Rights Action League.[34] The Hartford *Courant* posted NARAL recruiting notices.[35]

Instead of investigating, many newspapers still emphasized Laderist anti-Catholicism. When fire destroyed several abortion clinics in Ohio, a front-page headline in the Cleveland *Plain Dealer* proclaimed, "Catholics spur violence, pro-abortionist says"; a critic of that headline asked, "If an office of the Ku Klux Klan had been firebombed, would the press have reported as an immediately plausible fact the charge of a Klan leader that the NAACP had been responsible?"[36] In New York, the *Times* ignored scientific fact and contended that anti-abortion legislation would be "in apparent violation of the First Amendment" because it would "enact . . . the Roman Catholic view that life begins at the moment of conception."[37] The National News Council[38] then censured the *Times* for "implying that Catholic

Congressmen can be expected to respond almost automatically to the abortion issue on the basis of religious pressure," and for further implying that the City Council of Akron, Ohio, was "Roman-Catholic dominated" because it passed an anti-abortion ordinance.[39]

Despite the rebuff, the *Times* continued the Lader line not just verbally but pictorially as well. For example, its brief article on a January, 1979, anti-abortion march in which 60,000 persons took part was accompanied by a photograph of a nun carrying a "Right to Life" banner."[40] Other newspapers also received heated criticism from anti-abortionists for ignoring or playing down massive marches during the late 1970s, and some journalists agreed there was reason for concern. "No matter where you stand on the issue," Washington *Star* ombudsman George Beveridge acknowledged, a turnout of 60,000 "was news of broad general interest. Its treatment in the *Star*, unfortunately, invited the perception of a kiss-off."[41]

Instead of examining the typical, newspapers tended to highlight very unusual abortion cases. For example, the Detroit *Free Press* had massive coverage of a raped 11-year-old and a pregnant 13-year-old, without mentioning how unusual these situations were.[42] A Providence *Journal* article began by citing some abortion cases: "There was the 11-year-old victim of incest. There was the mother in her 40s who lacked the strength to raise a fifth child. There was the wife who discovered that her infant would be born deformed. . . . There was the woman who was raped by her brother-in-law."[43]

Traditionally, man-bites-dog stories such as these receive more attention than dog-bites-man — but what if 16,500 dogs are on the loose? A gripping story that received only minor attention was one of not a handful but 16,500 unborn child corpses found in a California dumpster.[44] That story began when the owner of a pathology lab in Los Angeles failed to make payments on a huge container in which he stored the remains of aborted unborn children. Owners of the container repossessed the container and workers sent to empty it discovered the bodies inside.

The Los Angeles *Times* buried the story on an inside page: "Investigators meticulously sorted through the contents of a shipping container holding 16,500 human fetuses Saturday to determine where they came from and whether any criminal violations were involved in their disposal."[45] The issue, for the *Times*, was whether any illegal abortions had taken place: "At least some of the fetuses — packed in formaldehyde-filled jars stuffed into boxes stacked eight feet high inside the container — may have been the products of illegal abortions."[46]

The story continued to play small, particularly because illegality could not be proven. Anti-abortion forces who tried to attract attention by photographing some of the corpses came under press attack; under a headline, "Release of Aborted-Fetus Photos May Be Illegal," the Los Angeles *Herald-*

Examiner cited "section 129 of the California Code of Civil Procedure, which prohibits photographs of autopsy victims except in court of law or for the education of forensic pathologists."[47] One of the truck drivers who repossessed the corpse-filled container, Hank Stolk, commented about the coverage: "They got all bent out of shape, saying there weren't supposed to be no pictures of dead people or murder victims. We kept trying to get the reporters to talk about something else — about the abortions and these babies that were killed. But they wouldn't listen or ask any questions about *that*."[48]

Press burying in 1982 and 1983 of the story of 16,500 abortion corpses contrasts with massive coverage of the bombing in 1983 and 1984 of some abortion businesses. Although illegal actions that lead to physical destruction clearly deserve sizeable coverage, the journalistic tradition is to devote more ink to death — and no one died in the abortion bombings. One reason for the departure from normal procedure may have been revealed in a survey that received considerable attention during the 1980s: Lichter and Rothman found that 90% of journalists surveyed at the most influential media outlets approved of unrestricted abortion.[49] But surveys were secondary means of showing which way the wind was blowing: The actual content of some abortion-related stories, and the absence of others, best shows the tilt.

For example, when both armies in the abortion war tried publicity offensives in 1985, differential coverage indicated the tilt. Anti-abortionists promoted *The Silent Scream*, a film developed by former abortionist Bernard Nathanson that examined the nature of fetal pain during abortion. The Philadelphia *Inquirer*, under the headline "A weapon for the foes of abortion," suggested that the film should be treated as propaganda.[50] The attack on the film included statements from the National Organization for Women and NARAL, but the key blow was struck by the reporter's citing of a Yale professor — "a "leading expert in neuroembryology" — who closed the argument by saying Nathanson's position is "not scientific."[51] Experts who believed otherwise were not quoted.

The Baltimore *Sun*'s debunking of the film was cruder. Five paragraphs of its story quoting Nathanson were followed by 32 paragraphs of sharp attack on the film. The article emphasized the views of three Baltimore doctors "who were shown the film by *The Sun*."[52] The three doctors were introduced in the story as supposedly neutral experts, but one was a board member of Planned Parenthood, the second was a part-time abortionist, and the third suggested that calling a newly conceived human a person is like calling "a pile of bricks a house."[53]

Despite press bias, *Silent Scream* was not choked off. Promoters of the film relied on sympathetic political leaders and the networking of anti-abortion groups. Newspapers, by reporting the controversy, informed more people of the existence of the film, and many of those who saw all or part of *Silent Scream* gained a heightened awareness of the issue.

Still, it is worth noting that the pro-abortion publicity offensive, "Silent No More" — a campaign to have women who had undergone abortions and were proud of themselves to come forward — received supportive treatment from the same two newspapers, and many others. The Philadelphia *Inquirer* declared that the women participating in the publicity campaign were courageous: "As difficult as it is for some women to forfeit their privacy, many volunteers are coming forward."[54] Thirty-one of the 36 paragraphs in the story were devoted to a defense of abortion. The Baltimore *Sun*, which had also slammed Nathanson's film, ran a story with 14 paragraphs of evocative specific detail about the pro-abortion campaign: "Anne Cross was a college senior when she got pregnant, 16 years ago," and then had a "difficult and degrading" experience in obtaining an abortion.[55] The Baltimore *Sun* "balanced" its coverage with one bland paragraph: "A group of representatives from the right to life movement held a news conference about the evils and dangers of abortion."[56]

Other major newspapers showed similar bias.[57] The Minneapolis *Star and Tribune* devoted 30 of the 32 paragraphs in its story to public relations material from two pro-abortion organizations and to "five Minnesota women [who] told painfully private stories in public."[58] The (Portland) *Oregonian* emphasized the NARAL position that "Over and over again, women who've had illegal abortions say they would have had them even if they had to go to a butcher. That's what will happen if abortion is [once again] illegal. Women will start dying again."[59] The final paragraph of the Portland story was even more like a press release: "Women may send letters, signed or anonymous (but with ZIP codes to ensure their getting to the proper Congressional representative) to Oregon NARAL, P.O. Box 4047, Portland 97240. Deadline is May 19."[60]

While newspapers were printing such press releases, the silence about life and death inside abortion businesses continued. Apparently, only the Miami *Herald* during the 1980s made an effort to break that silence; in 1983, beneath a headline "Fourth women dies after abortion at Miami clinic," the *Herald* told of the second fatality in 17 days at a Miami abortion business, the "Women's Care Center."[61] The *Herald* investigated and found that "one former clinic doctor . . . was legally blind in one eye" and "high on Quaaludes."[62] According to the *Herald*, the "Women's Care Center" was "a high-volume abortion mill where patients were left lying on the floor, doctors operated in blood-spattered clothes and basic medical rules were ignored."[63]

The *Herald* reported court documents' depiction of the center as "a place where unlicensed physicians performed 'innumerable' abortions without bothering to test for pregnancy, use sterilized instruments or wear surgical gloves."[64] The *Herald* reported that "one woman said she was injected with Valium while strapped to an operating table even after she changed her mind about having an abortion. The abortion continued."[65] Other conditions described in the article were reminiscent of those revealed in stories about back-alley butchers earlier in the century: A "doctor" with bloody clothes performing abortions, an unconscious woman left on the floor, then slapped in the face and told to get up, and women told they were pregnant when they were not.[66]

The Miami *Herald* emphasized the importance of advertising by such abortionists. The lead on one of its stories read, "The ads in the Yellow Pages are full of reassurance. 'Pregnant? We Care,' reads one. 'You are entitled to tender and compassionate care,' reads another."[67] Virtually every major newspaper ran such advertising from 1973 through the 1980s. Some ads asked questions ("WORRIED ABOUT BEING PREGNANT?"[68]) and some declared outright that their goal was "ABORTION."[69] Many ads used euphemisms such as "PREGNANCY TERMINATION" and others, designed to stop reproduction, gave themselves names such as the "CENTER FOR REPRODUCTIVE HEALTH."[70] Advertising was building abortion businesses again, as in the mid-19th century, and almost every major newspaper looked the other way.

One difference between the 19th century abortion campaign and its 20th century equivalent, however, is that abortionists did not have to buy space to make their ideological arguments: Latter-day journalists made them for free. A few enterprising reporters still played by the traditional journalistic rules: Do not manufacture news, but if you see a story, report it. For most, however, the desire to tell a story (and sell some newspapers at the same time) that led to the remarkable *Sun-Times* series was suppressed. The ideological commitment to abortion that reduced the impact of that series was triumphant. Many good stories were missed as ideology overran reporting, and many non-stories received front-page play.

Chapter 15

A Lap Dog for the Abortion Lobby

The grim articles of the Chicago *Sun-Times* series clearly showed that many women were pressured into abortions by parents or boyfriends, or by their own emotional need to act hastily — as if an abortion could be the end of thought about what might have been. In an age that made a hit out of a song with the lyrics "I am woman — I am strong — I am invincible," the admission of need often was suppressed; those who spoke of emotional scars often were called "sexist."

On one side sat an ideology of toughness, and on the other remained that *Sun-Times'* depiction of "an 18-year-old who wanted an abortion because her father, mother, and boy friend wanted her to have one. Did she want an abortion? She really didn't know."[1] The *Sun-Times* had described how an undercover investigator was reprimanded for asking a tearful and obviously troubled patient if she was sure she wanted an abortion: 'Don't ever ask them if they're sure, because they wouldn't be here if they didn't want it. We aren't supposed to ask them if they're sure."[2] The *Sun-Times* had quoted complaints: "I wasn't counseled at all. The nurse just took my name down and filled out the application. She gave a quick explanation of the procedure, but that's not counseling. I wasn't sure I wanted an abortion. I really wanted to talk to somebody about it."[3]

During the late 1960s and early 1970s, pro-abortion groups working to shake the societal consensus emphasized "counseling" for women in crisis.[4] After *Roe v. Wade*, however, those same groups minimized the importance of counseling and sometimes even opposed it; the New Haven *Register* quoted one pro-abortionist attack on counseling because "it often contributes to a feeling that there is something peculiar about a woman who seeks an abortion."[5] The New York *Post* reported the firing of counselors by abortionists, and quoted a statement by Alfred Moran, public relations head of Planned Parenthood of New York City, that "these patients have made a decision to get an abortion, and they must go through with it themselves. Besides, there is a nurse and doctor in the room who can provide all the support that's necessary."[6] Support for abortion did not mix well with questioning of it.

In the mid-1980s, however, counseling became an issue again. Hundreds of local anti-abortion groups began to provide counseling designed to foster what they saw as informed choice rather than pressured choice. The groups set up offices with names such as "crisis pregnancy center" or "pregnancy resource center" and began counseling women on fetal development, abortion consequences, abortion alternatives, and available social services. The anti-abortion hope, of course, was that some pregnant women who received such free counseling would decide not to have abortions.

That there was a need for such centers seemed apparent from a national survey conducted by David C. Reardon; he found that 91% of women who had abortions felt that their counselors and doctors failed to help them explore their decisions. Half of the women, according to Reardon's figures, said they were still hoping for an alternative even when approaching an abortion business.[7] The new alternative to abortion businesses grew rapidly during 1984 and 1985. By 1986, 3,000 such centers were said to exist in the United States.[8] These centers typically were small, with one low-paid director, volunteer counselors, and no public relations expertise. Most funds were raised from individual donors. The typical center received no government, corporate, or foundation support, and only small amounts from churches.[9]

The new anti-abortion strategy seemed to be working in two ways early in 1985. First, thousands of women who had been undecided or leaning toward abortion were deciding not to have abortions.[10] Second, some counseling centers received favorable publicity in small local newspapers for their "helpful" contribution to the process of developing "informed choice" on abortion.[11] One center director commented that by the end of 1985 her organization had "established credibility in the community as a very caring, responsible, helpful ministry."[12]

Pro-abortion organizations responded initially to the new challenge with open protests such as picketing. That produced some publicity but often seemed to rouse the anti-abortion side to greater efforts. At the end of 1985 the director of one counseling center said she looked forward to 1986 because she had heard that Planned Parenthood members were planning to picket her center; she planned to "take advantage of the free publicity."[13] Another director questioned at the end of 1985 said, "We're just helping pregnant women make an informed choice. The abortionists don't like it, but I don't think they're going to find an effective way to mount a big campaign against us."[14]

Public relations professionals hired by Planned Parenthood and other pro-abortion organizations found that "effective way," however. They initially charged 140 of the 3,000 counseling centers (those connected to the Pearson Institute, a St. Louis nonprofit organization) with "deception," and then widened their assault to include all the counseling centers, the vast majority of which had advertising and counseling policies very different from those of Pearson. The public relations professionals succeeded in placing stories filled with disinformation in *USA Today*, the New York *Times*, the Detroit *Free Press*, the (Portland) *Oregonian*, and many other newspapers throughout the United States, along with women's magazines such as *Vogue*, *Glamour*, *Self* and *Cosmopolitan*, and many television stations.[15]

The stories were rooted in examination of a controversial technique. According to Pearson Institute director Michael Byers, a woman who plans to "kill her unborn child" is like a Nazi during World War II knocking on a door and asking if there are any Jews inside: "We don't want to help her do evil."[16] Pearson affiliates were taught to be aggressive in attracting women planning abortion; for example, receptionists at Pearson affiliates were taught to insinuate over the telephone that they performed abortions. The receptionists were told to practice "mental reservation, which means that they were not to lie outright when asked about the availability of abortion at their center, but were to talk around the subject and mislead the caller so she would come for counseling. Byers said, "In the use of the telephone we do everything we can to get her into a center."[17]

Anti-abortion leaders from other groups said in interviews that they generally agreed with the Pearson end but disagreed with the means. The majority of counseling centers offered free pregnancy tests to draw clients, as many abortion businesses do, but they told callers that they do not perform abortions. Centers affiliated with larger anti-abortion organizations such as the Christian Action Council were encouraged to emphasize, in the words of one director, "the Christian duty of telling the truth." Interviews show that in order to obey one commandment against killing (with the implication that Christians should attempt to save the lives of others), anti-abortion volunteers generally were unwilling to engage in deception.[18]

Pro-abortion public relations workers lumped all anti-abortion counseling centers with Pearson and began working the press step by step. For example, Planned Parenthood/New York City public relations staffer Amy Sutnick began by handing her accusations to a pro-abortion reporter at the New York *Daily News*. The *Daily News* story, published in January, 1986, was written along the lines of one of Sutnick's press releases, even to the extent of sometimes using the same words ("plush" in a sentence describing the counseling center).[19] Sutnick then used that article to get the attention of other media outlets. With the *Daily News* article, her press kit, and telephone calls to pro-choice journalists, she soon had stories hitting the "deception angle" on virtually every New York television station, including the local network affiliates, and in many other New York newspapers.[20]

Sutnick then sent the *Daily News* article and her other materials to Planned Parenthood officials throughout the United States, so that many would contact allies on local newspapers and develop with them a regional version of the story. Sutnick also sent out "pitch letters" to women's magazines and spent considerable time on the telephone. As an example of her work, Sutnick pointed to a July, 1987 *USA Today* article. "I thought they'd be interested," she said, "so I called a reporter I had worked with once before. I had a sense she'd be sympathetic. I told her the story and she flew up the next day."[21]

Other pro-abortion public relations professionals also worked hard. Fredrica "Freddie" Hodges, executive director of the Religious Coalition for Abortion Rights (RCAR),[22] hosted a "bogus clinic" press conference in Washington on January 22, 1986. The press conference received extensive coverage and led to articles in *Vogue* and other publications. At the press conference William Schulz, president of the Unitarian Universalist Association, called counseling centers "a new and insidious stage" of the anti-abortion movement: "Like spiders, they lure their victims into their webs and then apply psychological terror."[23] The expressions "bogus clinics" and "lure" soon became standard in media coverage of the counseling centers. Hodges said local affiliates of RCAR were encouraged to attack counseling centers in their own cities, or, preferably "get reporters to go undercover to expose them."[24]

The National Abortion Federation (NAF), a trade association for abortion businesses, also made use of journalistic collaborators. According to the association's executive director, Barbara Radford, NAF tried several tactics, but "what worked best was to find someone in the local media who was interested, put them on to it, let them do the work."[25] Almost all reporters were sympathetic to her work, in Radford's experience: "You don't come right out and ask them if they are [pro-abortion]," she said, "but you get a sense that you can work with them."

Development of the "deception" article that probably had the greatest impact, the one in *USA Today*, showed the relationship of journalists and pro-abortion public relations professionals such as Sutnick. Marlene Perrin, author of the article, was regularly a reporter on the Gannett chain's *Iowa Press Citizen* in Iowa City, but during the summer of 1986 she was on loan to *USA Today* in Washington.[26] Sutnick and Perrin had talked when Perrin wrote a story on birth control, and Sutnick thought that Perrin would be useful on the counseling center story."[27] According to Perrin, "I didn't get a chance to do much with big stories that summer. The good stuff went to the regular staff . . . Amy called and said, 'Would you be interested?' "[28]

Sutnick handed Perrin the story; in Perrin's words,

> I went to New York to pick up materials from Amy. . . .I didn't get to talk to any of those fake abortion people. I got a lot of help from the Religious Coalition. . . . I couldn't get to the fake clinics, but I talked to clients who had been there. . . . The Planned Parenthood people were very helpful in providing them for me. . . . Amy had a lot of materials, like the Pearson manual.[29]

The July 23, 1986, *USA Today* story written by Perrin based on that research, "Anti-abortionists masquerade as clinics," could hardly have been better from the pro-abortion standpoint.[30] The article led off with a story of a woman who did not like the counseling she received at a center affiliated with the Christian Action Council; this client was provided by Sutnick. One-fourth of the story was direct quotation and paraphrase from Sutnick, who described her visit to two Manhattan counseling centers, where she was "overwhelmed by the brainwashing techniques and the lies."[31]

The *USA Today* story was typical of the genre. Rarely did reporters themselves go undercover into counseling centers; more often, they relied on reports provided by members of the National Organization of Women and employees of Planned Parenthood or abortion businesses. Journalists used as sources "dissatisfied clients" of the centers, sources frequently supplied to the reporter by pro-abortion groups. When the sources, as if on cue, attacked "misleading, emotionally disturbing" counseling, reporters accepted their accounts without challenge.[32] Newspapers such as the Detroit *Free Press* cited heads of pro-abortion and abortion trade organizations as expert authorities on the centers, and did not allow center representatives the opportunity to respond to charges.[33] Stories suggested that virtually *all* counseling centers, not just the 5% associated with the Pearson Institute, were "deceptive." A *Newsday* headline read, "Deception: It's No Way of Life/But right-to-lifers use it."[34]

A few exceptions to press pro-abortionism did emerge. The Milwaukee *Journal*, instead of merely accepting the offerings of pro-abortion public relations, sent undercover reporters to both counseling centers and abortion businesses, and then described in measured tones what the various groups offered.[35] A few newspapers quoted statements by counseling center representatives that their organizations were being criticized precisely because they were successful in meeting the needs of many women, and were thus cutting into the business of some abortionists and the power of some pro-abortion forces.[36] But the leads on even those articles that tried to bring in a bit of "balance" emphasized the deception angle. Not a single major newspaper ran a story that asked, "Who is behind the campaign to smear the counseling centers?"

A REFUSAL TO LOOK CLOSELY

Columnist Jack Anderson once complained that too many reporters were like lap dogs, writing stories that pleased those in power. This was certainly true about abortion coverage in the 1980s, with many reporters sitting in the laps of abortion high priests. Those who wanted to upset the abortion status quo were viewed as troublemakers; a Chicago *Sun-Times* reporter, Lynda Gorov, criticized Chicago anti-abortionists for demonstrating in front of an abortion business holding corpses of unborn children that the demonstrators had picked out of trash cans at the back of the business. "Sometimes concern about a problem takes an even uglier form than the problem," Gorov wrote.[37] "No one ever said abortion was pretty," she added, and quoted a spokesman for the abortion business saying, "What's horrifying is that those people broke into [trash bins] and stole private materials and invaded these women's privacy."[38]

Press coverage of that incident exemplified the problems anti-abortion groups faced when they offered vivid materials and statements to the press. Joseph Scheidler, executive director of the Pro-Life Action League, told reporters that "One little girl has her arm torn off at the shoulder, and the shoulder blade is still attached to it. They clipped the toes off of her left foot."[39] But the Associated Press would only quote him as criticizing, with much less vividness, "the abortion holocaust that is going on all over America today."[40] Monica Migliorino, director of Citizens for Life of Milwaukee, commented that "abortionists consistently refer to aborted babies as products of conception, blobs of blood and uterine scrapings. But these are little unborn children with arms, legs, heads and spinal columns."[41] Those comments were not quoted; instead, Gorov reported her uneasy feelings when confronted by the corpses. "Look closely, [an anti-abortionist] urged. Go ahead, look real close [sic]. I couldn't."[42]

In general, reporters would not "look close," and they played down stories and language that would help readers do their own looking. It was not surprising, given the overwhelmingly pro-abortion sentiment registered in the Lichter—Rothman survey, that coverage in the 1980s was biased.[43] Yet, some academic observers, even when acknowledging the import of such surveys, asked "so what?"—as if beliefs of reporters had no importance in the face of general codes of ethics concerning "objectivity."[44] *If one thing is clear from the history of press coverage of abortion, it is that journalists' beliefs, whether for or against abortion, do heavily influence coverage.*

Many reporters, trained to proclaim that they were "objective," did not want to deal with the influence of world views. In 1988, as in 1973, some journalists wrote of "consensus" on abortion even though there clearly was no peace; a New York *Times* headline claimed that "Broad Public Support for Right to Abortion Remains Undiminished."[45] The lead suggested "broad public support for preserving the right of women to obtain abortions," and gave as proof a survey commissioned by the National Abortion Rights Action League. Even material from this hardly-unbiased source, however, showed an interesting element not mentioned until the sixth paragraph of the story:

> Only a minority of the public, 39 percent, supported a right to abortion "for any woman who wants one," which is essentially the current state of the law, while 49% limited their support to particular circumstances such as a pregnancy that seriously endangered a woman's health.

Because 10% of those surveyed opposing abortion under any conditions, even this NARAL-sponsored poll showed 59% of Americans still opposed to the *Roe v. Wade* decision 15 years after its proclamation. With time tending to heal not only wounds but fights over Supreme Court decisions, it is remarkable, and unprecedented in American history,[46] that a decision, particularly one with so much media support, remains so unacceptable. But the New York *Times* chose not to remark on that.

FETAL TRANSPLANTS

In 1988 issues were emerging that would once again give reporters the chance either to "look real close," or to turn away. Fetal tissue transplants — using the brain tissues of an aborted unborn child to cure Alzheimer's and Parkinson's diseases or other neural disorders — received generally positive front-page treatment around the country. The technological advance signified a new economic development, however; because the most useful brain tissues could be taken only later in pregnancy, when the unborn child was more mature, the procedure would make abortions after the first trimester very economically profitable. Abortionists, who increasingly try to cut up the more mature unborn child in the womb in order to avoid live births, would be more likely to deliver him or her whole, so that the organs could be carefully removed. New Edelin or Waddill cases, this time involving almost-deliberate rather than inadvertent live births, seemed inevitable.

   With the exception of a few conservative columnists, however, the press seemed "open" to the new opportunity — and placid.[47] The likely comeback in 1988 of abortifacients — seemingly ready to emerge in quantities not seen since the 19th century — also brought slanted coverage; the Austin *American-*

Statesman headlined one story, "Abortion drugs heralded/Substances called safe, effective, easily distributed."[48] The accompanying article praised development of a "drug-induced, non-surgical abortion procedure . . . producing a 95 percent success rate with few side effects."[49] The unborn child was a non-person again, and the anti-abortion position was not mentioned until the 15th paragraph of a 15-paragraph story.

In 1988, overall, what John Noonan wrote a decade earlier concerning press bias was still largely accurate:

> If one were to enumerate all the anti-abortion testimony before Congress and the state legislatures which, as a consequence, went unreported to the public at large, one could compile an enormous dossier. If one were to tell of all the large anti-abortion rallies that, as a consequence, went unnoticed by television cameras or newspaper photographers, one could make a list as large. If one were to catalogue the number of anti-abortion articles rejected, the number of anti-abortion books unreviewed, the number of anti-abortion stories untold, the number of anti-abortion opinions unrecorded by the press, one could compose what would itself be a book. Buoyed by the currents of the time and creating those currents, self-confident and safe from challenge, the American press swept aside almost all signs that abortion as a liberty was unwelcome to the majority of Americans.[50]

And yet, even in the offices of the large publications, editors and reporters were not sovereign over their own consciences; qualms could deepen into questions about basic policy. For example, the Milwaukee *Journal* news pages did not entirely accept pro-abortionist attacks on crisis pregnancy centers; perhaps its caution was due to a debate among its top editors. That debate was reflected on its editorial page in 1985 under the headline "Abortion: A Re-evaluation":

> Any dynamic organization must from time to time re-examine past practices and traditional viewpoints to determine whether they fit current circumstances. We have done that with regard to The Journal's long-standing editorial views on the volatile subject of abortion — and found a need for some modification.
>
> Consequently, The Journal's clear pro-choice viewpoint on abortion has softened in recent years, and has hardly been expressed at all in the past two years. Now, after several months of careful re-evaluation, we find ourselves perhaps more strongly divided by individual views on abortion than on any other issue. Collectively, we fit into neither the pro-choice nor pro-life mold.[51]

The *Journal* proceeded to take a half-way position, supporting abortion to save a mother's health or in cases of rape, incest, or "birth defects serious enough to blight a child's life." It stated that the birth defect option "needed careful definition," and that abortion should also be allowed to preserve a mother's mental health "if certain standards, which we do not here presume to suggest, are met in judging mental-health risk." Pro-abortionists were dissatisfied that the *Journal* did not view abortion as "a woman's right," and anti-abortionists pointed out, among other objections, that a "mental health" clause provided a tank-sized opening to virtually unlimited abortion — yet, in an era of lap dog newspapers, the Milwaukee *Journal's* willingness to reconsider indicated that a more independent press could be a possibility.

The press, after all, has gone through many shifts in its relationship to abortion over the years. Madame Restell used the press to promote abortion, but the New York *Times* and the *National Police Gazette* helped to turn the tide. When those two newspapers dropped out of the war, others stepped in. As many newspapers were squeamish, uncaring, or lazy in their coverage of abortion early in the 20th century, pro-abortion forces began to regroup. Campaigns such as that of Amen in New York raised consciousness, but the gradualist approach of pro-abortion public relations encouraged a surrender through legalization to the problem of illegal abortion. Newspapers were key weapons in the pro-abortion drive before *Roe v. Wade* and key participants in the drive to smooth things over afterwards.

Overall, journalists frequently have demonstrated a cozy relation to power and a tendency to ignore the weak and helpless, particularly the most helpless — unborn children. This unattractive behavior has been particularly evident in the recent journalistic tendency to miss big stories, such as deaths at abortion businesses, and manufacture ones that fit ideological needs, such as the attack on crisis pregnancy centers.[52] The Springfield *Republican* editorial of a century ago is as applicable now as then: Concerning abortion, newspapers should "bear an honest testimony in the matter — without fear, favor, malice, or hope of reward."

The history of abortion and the press also suggests that the press helps to set public agendas and often grants legitimacy to various groups. At the same time, however, it is evident that wielders of ideas and power, including intellectuals and public relations men and women, set agendas for the press, which responds as frequently as it initiates. For example, reporters *were* setting the agenda in the 1960s, but they were responding to the strategies of masters of abortion public relations. In another sense, when *Time* in 1967 proposed that abortion be dealt with "not by moral absolutes toward unwanted pregnancy but by moral concern for each concrete situation,"[53] it *was* setting the agenda, but it was also repeating what situational ethicists had been saying for years.

The road to pro-abortion dominance became open early in the 20th century, as pro-abortionists laid the groundwork, anti-abortionists slept, and a cloud as small as a man's hand rose from the sea. The abortion power that has revealed itself is not easy to combat. Yet, in the long history of press response to abortion, editorial debate in a newspaper like the Milwaukee *Journal*'s illuminates once again a recurring theme: When there is life, there is hope.

Notes

INTRODUCTION

1. The most useful works are James Mohr, *Abortion in America* (New York: Oxford University Press, 1978); Germain Grisez, *Abortion: The Myths, the Realities and the Arguments* (New York: Corpus Books, 1970); and Joseph Dellapenna, "The History of Abortion: Technology, Morality, and Law," *University of Pittsburgh Law Review* 40 (1979), pp. 359+.

2. The gap may be due to lack of convenience: Until the 1970s only the New York *Times* was indexed consistently, and cranking microfilm in search of occasional stories wearies eyes and soul.

3. Westchester, IL: Crossway Books, 1988.

4. See chapters 3 and 4.

5. Except in those circumstances (extremely rare today) when the life of the mother is in imminent danger.

6. In addition, pro-lifers are not always pro-life: Most would shoot back at those invading their home or country, execute those who have murdered others, and kill animals when useful or necessary. The term *pro-choice* also grabs high ground but also embraces far too much: Most pro-choicers do not believe that rapists or thieves should not be punished, just because such criminals have consciously chosen to commit a particular crime.

7. "Politics and the English Language," *The Orwell Reader* (New York: Harcourt Brace and World, 1956) p. 363.

8. Ibid.

9. One exception: The term *fetal deformity* is used when other constructions would be awkward.

CHAPTER 1
MADAME RESTELL BUILDS A BUSINESS

1. Benjamin Wadsworth, *The Well-Ordered Family* (Boston, 1712), p. 45, quoted in John T. Noonan, Jr., *A Private Choice: Abortion in America in the Seventies* (New York: The Free Press, 1979), pp. 59–60. Wadsworth was president of Harvard College from 1725 through 1737.

2. Quoted in Dennis J. Horan and Thomas J. Marzen, "Abortion and Midwifery: A Footnote in Legal History," in Thomas W. Hilgers, Dennis J. Horan, and David Mall, *New Perspectives on Human Abortion* (Frederick, MD: University Publications of America, 1981), p. 199. The law was passed by the Common Council of New York City on July 27, 1716.

3. *An Essay on the Decalogue or Ten Commandments* (Boston, 1719), p. 89, quoted in Noonan, op. cit.

4. Many books and articles have examined Biblical views of abortion; three of the most useful are John J. Davis, *Abortion and the Christian* (Philadelphia: Presbyterian and Reformed, 1984); Harold O.J. Brown, "What the Supreme Court Didn't Know," *Human Life Review*, Spring, 1975, pp. 5–21; and John Warwick Montgomery, "The Fetus and Personhood," *Human Life Review*, Spring, 1975, pp. 41–49.

5. Lindsay Dewar, *An Outline of Anglican Moral Theology* (London: A. W. Mowbrey, 1968), p. 85; George Hunston Williams, "Religious Residues and Presuppositions in the American Debate on Abortion," *Theological Studies* 31 (1970), pp. 43–46; Noonan, p. 59.

6. *Calvin's Commentaries* (Grand Rapids, MI: Baker Book House, 1981), vol. 3, p. 42; translated from original Latin by Rev. Charles W. Bingham. Calvin added, "If it seems more horrible to kill a man in his own house than in a field, because a man's house is his place of most secure refuge, it ought surely to be deemed more atrocious to destroy an unborn child [Latin:foetus] in the womb before it has come to light."

7. See Dellapenna and Grisez, op. cit.

8. Mohr, op. cit., pp. 3–19.

9. During the 1820s, when a Christian newspaper such as the Boston *Recorder* was attacking all kinds of sins, it not once mentioned abortion as a problem. It is unlikely that the editors, forthright in so many other ways, would have covered up the abortion problem had it been a major one.

10. Alexis de Tocqueville, *Democracy in America* (New York: Knopf, 1945), vol. 1, pp. 314, 316 [orig. publication in 1835].

11. E. S. Turner, *The Shocking History of Advertising* (New York: E. P. Dutton, 1953), p. 135. The Boston *Daily Times*, put the new doctrine most precisely in 1837: "It is sufficient for our purpose that the advertisements are paid for. . . . One man has as good a right as another to have his wares, his goods, his panaceas, his profession, published to the world in a newspaper, provided he pays for it." [*Daily Times* quotation in Michael Schudson, *Discovering the News* (New York: Basic Books, 1978), p. 18.]

12. Frederic Hudson, *Journalism in the United States* (New York: Harper and Brothers, 1872), p. 286.

13. New York *Herald*, March 6, 1840, p. 1; April 13, 1840, p. 8; August 26, 1841, p. 3; February 15, 1842, p. 4; September 22, 1843, p. 4; January 17, 1845, p. 4.

14. Ibid.

15. Ibid.

16. Ibid.

17. The efficacy of any of these abortifacients is still in dispute, but apparently they did work on occasion. The *Journal of the American Medical Association* noted in 1909, "no medicine can be said to be sure to produce a miscarriage . . . nothing but mechanical means can be so relied on; but . . . many kinds of medicine may and do produce miscarriage." [*Journal of the American Medical Association*, vol. 52, no. 11 (September 11, 1909), p. 891.]

18. New York *Sun*, Sept. 27, 1840.

19. Ibid.

20. This would be particularly true in that pregnancy was sometimes a fearful occurrence in pre-20th century America; see Judith Walzer Leavitt, *Brought to Bed: Childbearing in America, 1750 to 1950* (New York: Oxford University Press, 1986).

21. New York *Sun*, May 9, 1839, p. 4.

22. Ibid., May 18, 1839, p. 4; June 12, 1839, p. 4; Aug. 17, 1839, p. 4; Sept. 11, 1839, p. 4.

23. Ibid., Dec. 11, 1839, p. 4. Also see New York *Herald*, March 6, 1840, p. 1; Aug. 26, 1841, p. 3; Sept. 22, 1843, p. 4; Jan. 25, 1844, p. 4; April 13, 1844, p. 4; Aug. 2, 1844, p. 4; Oct. 8, 1844, p. 4; Nov. 21, 1844, p. 4; Jan. 11, 1845, p. 4.

24. New York *Sun*, March 27, 1839, p. 1.

25. Ely van de Warker, "The Criminal Use of Proprietary Advertised Nostrums," *New York Medical Journal*, January, 1873, pp. 23–25.

26. Ed. P. Le Prohon, *Voluntary Abortion, or Fashionable Prostitution, with Some Remarks upon the Operation of Craniotomy* (Portland, ME, 1867); quoted in Mohr, p. 55.

27. For examples, see the New York *Herald*, March 6, 1840, p. 1; August 26, 1841, p. 3; September 22, 1843, p. 4; December 13, 1843, p. 4; April 13, 1844, p. 4; January 11, 1845, p. 4; and New York *Sun*, October 21, 1841, p. 4; February 24, 1842, p. 4; August 6, 1842, p. 1.

28. New York *Herald*, July 15, 1841, p. 4; Nov. 26, 1841, p. 4; Dec. 3, 1841, p. 4; Sept. 22, 1843, p. 4; Jan. 26, 1845, p. 4.

29. The first penny paper, New York's *Sun*, first published in September, 1833, was selling 15,000 papers a day by the end of 1835. The Philadelphia *Public Ledger* began publishing in March, 1836; by the end of 1837 it was selling 20,000 copies daily, at a time when the largest of the city's established newspapers sold about 2,000. (Schudson, p. 18.)

30. New York *Sun*, June 21, 1841, p. 2. The *Sun's* response indicates that one statement made by de Tocqueville just a few years earlier already was outmoded; de Tocqueville had written that, "Hitherto no one in the United States has dared to advance the maxim that everything is permissible for the interests of society, an

impious adage which seems to have been invented in an age of freedom to shelter all future tyrants." (*Democracy in America*, op. cit., vol. 1, p. 316.)

31. New York *Tribune*, December 20, 1841, p. 4.

32. New York *Sun*, June 26, 1839, p. 1.

33. New York *Herald*, March 6, 1840, p. 1; May 20, 1840, p. 1; Frank Luther Mott, *American Journalism* (New York: Macmillan, 1950), p. 230.

34. New York *Herald*, March 6, 1840, p. 4; January 15, 1845, p. 4.

35. Ibid., December 8, 1841, p. 4.

36. Abortion ads in many cities were equivalent to today's ads for escort services or massage parlors. Their meaning was widely known, but police and prosecutors could not or would not do much about the problem.

37. New York *Herald*, January 6, 1841, p. 4.

38. Ibid., February 25, 1841, p. 4.

39. New York *Sun*, September 14, 1840, p. 4.

40. Ibid.; also January 24, 1840, p. 4.

41. New York *Herald*, August 21, 1841, p. 4, etc.

42. Ibid., February 25, 1841, p. 4; March 6, 1840, p. 4; December 15, 1840, p. 4; New York *Sun*, March 16, 1840, p. 4.

43. Some may have exaggerated, but Mohr, pp. 46–85, provides ample evidence of the upsurge.

44. "Criminal Abortions," *Boston Medical and Surgical Journal*, XXX, No. 15 (May 15, 1844), pp. 302–303.

45. Mohr, op. cit., pp. 88–89.

46. *National Police Gazette*, February 14, 1846, p. 205.

47. Le Prohon quoted in Mohr, op. cit., p. 55.

48. Having an abortion, of course, is a much more serious matter than buying an automobile, but those who spend millions of dollars on political and ideological advertising argue that commercials can sell life-or-death ideas as well as products.

49. Quoted in *National Police Gazette*, November 15, 1845, p. 100.

50. Ibid.

51. Ibid.

52. Ibid.

53. The *Gazette* began publishing on September 13, 1845, with the stated goal of exposing criminals and vice. It was scorned by "respectable" citizens and feared by both crime lords and police who did not like criticism of corruption. In 1850 a criminal-led mob assaulted the *Gazette* plant; six people died and the plant was demolished. The newspaper resumed publication shortly thereafter.

54. *National Police Gazette*, February 14, 1846, p. 205.

55. Ibid.

56. Ibid.

57. Ibid., February 21, 1846, p. 218.

58. Ibid.

59. Ibid.

60. Ibid.

61. New York *Herald*, February 24, 1846, p. 1; New York *Tribune*, February 24, 1846, p. 2; New York *Morning News*, February 24, 1846, p. 1.

62. New York *Herald*, February 24, 1846, p. 1.

63. *National Police Gazette*, April 25, 1846, p. 284.

64. Ibid., February 14, 1846, p. 205.

65. New York *Tribune*, April 2, 1878, p. 1.

66. Ibid., September 3, 1855, p. 3. "Explicit directions" would be sent with the pills, which are "in sealed envelopes, and can be sent with the strictest privacy to any part of the United States."

67. New York *Herald*, May 19, 1961, p. 7.

68. New York *Times*, November 12, 1863.

69. New York *Herald*, April 1, 1865, p. 6.

70. For more statistical information, see Jeanine Halva-Neubauer, "Political Action, Social Change and Media Content," unpublished paper in the University of Minnesota Department of Mass Communication.

71. Frank Presbry, *The History and Development of Advertising* (New York: Greenwood Press, 1968), p. 230.

72. New York advertising dominance became clear during the Civil War when the federal government imposed a 30% tax on advertising. Of the $288,000 received by the government during the last fiscal year of the tax, ending June 30, 1867, $80,000 came from New York City. That was over double the total of five other large cities—Philadelphia, Boston, Cincinnati, Chicago, and New Orleans combined. (Presbry, p. 259)

73. Quoted in Alan Keller, *Scandalous Lady* (New York: Atheneum, 1981), p. 120.

74. New York *Times*, February 12, 1878, p. 8.

75. Keller, op. cit., p. 6.

CHAPTER 2
ABORTION ADVANCES, 1840–1870

1. New York *Herald*, December 15, 1840, p. 4.

2. Ibid.

3. Ibid., July 27, 1841, p. 4; Aug. 4, 1841, p. 4; Aug. 7, 1841, p. 4; Aug. 26, 1841, p. 4.

4. Ibid., December 6, 1841, p. 4; December 8, p. 4.

5. Ibid.

6. Ibid., December 8, 1841, p. 4.

7. Ibid., Dec. 10, 1841, p. 4; Dec. 17, p. 4; Jan. 6, 1842, p. 4; Feb. 4, 1842, p. 4; Feb. 27, p. 4; March 13, p. 4.

8. Ibid., March 14, 1842, p. 4.

9. Ibid.

10. New York *Sun*, June 31, 1842, p. 4; Aug. 1, p. 4; Sept. 15, p. 4.

11. New York *Herald*, Dec. 9, 1842, p. 4; Dec. 23, p. 4; Sept. 22, 1843, p. 4; Dec. 13, 1843, p. 4; Jan. 25, 1844, p. 4; April 13, 1844, p. 4.

12. New York *Sun*, Oct. 28, 1845, p. 4; Oct. 31, p. 4.

13. New York *Tribune*, Feb. 13, 1846, p. 1; Feb. 14, p. 1; Feb. 15, p. 1; Feb. 16, p. 1; Feb. 17, p. 1.

14. *National Police Gazette*, Feb. 28, 1846, p. 220; April 25, pp. 284–285; May 2, pp. 291, 293.

15. Connecticut *Courant*, June 19, 1847, p. 2.

16. Fort Smith *Herald*, January 3, 1849, p. 2.

17. New Orleans *Daily Crescent*, July 1, 1848, p. 1.

18. Ibid., p. 4. The ad was addressed to "Mothers and Married Ladies."

19. Louisiana *Courier*, November 16, 1855, p. 1.

20. Cleveland *Plain Dealer*, October 4, 1855; quoted in Kathleen L. Endres, " 'Strictly Confidential': Birth-Control Advertising in a 19th-Century City," *Journalism Quarterly*, vol. 63, no. 4 (Winter, 1986), pp. 748–751.

21. Ibid., November 15, 1858.

22. Ibid., May 24, 1855.

23. Ibid., May 26, 1858.

24. Cincinnati *Daily Commercial*, January 31, 1858, p. 1; March 21, p. 1.

25. *Indianapolis State Sentinel*, October 16, 1858; January 1 and 4, 1859; quoted in Mohr, p. 141.

26. Ads, it should be remembered, were news in papers around the country as they were news in New York. For example, the following ad for army volunteers appeared in the New Orleans *Daily Tropic* in 1845: "WHO'S FOR MEXICO? All those who may feel disposed to make a pleasant excursion to the frontiers of Mexico (and perhaps to explore some parts of that country) will find all the means and facilities requisite by enrolling themselves in the REGIMENT LOUISIANA VOLUNTEERS, now being recruited for the above stated objects." (August 22, 1845, p. 1.)

27. *National Police Gazette*, November 15, 1845, p. 100.

28. Mohr, p. 130.

29. Ibid., p. 132.

30. *National Police Gazette*, May 2, 1846, p. 293.

31. Hugh Hodge, *Foeticide, Or Criminal Abortion* (Philadelphia: University of Pennsylvania, 1869), reprinted in *Abortion in Nineteenth Century America* (New York: Arno Press, 1974).

32. Ibid., p. 76.

33. James C. Jackson, *The Sexual Organism, and Its Healthful Management* (Boston, 1862), pp. 261–263.

34. Quoted in Mohr, op. cit., p. 175.

35. Ibid., pp. 172–173.

36. E. Frank Howe, *Sermon on Ante-Natal Infanticide* (Terre Haute, IN: Allen & Andrews, 1869). Howe, in Terre Haute, Indiana, began his sermon with an interesting discussion of why he was speaking on abortion: "It is with extreme reluctance that I touch the subject, not simply because of its delicate nature, but because I cannot doubt that an evil so wide-spread has invaded my own church and congregation." He explained that "to talk of sins lying at the doors of those addressed, when these are friends loved and trusted, this is not so easy or pleasant a task." Howe predicted that "some will be disgusted at the introduction of so delicate a subject into the pulpit," while "the guilty, if such there be, may be angry." He also knew that "those who ever cry 'Peace, peace,' will doubtfully shake their heads." Yet, Howe said he would speak, and persevere. (p. 1)

37. Ibid., p. 2.

38. Ibid.

39. One reason for the lack of abortion stories may have been squeamishness — and yet, newspapers during that era regularly reported on murder and other bloody subjects. It seems likely that some newspapers were influenced by advertising clout.

40. *National Police Gazette*, February 21, 1846, p. 216.

41. Ibid.

42. Ibid., November 15, 1845, p. 100.

43. Ibid., November 22, 1845, p. 115. See also October 11, 1845, pp. 59, 67; November 15, pp. 98, 107; December 27, 1845, pp. 150, 155, 156; February 7, 1846, p. 197; February 14, pp. 200, 205, 208.

44. Ibid., February 21, 1846, p. 212.

45. Ibid., April 25, 1846, p. 285.

46. Ibid., May 2, 1846, p. 293.

47. Ibid., October 28, 1848, p. 3.

48. Ibid., September 14, 1867, p. 1.

49. Ibid.

50. New Orleans *Courier*, July 1, 1860, p. 1.

51. San Francisco *Daily Examiner*, January 1, 1860, p. 4.

52. Ibid.

53. Ibid.

54. Chicago *Daily Tribune*, February 20, 1864, p. 3. See also January 16, 1864, p. 3, etc.

55. Ibid., January 1, 1864, p. 3.

56. Ibid., January 16, 1864, p. 3.

57. Louisville *Courier*, July 15, 1865, p. 4.

58. Cleveland *Plain Dealer*, September 15, 1862; cited in Endres.

59. Ibid., July 29, 1861.

60. Ibid.

61. San Francisco *Daily Examiner*, June 12, 1865, p. 4; April 20, 1868, p. 3.

62. Springfield *Republican*, February 12, 1869, p. 1.

63. Ibid., June 26, 1869, p. 5.

64. Missouri *Republican*, August 3, 1869, p. 7.

65. Louisville *Daily Journal*, April 27, 1867, pp. 1, 4; March 5, 1867, p. 4.

66. Ibid., July 17, 1867, p. 4.

67. Ibid., August 26, 1867, p. 4.

68. Cleveland *Plain Dealer*, January 12, 1871, quoted in Endres, op. cit., p. 750.

69. Ibid., April 30, 1870, and January 3, 1871.

70. New Orleans *Daily Times*, March 20, 1870, p. 5.

71. Ibid., January 16, 1870; see also July 8, 1870, p. 7.

72. Ibid, January 16, 1870, p. 9.

73. Ibid., One month later, Urban, Luke and Pownall were still advertising, Wardle and Graham were not. The following month, Wardle was advertising again, Urban and Pownall were continuing, but Luke was not. Luke was back in April with his note about parlors arranged to secure perfect secrecy. (Feb. 17, 1870, p. 9; April 12, 1870, p. 9)

74. New Orleans *Daily Picayune*, Nov 21, 1871, p. 5.
75. Ibid., December 25, 1849, p. 1.
76. Ibid., November 5, 1865, p. 4.
77. New Orleans *Daily Times*, March 20, 1870, p. 5.
78. New Orleans *Daily Picayune*, October 31, 1871, p. 5.
79. Ibid.
80. Ibid.
81. *National Police Gazette*, Sept 28, 1867, p. 2
82. Ibid.
83. Ibid., November 30, 1867, p. 2.

CHAPTER 3
THE NEW YORK TIMES VERSUS ABORTION

1. New York *Times*, Jan. 12, 1863, p. 5; Jan. 21, 1863, p. 3; Sept. 28, 1865, p. 5; Sept. 29, 1865, p. 8; May 5, 1867, p. 6; May 28, 1867, p. 5; Aug. 25, 1867, p. 8; Aug. 26, 1867, p. 8; Nov. 24, 1867, p. 5; Aug. 29, 1868, p. 8; Aug. 30, 1868, p. 8; Sept. 4, 1868, p. 2; Sept. 9, 1868, p. 2; March 19, 1869, p. 8; March 24, 1869, p. 11; March 25, 1869, p. 2.
2. Ibid., May 28, 1867, p. 5.
3. Ibid., August 25, 1867, p. 8.
4. Ibid., July 1, 1867, p. 1; July 3, 1868, p. 7; January 2, 1869, p. 7; etc.
5. Ibid.
6. Ibid.
7. Quoted in Mohr, p. 216.
8. See law of May 6, 1869, chapter 631, [1868] N.Y. Laws.
9. Jones also showed gumption in other ways. When the *Times* uncovered evidence that would expose the New York political machine known as the Tweed Ring, he turned down Tweed's offer of $5 million to sit on the story, and commented that "the Devil" never again would offer him so high a price. [Elmer Davis, in *History of the New York Times, 1851–1921* (New York: The New York Times Co., 1921), p. 103, discusses the Tweed Ring story.]
10. New York *Times*, November 3, 1870, p. 4.
11. Ibid., January 27, 1871, p. 3.
12. Ibid.
13. Ibid., August 23, 1871, p. 6.
14. Ibid.
15. Ibid.
16. Ibid.
17. Ibid., August 27, 1871, p. 1.
18. Ibid.
19. Ibid., Aug. 28, 1871, p. 8; Aug. 29, p. 8; Aug. 30, p. 8.
20. Ibid., August 29, 1871, p. 8.
21. Ibid., August 30, 1871, p. 4.
22. Ibid.
23. Ibid.

24. Ibid., p. 8.
25. Ibid.
26. Ibid.
27. Ibid.
28. Ibid., September 2, 1871, p. 8.
29. Ibid., September 6, 1871, p. 8.
30. Ibid., September 8, 1871, p. 8.
31. *Transactions of the American Medical Association*, vol. 22 (1871), p. 258.
32. Ibid.
33. New York *Times*, September 3, 1871, p. 8.
34. New York *Tribune*, August 30, 1871, p. 4.
35. Ibid.
36. New York *Times*, October 26, 1871, p. 2.
37. Ibid., October 30, 1871, p. 1.
38. Ibid., December 8, 1871, p. 2.
39. Ibid., December 15, 1871, p. 1.
40. Ibid.
41. Ibid., January 12, 1872, p. 4.
42. Ibid.
43. Ibid.
44. Chapter 181 [1872], N.Y. Laws.

45. San Francisco *Daily Examiner*, August 30, 1871, p. 3; see also Aug. 31, 1871, p. 3; Sept. 1, 1871, p. 3.

46. Chicago *Tribune*, August 28, 1871, p. 2; see also Aug. 29, 1871, p. 1, and Aug. 31, p. 1.

47. New Orleans *Daily Picayune*, Aug. 30, 1871, p 8.

48. Galveston *Daily News*, September 6, 1871, p. 1; see also August 30, p. 1.

49. "Advertising to produce miscarriage," *The Penal Code of the State of California* (San Francisco: Bancroft-Whitney Co, 1915), section 317. See judicial narrowing of statute in *People vs. McKean*, 243 Pac. R 898.

50. *Consolidated Laws of New York* (Brooklyn: Edward Thompson Co., 1917), Article 106, Section 1142, paragraph 318, p. 591; includes minor 1887 amendments.

51. New York *Times*, November 3, 1870, p. 4.

52. Cyril C. Means, Jr., "The Law of New York Concerning Abortion and the Status of the Foetus, 1664-1968: A Case of Cessation of Constitutionality," *New York Law Forum*, Fall, 1968, pp. 455-487.

53. Ibid.

54. Norman Dorsen, Roy Lucas, Sarah Weddington et al., "Brief for Appellants in the Supreme Court of the United States, 70-18, 1971 Term. Because there are no minutes of legislative discussion of abortion bills extant, pro-abortion lawyers emphasized the "circumstances" under which legislation was passed, but evidently did not pay attention to the press circumstances.

55. See chapter 4 for additional examples of 19th century concern for unborn children.

56. New York *Times*, August 23, 1871, p. 6.

57. Ibid., February 12, 1878, p. 8.

58. Ibid., February 14, 1878, p. 8.

59. New York *Tribune*, Feburary 15, p. 8; see also New York *Times*, February 12, 13, 14, 15, 16, 24, 28; March 2, 6, 8, 13, 30; April 2, 3, 4, 5, 1878.

60. Ibid.

61. Ibid.

62. New York *Tribune*, April 2, 1878, p. 1; New York *Times*, April 2, p. 1.

63. Ibid.

64. New York *Times*, April 2, 1878, p. 1.

CHAPTER 4
DANGER AND DOLLARS, 1878–1898

1. New York *Times*, February 12, 1879, p. 5; February 13, p. 8; February 14, p. 2; March 28, p. 3; March 29, p. 8; April 1, p. 8; April 3, p. 8; April 15, p. 3.

2. Ibid., July 2, 1879, p. 8; July 12, p. 1.

3. Ibid., May 19, 1880, p. 1; July 12, p. 1; December 29, 1882, p. 1; February 22, 1883, p. 1.

4. Ibid., March 14, 1880, p. 12; January 7, p. 2; May 19, p. 1; January 10, p. 3; August 2, p. 1; March 25, 1881, p. 1; April 6, p. 1; April 30, p. 8.

5. Ibid., June 21, 1883, p. 1.

6. Ibid., June 24, 1883, p. 1; June 28, p. 1.

7. Ibid., January 5, 1884, p. 2. The complainant was Annie Riley, a single "beautiful blonde, 17 years of age, who said one of the doctors had "betrayed her" (impregnated her in his medical office) and then sent her to a colleague for an abortion. The reporter wrote that "Miss Riley told her story in court with modesty and an air of truthfulness that carried weight with it." With policemen concealed in a room, she had confronted the two doctors; they had offered her a bribe for silence.

8. Ibid.

9. Ibid., July 8, 1886, p. 2.

10. Ibid., January 22, 1887, p. 2.

11. Ibid., November 5, 1880, p. 6.

12. Ibid.

13. Ibid., November 13, 1880, p. 2; January 4, 1881, p. 8. See also stories on November 6, 1880, p. 8; November 7, p. 2; November 12, p. 2; November 14, p. 2.

14. Ibid., April 12, 1881, p. 1.

15. Ibid., September 7, 1882, p. 5. The doctor, Theodore Kinne, claimed the child was stillborn, and he eventually was acquitted for lack of proof that he had actually killed the child through abortion, although that was the husband's intention. (September 8, p. 8; September 9, p. 8; September 10, p. 7).

16. Ibid., January 19, 1884, p. 1, and January 24, p. 1; see also January 18, p. 3.

17. Ibid., January 28, 1884, p. 8: "Jacob was very intimate with Margaret, and her ruin and death were the results of this intimacy." She is an "unfortunate girl."

18. Ibid., March 5, 1887, p. 3; March 8, p. 2; March 12, p. 2; March 15, p. 2. See also "City Lights and Shadows," April 4, 1884, p. 2.

19. *National Police Gazette*, May 21, 1878, p. 14

20. Ibid., October 6, 1878. See also August 10, p. 10; September 28, 1878, p. 6; October 5, p. 6; October 12, p. 7; and October 19, p. 11.

21. *National Police Gazette*, January 3, 1880, p. 2.

22. Ibid., October 16, 1880, p. 7.

23. Ibid.

24. Ibid. The doctor added, "Many of the women who practice this enormous crime of Foetal murder, move in the best society; are looked upon as christian women, yet in secret they perpetrate a heinous sin, forgetting that they are seen by one to whom darkness and light are the same."

25. Ibid., September 11, 1880, p. 10.

26. Ibid.

27. The *Gazette* at times criticized the motives of those having abortions. In "Mrs. Foley, an Abortionist's Victim," the newspaper reported on "the latest abortion sensation in Chicago. The victim was a married woman, is represented as quite handsome & seems to have had no object in subjecting herself to the abortionist, except a dread of childbearing, in which she was probably stimulated by a too-prevalent female vanity & love of pleasure." Another story, "Passion's Slaves," told of how a "child was made away with by some unnatural mother." (December 6, 1879, p. 7; April 10, 1880, p. 10.) See also "A Singular Case," concerning a Sharon, Pennsylvania, abortion, October 2, 1880, p. 11.

28. Ibid., October 12, 1878, p. 7.

29. Ibid., October 25, 1879, p. 11.

30. Ibid., September 11, 1880., p. 5.

31. Ibid., June 26, 1880, p. 5; December 6, 1879, p. 7.

32. Ibid., April 10, 1880, p. 3.

33. Ibid., January 24, 1880, p. 11.

34. Ibid., March 13, 1880, p. 11; October 9, p. 10; November 5, p. 11.

35. Ibid., February 7, 1880, p. 11.

36. Ibid., January 10, 1880, p. 6.

37. Ibid., November 29, 1879, p. 11.

38. *National Police Gazette*, February 28, 1882, p. 13; October 25, 1879, p. 11; November 15, 1879, p. 13; January 17, 1880, p. 10; May 15, p. 10; July 17, p. 11; November 6, p. 7; April 9, 1881, p. 11; May 29, p. 14; October 15, p. 7; December 31, p. 12.

39. Ibid., July 14, 1883, p. 7.

40. Ibid.

41. For example, see stories of April 23, 1881, p. 11; June 11, p. 3; September 3, p. 2; October 15, p. 11; September 23, 1882, p. 2; September 30, p. 13; October 28, p. 10; November 18, p. 6; January 27, 1883, p. 3; September 15, pp. 2, 4.

42. *National Police Gazette*, February 9, 1884, p. 2.

43. Springfield *Daily Republican*, August 21, 1880, p. 4.

44. Ibid.

45. Ibid.

46. Washington *Post*, August 28, 1880, p. 1.

47. September 21, 1886, quoted in Endres, op. cit., p. 750.

48. Quoted in Jeanine Halva-Neubauer, "Political Action, Social Change and Media Content: A Case Study," University of Minnesota unpublished paper.

49. New York *Times*, March 17, 1875, p. 7.

50. Ibid., March 19, 1875, p. 6.

51. New Orleans, toward the close of the 19th century, became the abortion depot of the south. With railroad competition increasing the number of trains and routes while decreasing ticket prices, it was not hard for a woman to go to a place where she was not known. Newspaper ads frequently proclaimed the willingness of abortionists to treat out-of-town patients and to even provide lodging for them if requested. One New Orleans abortionist, Dr. Mason, even advertised in the Houston *Post* (December 7, 1891, p. 6).

52. New Orleans *Picayune*, September 30, 1887, p. 5. Also July 10, 1888, p. 3; July 13, 1890, p. 5; September 4, 1891, p. 6, etc.

53. Ibid.

54. Ibid., July 4, 1892, p. 8.

55. Ibid., August 14, 1897, p. 5.

56. Ibid., August 16, 1897, p. 5; August 17, 1897, p. 3.

57. Ibid., August 16, 1897, p. 5.

58. San Francisco *Examiner*, January 13, 1889, p. 7.

59. Ibid., January 1, 1890, p. 8.

60. Ibid.

61. Ibid., March 24, 1893, p. 10.

62. Ibid., March 24, 1893, p. 10.

63. Ibid., January 1, 1890, p. 10.

64. Ibid., July 29, 1898, p. 8.

65. Ibid., November 1, 1894, p. 10.

66. Ibid.

67. Ibid., November 1, 1894, p. 10.

68. Chicago *Tribune*, January 1, 1876, p. 5.

69. Ibid., January 3, 1876, p. 5.

70. Ibid., July 1, 1876, p. 7; July 8, p. 7.

71. Ibid.

72. Ibid., August 12, 1876, p. 7. By November Dr. Clarke was also gone but "Dr. J. H. CLARK — THE OLD AND RELIABLE" was advertising, and at a different address from Clarke with an "e." This Dr. Clark maintained that "Thirty years" practice ought to inspire confidence. . . . He will not deceive you." (November 1, 1876, p. 7)

73. Ibid., November 1, 1876, p. 7.

74. *Missouri Republican*, May 21, 1878, p. 3.

75. Galveston *Daily News*, April 19, 1884, p. 1.

76. J.E. Kelly, "The Ethics of Abortion, as a Method of Treatment in Legitimate Practice," *Journal of the American Medical Association*, November 6, 1886, pp. 506–507.

77. Ibid., p. 508. Strong statements such as those of Kelly lead me to doubt Mohr's theory (in *Abortion in America*) that a prime reason for the physicians' anti-abortion crusade was the desire to protect their own medical bailiwick against "irregulars," including abortionists. Materialist considerations undoubtedly figured in the calculations of some anti-abortion doctors, but my reading of the period's history is that ideas, and ideals, had consequences.

78. Marion Harland, *Eve's Daughters* (New York: John R. Anderson & Henry S. Allen, 1883), p. 433.

79. Ibid.
80. Ibid., p. 434.
81. Ibid.

CHAPTER 5
DRIVING ABORTION UNDERGROUND

1. *National Police Gazette*, July 5, 1884, p. 15.
2. Ibid.
3. Ibid.
4. Ibid.
5. Ibid, December 4, 1886, p. 11.
6. Ibid.
7. Ibid., April 5, 1886, p. 15.
8. Ibid.
9. Ibid., December 4, 1886, p. 11.
10. Ibid., September 19, 1885, p. 15; October 2, 1886, p. 15.
11. Ibid.
12. *National Police Gazette*, September 19, 1885, p. 15.
13. Ibid.
14. Ibid.
15. Ibid., March 20, 1886, p. 15.
16. Ibid., May 29, 1886, p. 7.
17. Ibid., July 23, 1887, p. 6.
18. Ibid., June 18, 1887, p. 14.
19. Ibid., May 7, 1887, p. 14.
20. The publisher of the *Gazette* during the 1880s was Richard K. Fox, who turned his newspaper from exposure of crime and vice to promotion of burlesque queens in tights. In the 1890s the *Gazette* was not available at reputable newsstands but could be found, printed on pink paper, in barrooms and barber shops throughout the United States. In the 20th century the *Gazette* fell into declining circulation and eventual bankruptcy.
21. New York *Times*, July 23, 1890, p. 8.
22. Ibid.
23. Ibid., July 24, 1890, p. 2. Also see July 25, p. 8; July 26, p. 2; July 27, p. 13; July 28, p. 8; July 29, p. 8; July 30, p. 8; July 31, p. 8; September 19, p. 8; September 23, p. 8; September 24, p. 9; September 25, p. 3; September 26, p. 2; September 27, p. 8; October 1, p. 8; October 2, p. 9; October 3, p. 3; October 4, p. 1; October 16, p. 9 (reporting McGonegal's sentencing to 14 years in prison for first degree manslaughter).
24. Ibid., March 25, 1894, p. 13
25. Ibid., October 24, 1894, p. 16; December 5, 1894, p. 16; September 28, 1896, pp. 5, 8; October 9, 1896, p. 2. See also March 7, 1896, p. 15; April 9, p. 2; June 12, p. 1; June 30, p. 6.
26. The *Times* at this point, both in its stories and its indexing, was using eu-

phemisms such as "medical malpractice" or "illegal operation." No listings from 1898 through 1916 were found under those or a dozen other possible listings.

27. It is possible that stories were present and the indexer did not include them, but I have not run across any. It is also possible that the incidence of abortion had declined so sharply in New York that it was no longer a problem, but that also seems unlikely. The more likely reason is that the *Times* simply stopped covering abortion.

28. Davis, *History of the New York Times*, op. cit., pp. 199–200.

29. Quoted in J. H. Kellogg, *The Home Hand-Book of Domestic Hygiene and Rational Medicine* (Des Moines, IA: Condit & Nelson, 1887).

30. Ibid.

31. Ibid.

32. Ibid.

33. Dr. J. H. Kellogg, *Ladies' Guide in Health and Disease* (Battle Creek, MI: Modern Medicine Publishing Co., 1893), pp. 366–367.

34. *Rocky Mountain News*, January 28, 1896, p. 7.

35. Washington *Post*, September 30, 1898, p. 5.

36. Houston *Post*, January 2, 1902, p. 9.

37. Dallas *Morning News*, September 25, 1899, p. 7.

38. Ibid.

39. Ibid.

40. Houston *Daily Post*, September 6, 1898, p. 9.

41. Atlanta *Constitution*, November 21, 1897, p. 31; November 24, p. 9.

42. New York *Journal*, October 2, 1895, p. 15.

43. Ibid., December 1, 1895, p. 15.

44. Ibid., June 2, 1899, p. 11.

45. Ibid., January 1, 1900, p. 7.

46. Ibid., August 6, 1900, p. 11.

47. Ibid., February 1, 1901, p. 11.

48. Minutes of the Chicago Medical Society, vol. 16, 1903–1904. The committee was established at a special "Symposium on Criminal Abortion" at which several doctors, including Rudolph W. Holmes, read papers about abortion; Holmes' was entitled "A Brief Consideration of Criminal Abortion in its Relation to Newspaper Advertising."

49. Ibid.

50. Ibid.

51. Ibid.

52. Ibid.

53. Chicago *Tribune*, March 1, 1905, p. 13.

54. Ibid.

55. Minutes of the Chicago Medical Society, vol. 17, October, 1905–June, 1907.

56. Act of March 4, 1909, Chapter 321, Section 211, *U.S. Statutes at Large* (Washington, DC: Government Printing Office, 1909), vol. 35, part 1, p. 1129. The crucial provision read: "Every article or thing designed, adapted, or intended for preventing conception or producing abortion . . . every written or printed card, letter, circular, book, pamphlet, advertisement, or notice of any kind giving information directly or indirectly, where, or how, or from whom, or by what means any of the hereinbefore-mentioned matters, articles, or things may be obtained or

made, or where or by whom any act or operation performed . . . and every paper, writing, advertisement, or representation that any article, instrument, substance, drug, medicine, or thing may, or can be, used or applied for preventing conception or producing abortion . . . is hereby declared to be nonmailable matter."

57. The *Journal*, owned by William Randolph Hearst, had in 1914 the largest daily circulation in the United States (about 800,000).

58. New York *Journal*, May 10, 1909, p. 5.

59. Ibid.

60. Circulation of about 100,000 in 1908.

61. San Francisco *Examiner*, September 24, 1910, p. 1.

62. Ibid.

63. Ibid.

64. Ibid.

65. Ibid., p. 2.

66. Ibid.

67. Ibid., pp. 2, 3.

68. Ibid., p. 2.

69. Ibid., September 27, p. 1.

70. Los Angeles *Times*, September 25, 1910, p. 3.

71. Ibid., September 26, 1910, p. 1.

72. Ibid., September 29, p. 4.

73. See, for example, Washington *Post*, September 25, 1910, p. 7; September 26, p. 1.

74. New York *Herald*, October 3, 1910, p. 1.

75. Los Angeles *Times*, September 28, 1910, p. 1.

76. Ibid.

77. Ibid.

78. San Francisco *Examiner*, September 30, 1910, p. 13.

79. Ibid.

80. Ibid.

81. Ibid., September 11, 1910, p. 5, etc. Apparently, there was no Mary Grant, but some potential clients might be attracted by the promise of a female partner.

82. The *Examiner*, assuming in this case that a person was guilty before proven so in a court of law, called Thompson a "monster," but noted that he was not as cool as he appeared publicly: "Although he managed to keep a semblance of a repressed countenance yesterday, Grant spent a nervous night in his cell at police headquarters. He kept pacing up and down his cramped quarters until the gray light of dawn began to filter down the corridors, swinging his hands and gulping cold draughts of water continually." (September 27, p. 1)

CHAPTER 6
SOUNDS OF SILENCE

1. Los Angeles *Times*, March 2, 1911, p. 7.

2. Atlanta *Constitution*, September 1, 1911, p. 10.

3. San Francisco *Examiner*, March 1, 1911, p. 13; March 4, p. 15; March 7, p. 11; May 1, p. 13.

4. Margaret Sanger, *An Autobiography* (New York: Maxwell Reprint Co., 1970), pp. 86–92.

5. James Reed, *From Private Vice to Public Virtue* (New York: Basic Books, 1978), p. 441.

6. For an example of the "steady demand" hypothesis, see Kristin Luker, *Abortion and the Politics of Motherhood* (Berkeley, CA: University of California Press, 1984), pp. 50–51.

7. New York *Times*, January 14, 1916, p. 5.

8. Ibid.

9. The *American* was William Randolph Hearst's morning and Sunday newspaper in New York. In 1914 it had the largest Sunday circulation in the United States (about 750,000).

10. New York *American*, January 14, 1916, p. 11.

11. Ibid.

12. Ibid., January 15, 1916, p. 9.

13. Ibid.

14. Ibid., January 16, p. 2.

15. New York *American*, January 19, 1916, pp. 3, 5.

16. Ibid., January 18, p. 5. The dinner was attended by "nearly 150 men and women — most of them prominent in the literary, educational, medical or political world."

17. *People v. Hager* (1917) 181 App. Div. 153, 168 N.Y.S. 183: "If defendant, on being consulted as to a supposed pregnancy which was indicated by a cessation of the menses, furnished a drug with the statement that it would bring on the menses, though actually the drug would not have caused an abortion, he was guilty of violating provisions of this section prohibiting any person from holding out representations that a drug or medicine can be used or applied to cause an unlawful abortion."

18. Sanger, *An Autobiography*, p. 217. For other anti-abortion statements see Sanger's magazine *Woman Rebel*, April, 1914, p. 10; May, 1914, p. 24; June, 1914, p. 32; and *Birth Control Review*, November, 1918, pp. 3–4. Also see Ira Wile, "Discussion of 'Birth Control in its Medical, Social, Economic, and Moral Aspects,' " *The American Journal of Public Health*, vol. 7, no. 1 (January, 1917), p. 165; Wile argued for a distinction "between the prevention of conception, which carries practically no morbidity and certainly no mortality, and abortion, which may cause destruction of two lives."

19. New York *Times*, November 8, 1919, p. 6.

20. New York *Journal*, November 8, 1919, p. 5.

21. Ibid.

22. New York *Times*, June 25, 1920, p. 18; June 26, p. 9. Hammer received 3½ to 15 years.

23. Ibid., June 26, 1920, p. 1.

24. Ibid.

25. New York *Journal*, June 25, 1920, p. 2.

26. New York *Times*, June 25, 1920, p. 18; June 26, p. 9. Hammer received 3½ to 15 years.

27. New York *Times*, May 6, 1923, p. 26.

28. San Francisco *Examiner*, December 5, 1920, p. 17.

29. Los Angeles *Times*, May 1, 1929, p. 8.

30. Quoted in Germain Grisez, *Abortion: The Myths, the Realities and the Arguments* (New York: Corpus Books, 1970), pp. 224–225.

31. Ibid., p. 225.

32. Ibid.

33. Ibid.

34. *JAMA*, vol. 82, no. 22 (May 31, 1924), p. 1806.

35. Ibid.

36. New York *Times*, August 9, 1924, p. 5; August 10, p. 14; August 14, p. 17.

37. New York *Journal*, August 8, 1924, p. 4; August 10, p. 5.

38. Ibid., August 10, p. 5.

39. New York *Journal*, April 10, 1925, p. 1. The *Journal* did not use the Latin word "fetus."

40. Ibid., p. 2. Moloch was the Ammonite god mentioned 15 times in the Old Testament, in passages such as "Do not give any of your children to be sacrificed to Moloch" (Leviticus 18:21). The Hebrew prophets vigorously protested such human sacrifice.

41. Ibid.

42. Ibid.

43. Ibid.

44. Ibid.

45. Ibid., July 13, 1926, p. 2.

46. Ibid., July 14, 1926, p. 1.

47. New York *Times*, July 14, 1926, p. 26. The *Times* story, noting that evidence pointed to "illegal surgery," did include a description of body parts, wrapped in paper, with the medical examiner quoted as saying, "Whoever dismembered it had done it skillfully . . . apparently an expert surgeon." The dead woman was an "attractive 25-yr.-old, 5'6", with bobbed black hair and dark brown eyes."

48. New York *Journal*, July 14, 1926, p. 1.

49. Ibid., July 15, 1926, p. 1.

50. Ibid., July 16, 1926, p. 1.

51. New York *American*, July 16, p. 5.

52. Ibid., July 20, p. 2.

53. For another example of coverage, concerning the arrest of Dr. Jacques Alper, see New York *Journal*, August 23, 1926, p. 1.

54. The *Daily News* was a tabloid featuring photographs and short, sometimes hard-hitting articles, many of which featured crime and sex. In 1924 the *Daily News* attained the highest daily circulation in the United States (750,000); circulation grew to 1,320,000 in 1929 and peaked in 1947 at 2,400,000 daily.

55. *Journal of the American Medical Association*, vol. 92, no. 7 (February 16, 1929), p. 579.

56. New York *Daily News*, September 7, 1928; clipping in *Journal-American* archives.

57. Ibid., September 8, 1928.

58. Ibid., September 27 and 28, 1928.

59. Ibid., October 2, 1928.
60. Ibid., September 5, 1928.
61. Ibid. Such self-promotion was similar to that of the New York *Times* following its abortion expose in 1871.
62. Ibid., January 12, 1929.
63. Ibid., January 9, 1929.
64. Ibid., January 12, 1929.
65. New York *Journal*, November 19, 1929. See also New York *Times*, January 19, 1929; New York *World*, September 27, 1928' New York *Daily News*, March 16, 1929; all of these articles in the *Journal-American* archives.
66. *Journal of the American Medical Association*, February 16, 1929, p. 579.
67. New York *Times*, January 24, 1929, p. 15. The complaint was brought by Mrs. Hazel Potter who, one week after her abortion, went to a hospital for "a second operation . . . to save her life."
68. Ibid, January 25, 1929, p. 48; January 29, p. 20; January 30, p. 13. For contemporary accounts of those events and summaries at the time of the trial, see New York *Tribune*, November 15, 1910; New York *Daily News*, December 2, 1928, and New York *American*, October 22, 1922. These and following Carman stories from the *Journal-American* archives.
69. New York *Journal*, November 25, 1928.
70. New York *Daily News*, December 2, 1928.
71. Ibid., December 2, 1926.
72. New York *Journal*, January 24, 1929; New York *American*, January 30, 1929.

CHAPTER 7
GREED AND CORRUPTION, 1930–1939

1. New York *Evening World*, March 18, 1930, p. 16.
2. Ibid.
3. New York *American*, March 27, 1930. This article, and all others in this chapter without page numbers, are from the *Journal-American* archives.
4. Ibid.
5. Ibid, n.d.
6. Original story in New York *World*, November 26, 1914.
7. Compare New York *Times*, December 26, 1934, p. 12, and December 27, p. 42, with New York *Journal*, December 26, p. 1.
8. New York *Journal*, Oct. 13, 1936, p. 3, and Oct. 15, p. 3. New York *Times*, Jan. 1, 1936, p. 52; Feb. 8, p. 18; Aug. 19, p. 10; Aug. 26, p. 10; Sept. 24, p. 24; Oct. 12, p. 3; Oct. 23, p. 24; March 4, 1937, p. 5.
9. New York *Times*, April 30, 1937, p. 14.
10. New York *Journal*, April 15, 1936. The *Journal* also noted of Alper, "His history of trouble goes back to August, 1927, when a lovely young woman of 18 died in his office."
11. "Physicians Accused by Girl Dancer," Los Angeles *Times*, May 1, 1929, p. 8.
12. See, for example, Los Angeles *Times*, May 1, 1931, p. 4.
13. Quoted in Grisez, pp. 225–226.

14. Grisez, loc. cit., pp. 225–226,

15. See Grisez, p. 225.

16. "Ten years of Legalized Abortion in the Soviet Union," *American Journal of Public Health*, September, 1931, p. 1043.

17. William J. Robinson, *The Law Against Abortion* (New York: Eugenics Publishing Co., 1934), p. i.

18. Ibid., p. 115.

19. Ibid., p. 116.

20. Quoted in Grisez, loc. cit., p. 225.

21. Ibid., p. 226.

22. Similar to Fabian tactics in 20th century socialist economics, or the "salami tactic" — slice-by-slice — which Marxists occasionally praised.

23. Robinson, op. cit., p. 13.

24. Ibid., p. 114.

25. See chapter 9 for further discussion of statistics on incidence of abortion.

26. Frederick J. Taussig, *Abortion* (St. Louis: C.V. Mosby, 1936), p. 25.

27. Ibid., p. 449.

28. Ibid., p. 448.

29. Ibid., p. 25.

30. Ibid.

31. Ibid., p. 26.

32. Ibid., p. 28.

33. *Time*, March 16, 1936, p. 52.

34. Ibid.

35. Ibid. *Time* did use the word "abortion," at a time when newspapers still referred to "illegal operation."

36. Ibid. A few years later abortion in cases of probable infant deformity, women's mental health, and family poverty would become part of the liberalization package that pro-abortion forces would demand.

37. *Time*, October 19, 1936, pp. 70–71.

38. Ibid. In a reference that sounds hauntingly like some that emerged from Germany in 1945 as concentration camps were discovered, *Time* noted that one Rankin business "was reported so busy it maintained an ever-burning furnace in which abortions were incinerated."

39. Ibid.

40. Ibid.

41. Los Angeles *Times*, October 25, 1936, pt. 2, p. 2; the lead read, "Five leaders of the so-called syndicate conducting a chain of clinics on the Pacific Coast for the performance of illegal surgical abortions yesterday drew sentence of from ten to 25 years each in San Quentin Penitentiary." Nurses were allowed to file applications for probation. For other Los Angeles *Times* coverage, see October 17, 1936, pt. 2, p. 3; October 22, p. 2; October 23, pt. 2, p. 2; October 24, pt. 2, pg. 3; November 3, pt. 2, p. 3.

42. Quoted in London *Times*, July 20, 1938, p. 9a.

43. New York *Times*, July 20, 1938, p. 4. See also *Newsweek*, August 1, 1938, p. 29, and *Time*, August 1, p. 17.

44. A. J. Rougy, "Abortion: The $100,000,000 Racket," *American Mercury*, February, 1937, pp. 145–150.

45. *Forum*, July, 1938, pp. 33–37.

46. Ibid.

47. The morning and afternoon Hearst newspapers were combined into one on June 24, 1937. In the 1940s the newspaper sold about 700,000 copies each evening and 1.3 million on Sunday.

48. New York *Journal-American*, July 12, 1937.

49. The *Daily Mirror* was a sensational picture tabloid founded by William Randolph Hearst in 1924 to compete with the *Daily News*.

50. On July 7, 1937, the *Daily News* suggested that Duke's "jousts with the law on charges of performing illegal operations in the past have given him a clean bill of health" because of Rudich's protection, and the *Daily Mirror* noted that Duke after one recent arrest was released by "Rudich, who, two years ago, freed Dr. Duke when he was arraigned before him on a similar charge."

51. New York *Daily Mirror*, July 12, 1937, p. 8.

52. Attacking abortion was only one of Amen's assignments; he also examined corruption in the fur industry, in bail procedures, and in other areas.

53. New York *Journal-American*, March 16, 1939, p. 1.

54. Ibid., February 16, 1939. The New York *Sun* struck a low blow in describing how Rudich was dressed when responding to his accusers in court: "The accused man, who is only about 5 feet tall, was flushed and ill at ease as he took the witness chair. He was dressed in a brown suit, with white shirt, green tie, blue socks and tan shoes." (March 22, 1939)

55. Ibid., April 21, 1939.

56. Ibid., March 10, 1939, p. 1.

57. New York *Times*, March 11, 1939, p. 1; see also May 3, p. 1, and June 1, p. 1.

58. New York *Journal-American*, March 12, 1939, p. 1.

59. Ibid., March 12, 1939, p. 1.

60. Ibid., December 10 and 11, 1938.

61. Ibid., March 11, 1939, p. 1.

62. Ibid., May 28, 1939, p. 1; May 29, p. 1; June 1, p. 1.

63. New York *World-Telegram*, May 27, 1939, p. 1.

64. New York *Times*, May 28, 1939, p. 1.

65. Ibid., May 30, 1939.

66. New York *Journal-American*, May 28, 1939, p. 1.

67. Ibid., May 29, 1939, p. 1.

68. New York *World-Telegram*, May 29, 1939, p. 1.

69. "Madden Charged With Taking $9,000 Bribes to Protect Medical Racket," New York *Times*, April 22, 1939, p. 1.

70. New York *Journal-American*, May 6, 1940. See also Brooklyn *Eagle*, May 7, 1940, and May 9, 1940.

71. Ibid., April 5, 1939.

72. New York *Mirror*, May 2, 1940.

73. Typescript AP biography in *Journal-American* archives.

74. New York *World-Telegram*, March 11, 1939.

75. "Prober Praises Aid of *Journal-American*," *Editor & Publisher*, December 23, 1939.

CHAPTER 8
BUILDING THE ABORTION RATIONALE

1. "Hunt Poison Death of Amen Witness," New York *Times*, August 15, 1939, p. 1; also see Brooklyn *Eagle*, August 15, 1939, p. 1.

2. New York *Daily Mirror*, May 8, 1939. Other stories without page numbers in this chapter are from the *Journal-American* archives.

3. New York *Journal-American*, March 10, 1939. That move fell through, but problems in the grand jury system itself were evident. When Amen found that nine grand jury panel members in Brooklyn had criminal records, the New York *Times* reported on the "almost unbelievable condition of convicted criminals being in a position to rule on the merits of criminal evidence presented before them as grand jurors and also to pass on to their associates the secret deliberations of the grand jury and thus permit prospective defendants to flee the jurisdiction before their indictment." (*Times*, January 12, 1939)

4. New York *Journal-American*, June 3, 1939. See also New York *Sun*, May 29, 1939.

5. Defense attorneys for Ullman, Martin, and Madden all used this technique. Ironically, scorn for abortion may have hindered Amen's ability to fight abortion in another way. To encourage other abortionists to confess, Amen wanted Doctor Louis Duke to be able to practice medicine following the conclusion of his testimony. The Brooklyn *Eagle* was not so cooperative, however. In May, 1939, it published a photograph of a small sign announcing Duke's resumption of practice, and suggested over the next 2 months that it was not right for him to do so. Medical societies, prompted by the press, began hearings, and the *Eagle* eventually was able to announce that Duke's license had been revoked, over Amen's objections. (*Eagle*, May 29, 1939; July 13, 1939; April 18, 1941)

6. New York *Journal-American*, July 29, 1942.

7. H. L. Mencken, "Newspaper Morals," *Atlantic*, March, 1914, p. 292.

8. Ibid., p. 293.

9. On May 16, 1940, the *Journal-American* reported a raid on an abortionist's house that had "pink statues of storks on the front lawn," but more often irony had to be hidden.

10. New York *Times*, July 17, 1941, p. 20, and August 13, 1941.

11. Ibid., June 13, 1942, p. 21; June 26, p. 12; October 28, p. 17; November 27, p. 25; December 2, p. 52; December 11, p. 13; December 16, p. 16; etc. See also "Inquiry Involves 21 Bronx Doctors," New York *Sun*, October 21, 1942, and articles in New York *Journal-American*, April 1 and October 15, 1942.

12. The *Times*, for example, had harshly attacked Bruno Hauptmann when he was accused (and later convicted) of the kidnapping and murder of the Lindbergh baby.

13. *The Abortion Problem: Proceedings of the Conference Held Under the*

Auspices of the National Committee on Maternal Health, Inc. (Baltimore, MD: Williams & Wilkins, 1944), pp. 50–52, 104.

14. Ibid.

15. Ibid., p. 144.

16. Ibid., pp. 100–101.

17. New York *Times*, January 31, 1942, p. 30.

18. Ibid.

19. New York *Journal-American*, November 22, 1953.

20. Ibid., November 21, 1953.

21. New York *World-Telegram*, March 31, 1942. The New York *Journal-American* called the abortion office "a Park Avenue abortion headquarters, catering to a limousine clientele." (April 1, 1942).

22. See New York *Times* articles of March 31, 1942, p. 32, April 2, p. 13; April 9, p. 40; August 11, p. 21; September 10, p. 20; October 16, p. 40; October 21, p. 13; October 22, p. 17; October 23, p. 23.

23. New York *World-Telegram*, March 18, 1942.

24. 'What Everyone Should Know About Abortion," *American Mercury*, August, 1941, pp. 194–200.

25. "Death Before Birth," *Collier's*, January 22, 1944, p. 11.

26. *Time*, March 6, 1944, p. 60.

27. For instance, New York *World*, February 25, 1943.

28. Among Sanger's many expressions of this position, see particularly "Birth Control—Past, Present and Future," *Birth Control Review*, August, 1921, pp. 19–20; *Woman of the Future* (London: Birth Control International Information Centre, 1934); and "Japan Wants Birth Control," *Nation*, December 13, 1952, pp. 553–555.

29. New York *Times*, April 11, 1939, p. 17.

30. James Reed, *From Private Vice to Public Virtue* (New York: Basic Books, 1978), p. 118.

31. Many have been dubious about Sanger's anti-abortionism, seeing it only as public relations; on the other hand, Rosalind Petchesky, *Abortion and Woman's Choice: The State, Sexuality, and Reproductive Freedom* (New York: Longman, 1984), written from a radical feminist position, criticizes Sanger for what the author sees as her anti-abortionism.

32. Sanger quotations used in Lawrence Lader, *Abortion* (Indianapolis: Bobbs-Merrill, 1966), p. 167.

33. Because the Comstock Act of 1873 had attacked both birth control and abortion, legitimation of the first emboldened partisans of the second to increase their legal efforts as well. In *United States v. One Package*, 86 F. 2d 737 (2d Cir. 1936), the US Court of Appeals acquitted Sanger's clinic manager Hannah Stone of a criminal act in importing a package of contraceptive diaphragms from abroad; the diaphragms were intended for a physician to use in the treatment of a patient.

34. New York *Times*, January 7, 1944, p. 19. Just a few years before a refusal to condemn abortion would have been considered akin to a refusal to condemn racism today. (Sentences such as, "The problem is not racism but the unscrupulous racist," are not generally accepted now.)

35. Ibid., April 1, 1943, p. 25; April 22, p. 21; April 21, 1944, p. 21; May 12, 1944, p. 21.

36. Ibid., April 20, 1943, p. 18.

37. Ibid., January 29, 1944, p. 7.

38. Ibid., January 27, 1944, p. 21; January 28, p. 10; February 3, 1944, p. 20; February 4, p. 17; February 20, 1944; February 24, p. 17; March 5, p. 37; June 1, p. 21; July 6, p. 17; July 19, p. 21.

39. New York *Daily News*, Sept. 15, 1946, p. 20.

40. Ibid.

41. Ibid.

42. San Francisco *Examiner*, May 22, 1946, p. 8.

43. Ibid., May 29, 1946, p. 3. See also May 13, 1946, p. 6; May 14, p. 8; May 15, p. 8; May 16, p. 28; May 17, p. 5; May 18, p. 22; May 20, p. 24; May 21, p. 10; May 23, p. 5; May 24, p. 28; May 25, p. 5; May 27, p. 24; May 28, p. 15; May 30, p. 11; June 4, p. 13; June 5, p. 28; June 6, p. 30; June 7, p. 30; June 10, p. 9; June 11, p. 26; June 13, p. 32; June 18, p. 26; June 19, p. 24; June 21, p. 28; July 2, p. 30; July 4, p. 13; July 10, p. 28; July 11, p. 7; July 13, p. 1; July 14, p. 14.

44. See, for instance, "Four Seized in Alleged Illegal Operation Raids," Los Angeles *Times*, September 30, 1948, p. 2.

45. New York *World-Telegram*, March 18, 1942.

46. New York *Times*, February 16, 1946, p. 15.

47. New York *Journal-American*, July 8, 1945.

48. Ibid.

49. New York *Daily News*, March 4, 1945.

50. Ibid., September 5, 1947.

51. New York *Journal-American*, September 4, 1947.

52. *Time*, September 15, 1947, pp. 49–50.

53. New York *Times*, September 4, 1947, p. 52; September 5, p. 11; September 6, p. 30.

54. New York *Journal-American*, January 4, 1947; September 4, 1947.

55. Ibid., August 23, 1946.

56. New York *Times*, June 14, 1949, p. 11.

57. New York *Daily News*, March 20, 1951.

58. New York *World-Telegram*, May 5, 1947.

59. See, for example, New York *Times*, January 2, 1947: New York *Tribune*, January 27, 1947; New York *Journal-American*, June 18, 1947, and March 14, 1948; New York *World-Telegram*, March 30, 1948; Brooklyn *Eagle*, March 30, 1948.

60. New York *Journal-American*, January 29, 1948, p. 1; New York *Times*, November 29, 1947, p. 8; July 15, 1948, p. 24; November 20, 1948, p. 28; December 30, 1949, p. 12.

61. New York *Tribune*, February 22, 1948.

62. New York *Journal-American*, July 23, 1948.

63. There were over 5,000 maternal deaths annually from abortion during the 1930s; see the end of chapter 10 for a further statistical discussion, and see Thomas W. Hilgers, "The Medical Hazards of Legally Induced Abortion," in *Abortion and Social Justice* (New York: Sheed & Ward, 1972), pp. 57–88.

CHAPTER 9
HEADING TOWARD THE MOON, 1950–1959

1. Houston *Post*, April 15, 1950, p. 1.
2. Ibid.
3. Ibid., p. 2.
4. Los Angeles *Times*, May 28, 1952, p. 2.
5. Ibid.
6. Ibid.
7. See "Illegal Operation Nets M.D. 3 Years," New York *Journal-American*, May 5, 1950; also September 6, 1951; November 21, 1951; March 30, 1952; and July 14, 1952. See also "3 Doctors and 4 Others Plead Guilty of Abortion," New York *Tribune*, February 18, 1952. All articles without page numbers in this chapter were found in the *Journal-American* archives.
8. New York *Sun*, November 22, 1953.
9. New York *Journal-American*, November 21, 1953.
10. New York *Tribune*, August 23, 1951; New York *World-Telegram and Sun*, August 22, 1951; August 31, 1951. For additional stories of certified doctors performing abortions, see also New York *Daily News*, January 13, 1951; New York *Journal-American*, January 24, 1950; July 2, 1950; September 6, 1951; March 29, 1952; January 1, 1953; New York *Times*, November 22, 1953, p. 35.
11. New York *Journal-American*, August 2, 1951; see also New York *Times*, July 3, 1951, p. 9.
12. New York *Times*, April 5, 1954, and June 18, 1954, p. 48.
13. "Charges MDs, Hospitals Hush Abortion Cases," New York *Post*, December 10, 1953.
14. New York *Daily News*, April 4, 1951. See also New York *Times*, April 4, 1951, p. 25; April 5, p. 26; May 11, p. 19; February 16, 1952, p. 8.
15. New York *Journal-American*, May 2, 1955. Blank, after cooperating with the Amen investigation and receiving a pardon, had returned to the abortion business and enjoyed an estimated annual income of $115,000.
16. New York *Journal-American*, June 28, 1954.
17. Max Lerner, "Death and Abortion," New York *Post*, April 9, 1954.
18. Harold Rosen, *Therapeutic Abortion* (New York: Julian Press, 1954); republished as *Abortion in America* (Boston: Beacon Press, 1967).
19. Joseph Fletcher, *Morals and Medicine* (Princeton: Princeton University Press, 1954).
20. Fletcher became better known following publication of his mid-1960s book, *Situation Ethics, the New Morality*.
21. Glanville Williams, *The Sanctity of Life and the Criminal Law* (New York: Alfred A. Knopf, 1957).
22. Williams argued that laws against murder are essential because anarchy would prevail if adults could kill each other at will; laws against abortion are not necessary because abortion cannot lead to such anarchy, apparently because unborn children cannot shoot back.

23. Williams wrote that no foetal electroencephalograms were posssible before the 28th week, so there was no person there; EEGs are now possible by the 8th week of pregnancy. Joseph Dellapenna provides information on this and other technological developments in "The History of Abortion: Technology, Morality, and Law," *University of Pittsburgh Law Review*, vol. 40 (1979), p. 410.

24. Mary Calderone, ed., *Abortion in the United States* (New York: Hoeber-Harper, 1958), pp. 9–11.

25. Ibid., p. 162.

26. Ibid., p. 164.

27. Ibid., p. 164. Taylor added, "We ought to decide whether we are talking about the indications for therapeutic abortion, or are hoping to do something to diminish the one hundred times as frequent illegal abortions for which there cannot possibly be a medical reason."

28. Ibid., p. 165.

29. Ibid.

30. Ibid., p. 166.

31. Ibid.

32. Ibid., p. 167.

33. Ibid.

34. Ibid., p. 169.

35. Ibid., p. 183. Guttmacher insisted that participants "include humanitarian reasons in our statement." Taylor argued that "to include this indication makes it so completely uncontrollable that such a recommendation is unrealistic" (p. 175). Guttmacher won.

36. Ibid., p. 184.

37. *Time*, June 2, 1958, p. 70; *Coronet*, June, 1958, pp. 78–86. Publication of books also helped pro-abortion doctors, lawyers, and liberal theologians to become known as the "experts" who would then be quoted by reporters in "objective" abortion stories.

38. New York *World-Telegram and Sun*, July 6, 1957.

39. New York *Tribune*, January 31, 1956.

40. New York *Times*, Jan. 12, 1956, p. 56; Jan. 14, p. 38; Jan. 20, p. 26; May 20, p. 40; June 27, p. 62; June 28, p. 58.

41. New York *Mirror*, December 1957.,

42. New York *Journal-American*, December 20, 1957.

43. New York *Herald Tribune*, June 27, 1954.

44. Ibid.

45. Washington *Post*, June 28, 1954, p. 7.

46. New York *News*, March 10, 1956.

47. Los Angeles *Times*, December 1, 1954, p. 2.

48. Ibid. The story made coast-to-coast headlines, sometimes with errors. The December 1, 1954, New York *Herald Tribune*, under a headline "Death of Movie Aspirant is Blamed on Abortion," incorrectly identified Virginia Watson as the sister of movie swimming star Esther Williams. See also "Swimming Star Dead: Abortion to Aid Film Career Fatal to Virginia Hopkins," New York *Times*, December 1, 1954, p. 36.

49. New York *Daily News*, January 11, 1956. See also New York *Herald Tribune*, September 2, 1955.

50. New York *Journal-American*, February 22, 1956.

51. Ibid., July 7 and July 14, 1957.

52. New York *Journal-American*, *July 15, 1957*.

53. See Paul H. Gebhard, Wardell B. Pomeroy, Clyde E. Martin, and Cornelia V. Christenson, *Pregnancy, Birth and Abortion* (New York: Hoeber-Harper, 1958).

54. New York *Times*, November 9, 1958, p. 86. See also New York *Journal-American*, February 24, 1958; this story noted that the median price of abortions, $76 in the 1920s, jumped to $143 in the 1940s and had since gone higher.

55. New York *Times*, Jan. 20, 1956, p. 26.

56. New York *Journal-American*, July 7, 1957.

57. *Time*, June 2, 1958.

58. Calderone, ed., op. cit., p. 180: "Taking into account the probable trend of the abortion ratio during the interwar period, a plausible estimate of the frequency of induced abortion in the United States could be as low as 200,000 and as high as 1,200,000 per year, depending upon the assumptions made as to the incidence of abortion in the total population as compared with the restricted groups for which statistical data are available, and upon the assessment of the direction and magnitude of bias inherent in each series of data. There is no objective basis for the selection of a particular figure between these two estimates . . . "

59. Rosen, *Therapeutic Abortion*, p. 267. Jerome Bates and Edward Zawadski, in their book *Criminal Abortion* (Springfield, IL: C.C. Thomas, 1964), noted that they could not provide an accurate figure on the number of abortions, but preferred "a fairly conservative, commonly agreed upon, although admittedly rough figure." (p.3)

60. See Dr. and Mrs. J. C. Willke, *Abortion Questions and Answers* (Cincinnati, OH: Hayes Publishing, 1985), p. 165.

61. New York *Times*, November 9, 1958, p. 86, and other publications.

62. New York *Herald Tribune*, November 9, 1958.

63. New York *Post*, June 2, 1958; June 28, 1959.

64. It would be virtually impossible for the prosecution to prove that the doctor had not believed — even if incorrectly — that the mental health of the mother was in danger.

65. Robert Hall, "The Abortion Revolution," *Playboy*, September, 1970, p. 112.

66. New York *Times*, July 28, 1959, p. 29.

CHAPTER 10
FROM MURDER TO LIBERATION

1. Dr. X as told to Lucy Freeman, *The Abortionist* (New York: Grove Press, 1962), p. i.

2. The abortionist evaded police but eventually was captured in France and extradited. See "Queen's M.D. Admits Girl's Abortion Death," New York *World-Telegram and Sun*, September 12, 1962, p. 1, and "Runaway M.D. is Indicted in Death of Coed," New York *Journal-American*, September 26, 1962, p. 1.

3. *Arizona Republic*, July 23, 1962, p. 1.

4. Los Angeles *Times*, August 3, 1962, p. 1.

5. Eight major newspapers were examined closely for this chapter: Los Angeles *Times*, San Francisco *Examiner*, Arizona *Republic*, Chicago *Tribune*, Atlanta *Constitution*, Washington *Post*, New York *Times*, New York *Post*, New York *Journal-American*.

6. Washington *Post*, August 3, 1962, p. A4.

7. *Newsweek*, August 13, 1962, p. 52.

8. Arizona *Republic*, July 16, 1962, p. 1.

9. *Ibid*, July 23, 1962, p. 1.

10. Los Angeles *Times*, August 4, 1962, p. 15.

11. Arizona *Republic*, July 24, 1962, p. 1.

12. Chicago *Tribune*, July 31, 1962, p. 1.

13. *Ibid*, July 28, 1962, p. 2.

14. Los Angeles *Times*, August 1, 1962, p. 1., Chicago *Tribune*, August 1, 1962, p. 3.

15. Washington *Post*, July 31, 1962, p. A3.

16. Los Angeles *Times*, July 31, 1962, p. 1.

17. New York *Times*, August 1, 1962, p. 19.

18. Washington *Post*, August 1, 1962, p. A6; Chicago *Tribune*, August 1, 1962, p. 3.

19. New York *Times*, August 5, 1962, p. 64.

20. Arizona *Republic*, August 21, 1962, p. 1.

21. Washington *Post*, August 5, 1962, p. A3.

22. New York *Times*, August 13, 1962, p. 62; Arizona *Republic*, August 3, 1962, p. 1.; Washington *Post*, August 3, 1962, p. A4.

23. See Washington *Post*, August 5, 1962, p. A3.

24. For example, see New York *Times*, August 13, 1962, p. 16; Washington *Post*, August 3, 1962, p. A4.

25. Los Angeles *Times*, August 4, 1962; p. 1.

26. Chicago *Tribune*, August 4, 1962, p. 5, and August 5, 1962, p. 1.

27. Atlanta *Constitution*, August 18, 1962, p. 30.

28. New York *Journal-American*, July 25, 1962, p. 1.

29. Washington *Post*, July 31, 1962, p. A3.

30. New York *Times*, August 5, 1962, p. 64.

31. Ibid., August 1, 1962, p. 19.

32. Los Angeles *Times*, August 1, 1962, p. 1.

33. Paul Coates, *ibid*, August 4, 1962, p. 1.

34. New York *Journal-American*, August 18, 1962.

35. See, for example, Chicago *Tribune*, July 27, 1962, p. 12.

36. See, for example, New York *Times*, August 5, 1962, p. 12, and August 19, p. 12; New York *Journal-American*, August 18.

37. George Orwell, "Politics and the English Language," *The Orwell Reader* (New York: Harcourt Brace and World, Inc., 1956) p. 363.

38. New York *Journal-American*, August 5, 1962, p. 1.

39. New York *Post*, July 31, 1962, p. 24.

40. Ibid.

41. Ibid., August 20, 1962, p. 23.

42. Los Angeles *Times*, August 4, 1962, p. 15; see also Chicago *Tribune*, July 27, 1962, p. 4.

43. Ibid., August 4, 1962, p. 15.

44. New York *Journal-American*, August 17, 1962.

45. Los Angeles *Times*, August 4, 1962, p. 15.

46. *The Gallup Poll, Public Opinion 1935-1971* (New York: Random House, 1972). p. 1984.

47. New York *World-Telegram and Sun*, March 18, 1964.

48. "Agony of mothers about their unborn," *Life*, June 4, 1965, pp. 24-31; "Major tragedy feared: defective births are on the rise," *U.S. News and World Report*, May 3, 1965, p. 11. See also "Tragic pregnancy: Case of German Measles," *Good Housekeeping*, January, 1966, p. 12.

49. Cited in Grisez, p. 241.

50. Ibid.

51. "Abortion, Legal and Illegal," *Time*, December 25, 1964, p. 53.

52. "More Abortions: The Reason Why," *Time*, Sept 17, 1965, p. 82.

53. "The Abortion Epidemic," *Newsweek*, November 14, 1966, p. 92.

54. For additional discussion of this and other magazine estimates, see Susan and Marvin Olasky, "Correcting the Abortion Record," *Presbyterian Journal*, January 15, 1986, pp. 6-7.

55. See James T. Burtchaell, *Rachel Weeping* (Kansas City: Andrews & McMeel, 1981).

56. Department of Health and Human Services, Center for Disease Control, *Abortion Surveillance*, November, 1980; quoted in Willke, p. 164. The number of maternal deaths continued to go down while abortion was still illegal, and by 1973 the official figure was down to 45.

57. Quoted in Burtchaell, p. 65. The official figures may have underestimated the problem, but evidence suggests that the official figures could not have been as far off as pro-abortionists suggested. For example, Burtchaell noted that beginning in the 1950s Minnesota obstetricians and gynecologists deployed medical teams to check carefully all reports of female deaths that might be maternal. The teams found there were 28 maternal deaths from abortion in Minnesota during 24 years, or 1.2 per year; that was about 1% of the death rate from illegal abortion then being claimed by abortion advocates.

CHAPTER 11
THE TRIUMPH OF PUBLIC RELATIONS

1. See Reed, *From Private Vice to Public Virtue*, pp. 377-379.

2. New York *World-Telegram and Sun*, March 22, 1965.

3. Lawrence Lader, *Abortion* (Indianapolis, IN: Bobbs-Merrill, 1966).

4. Ibid., p. 29.

5. Ibid., pp. 167-175.

6. Lawrence Lader, *Abortion II: Making the Revolution* (Boston, MA: Beacon Press, 1973), p. ix. Lader wrote of his public relations planning when the revolution was won.

7. Quoted by Bernard Nathanson in *Aborting America* (Garden City, NY: Doubleday, 1979), pp. 51–52.

8. Ibid.

9. Lader, *Abortion II*, p. 92.

10. Following *Roe v. Wade* NARAL kept its initials by changing its name to the National Abortion Rights Action League.

11. Lader, loc. cit.

12. Ibid., p. 97.

13. Arlene Carman and Howard Moody, *Abortion Counseling and Social Change, from Illegal Act to Medical Practice: The Story of the Clergy Consultation Service on Abortion* (Valley Forge, PA: Judson Press, 1973), p. 18.

14. Ibid.

15. Ibid.

16. Ibid. See Edward B. Fiske, 'Clergyman Offer Abortion Advice: 21 Ministers and Rabbis Form New Group—Will Propose Alternatives," New York *Times*, May 22, 1967, p. 1.

17. Carman and Moody, p. 45.

18. Lader, *Abortion*, p. 148.

19. *Playboy*, September, 1970, pp. 112–115, 272–276.

20. Ibid.

21. Ibid.

22. Mary Calderone, "Illegal Abortion as a Public Health Problem," *American Journal of Health*, July, 1960, p. 949. It might be noted that the Kinsey study in the 1950s, although dubious on some methodological grounds, had contended that 84 to 87% of illegal abortions were done by "reputable physicians in good standing in their local medical association."

23. These individuals supported each other's themes, of course; Hall, in his *Playboy* article, also emphasized Lader's attacks on Catholic leaders and perceived unfairness to the poor.

24. Lader, *Abortion*, p. 148.

25. Rockefeller was chairman of the board of trustees of the Population Council, which in February, 1969, devoted an entire issue of its magazine to the topic, "Beyond Family Planning." Articles examined proposals to limit population that went "beyond present programs of voluntary family planning"—proposals such as legalization of abortion and mandatory abortion of all illegitimate pregnancies—and suggested that extreme measures be proposed, even if they could not be accepted: "More extreme or controversial proposals tend to legitimate more moderate advances, by shifting the boundaries of discourse." A leadership group as close to the governmental and economic "establishment" as could be found was now committed to pushing the abortion debate as far as it could go, with the goal of ening up with abortion liberalization.

26. Lader, *Abortion II*, p. 32.

27. Ibid., p. 34.

28. Washington *Post*, September 7, 8, 9, 1967.

29. Lader, *Abortion*, p. 39.

30. See Tom Wolfe, *Radical Chic and Mau-Mauing the Flak-Catchers* (New York: Farrar, Straus & Giroux, 1970).

31. Nguyenphuc Buutap, "Legislation, Public Opinion, and the Press: An Interrelationship Reflected in the New York Times Reporting of the Abortion Issue" (doctoral dissertation, University of Chicago, 1979), p. 117.

32. Ibid.

33. New York *Times*, February 13, 1965, p. 20.

34. Ibid., April 7, 1965, p. 42

35. Ibid.

36. Lawrence Lader, "The Scandal of Abortion Laws," New York *Times*, April 25, 1965, Section VI, p. 32.

37. New York *Times*, December 8, 1965, p. 46.

38. Ibid., March 7, 1966, p. 26.

39. Ibid., January 3, 1967, p. 36; January 7, p. 26; January 13, p. 22.

40. Ibid., February 14, 1967, p. 42.

41. Ibid., Actually, only 79 expectant mothers died in New York City during 1964, with 35 of those deaths attributed to abortion. Even if that figure was doubled to compensate for cover-ups, and even if the *Times* editorial was referring to the state of New York rather than the city, the *Times* editorial numbers were grotesquely exaggerated.

42. Ibid., April 27, 1967, p. 34. Burtchaell, op. cit., observes that in 1967, concerning abortion-related maternal mortality, the New York *Times* was off by only 3,000%.

43. Martin Gansberg, "Marchers Favor Abortion Reform," New York *Times*, March 13, 1967, p. 40.

44. Ibid.

45. New York *Times*, January 8, 1968, p. 28.

46. Ibid. The article also played up the story of a South Dakota abortionist who stayed in business for 30 years without legal hindrance. That happened in some places because of bribery and favor-swapping, but to generalize as did the *Times* by stating that abortion has been accepted "in cities and towns throughout the country for many years" goes far beyond the evidence.

47. Nineteenth century euphemisms were returning.

48. New York *Times*, January 8, 1968, p. 28. The article's prognosis also showed incomprehension of what has become known as "post-abortion syndrome." Not knowing does not yield peace of mind.

49. The article summarized the Catholic position and then observed: "Until recently, Protestants also tended to oppose abortion, and it was Protestants, not Catholics, who put rigorous anti-abortion laws on the books of most states . . . during the 19th century. The Protestants, however, never shared the Catholic belief that human life began at the point of conception. . . . Characteristic Protestant individualism also led to the conclusion that the morality of abortion was a matter for the individual to decide for himself." Bible-believing Protestants did not come to such a conclusion. The eleventh paragraph of the story does mention that Protestants have been "far from unanimous" in adopting a pro-abortion position, but that acknowledgement is skipped by without further discussion.

50. New York *Times*, December 29, 1968, Section VI, p. 10.

51. Ibid.

52. Ibid., April 18, 1969, p. 1.

53. See, for example, New York *Times*, January 11, 1968, p. 36, and April 6, 1968, p. 38.

54. New York *Times*, January 26, 1969, p. 44; January 29, 1969, p. 40.

55. Ibid., May 25, 1969, p. 34; May 30, 1969, p. 26.

56. See "The Legislature's Failure," ibid., May 3, 1969, p. 34.

57. Ibid., p. 96.

58. Ibid., May 26, 1969, p. 12.

59. Betsy Bliss, "Should We Change Our State Abortion Laws?" Chicago *Daily News*, March 1, 1967, p. 29. All articles from the Chicago *Sun-Times* and Chicago *Daily News* were found in the *Sun-Times* morgue in Chicago.

60. Ibid. The articles, although giving a green light to those contemplating abortion, also tended to trivialize the act: "Contrary to what most people believe, an abortion is safe (safer than a tonsillectomy), quick and relatively inexpensive—if performed by a competent physician under hospital conditions before the end of the third month of pregnancy."

61. Chicago *Sun-Times*, November 17, 1968, p. 8.

62. Ibid., November 18, 1968, pp. 1, 32.

63. Ibid., p. 32.

64. A *Sun-Times* series 10 years later, discussed in chapter 13, showed that the risk to women also may not correlate with illegality.

65. Ibid., February 8, 1969; CST Morgue. The Chicago *Daily News* on February 2, 1969, also gave the figure of 5,000.

66. Chicago *Sun-Times*, January 26, 1969.

67. Ibid., February 23, 1969, section 4, p.1.

68. Ibid., December 14, 1969, section 4, pp. 1, 22.

69. Ibid., February 9, 1969, section 4, p. 1.

70. *Playboy*, July, 1974, p. 164. According to *Playboy*, "as the song was played over and over, therapist Myers danced to the music, kicking up her heels."

71. As in Chicago, two newspapers under common ownership.

72. San Diego *Tribune*, June 21, 1965.

73. Ibid., October 27, 1967.

74. San Diego *Union*, September 7, 1967.

75. Ibid., January 9, 1966.

76. See Tatalovich, pp. 91–93. Tatalovich et al. concluded their examination of magazine articles by noting "how consistent the arguments in favor of therapeutic abortions were. Moreover, it shows how much media impact a relatively small number of committed pro-abortion activists had." (p. 93)

77. Grisez summarized the new laws on pp. 244–250; Lader, *Abortion*, has a chapter on "The Campaign for New Laws," pp. 56–71.

76. Tatalovich, p. 33.

CHAPTER 12
PULPITS FOR ABORTION, 1970–1974

1. Hall, loc. cit.

2. Ibid.

3. Cleveland *Plain Dealer*, March 29, 1970, in Pro-Life Action League files. All newspaper articles cited without page numbers in this chapter are from the libraries of the Chicago *Sun-Times* or the San Diego *Union*, or from the Pro-Life Action League.

4. Detroit *Free Press*, January 20, 1970.

5. For example, St. Louis *Post-Dispatch*, April 12, 1970, 21C8. The last piece of information, 21C8, means for this and upcoming citations that the article was found in NewsBank, a microfiche collection of articles [1970–present] selected from over 100 local newspapers throughout the United States. NewsBank must be used only as a supplement to other research, or else the reader is at the mercy of the NewsBank article selectors, but when used properly it is an excellent tool. The notation 21C8 indicates that the article was found on fiche 21 for the year in question [here, 1970], row C, position 8.

6. Chicago *Sun-Times*, July 31, 1970. The *Sun-Times* also used bandwagon appeals, noting that "the list of states with modernized abortion laws is growing. . . . We believe Illinois, a supposedly enlightened state, should not be at the tag end of this particular parade."

7. Omaha *World-Herald*, October 4, 1970, 40D12.

8. *Long Island Press*, December 20, 1970.

9. Ibid.

10. Hartford *Courant*, October 9, 1970, 42B4.

11. *Oregonian*, March 1, 1970, 16B1.

12. San Francisco *Chronicle*, May 5, 1970, 24C10.

13. Ibid., April 11, 1970, 21B9.

14. Ibid., November 6, 1970, 50B10.

15. Ibid.

16. Ibid.

17. Memphis *Commercial Appeal*, October 3, 1970, 40C10.

18. Newark *Evening News*, March 11, 1970, 17B7.

19. Washington *Post*, September 18, 1970, 35E10.

20. Baltimore *Sun*, April 24, 1970, 22B6.

21. San Francisco *Chronicle*, May 5, 1970, 24C10.

22. Ibid., May 6, 1970.

23. See, for example, San Diego *Union*, January 29, 1970, and San Diego *Tribune*, December 15, 1971.

24. New York *Times*, April 9, 1970. This comment about Constance Cook was contained in a puff piece "Woman in the News" profile.

25. Houston *Post*, September 27, 1970; series by Miriam Kass, Post Medical Writer.

26. Ibid., September 29, 1970, p.

27. Ibid. Those ideologies were not specified, but the series' concluding article made several striking theological points. Kass wrote on October 2 (40c2), "We want to control pollution, control population, control crime. In short, control our own lives. Some might say this is presumptuous, that our future must lie in the power of forces greater than ourselves. Others say we have been given our brains by this

power and we have the responsibility to use them for the betterment of life on earth. Abortion is one way of controlling . . . a way of controlling how many and what kind of people will live on the earth with us."

28. Dallas *Morning News*, November 15, 1970; series written by Carolyn Dunnigan.

29. Ibid.

30. Ibid., November 16, 1970.

31. Ibid., November 25.

32. Indianapolis *Star*, September 13, 1970, 35C2.

33. Mildred Spencer, "877 Fetal Deaths Are Reported," Buffalo *Evening News*, September 29, 1970, 39E7.

34. Lynn Sherr, "Abortion Law Reforms Still Leave Some Problems," Cincinnati *Enquirer*, September 27, 1970, 39B4.

35. John Noonan, *A Private Choice: Abortion in America in the Seventies* (New York: The Free Press, 1979).

36. Noonan (pp. 41–45) discusses the Nixon administration's role in abortion.

37. Head of the Population Affairs section of the Agency for International Development.

38. Commission on Population Growth and the American Future, *Population and the American Future* (Washington, DC: Government Printing Office, 1972), pp. 5–6. A dissenting member of the Rockefeller Commission, Grace Olivarez, wrote that "To talk about the 'wanted' and the 'unwanted' child smacks too much of bigotry and prejudice. Many of us have experienced the sting of being "unwanted" by certain segments of our society. . . . Those with power in our society cannot be allowed to 'want' and 'unwant' people at will. . . . The poor cry out for justice and equality, and we respond with legalized abortion." (p. 161)

39. *California Medicine*, September, 1970, pp. 67–68. The article urged doctors to adopt pro-abortion standards in order to become leaders "in what is almost certain to be a biologically oriented world society."

40. Judith Blake, "The Supreme Court's Abortion Decisions and Public Opinion in the United States," *Population and Development Review* 3 (1977), p. 52.

41. Ibid.

42. New York *Times*, January 24, 1973, reprinted in Lauren R. Sass, ed., *Abortion: Freedom of Choice & the Right to Life* (New York: Facts on File, 1978). The editorial writer evidently did not read Blackmun's decision very closely, nor did he read his own newspaper's clip files; the writer argued incorrectly that "the spur to the initial adoption of state laws banning abortion nearly a century ago was the great risk of maternal death involved in the surgical procedures then used."

43. St. Louis *Post-Dispatch*, January 28, 1973; reprinted in Sass, p. 9.

44. *Christian Science Monitor*, January 29, 1973, and Sass, p. 7.

45. Indianapolis *News*, January 26, 1973, Sass p. 4: "In this decision the major issues of life and death are blandly ignored or handled in parentheses, while secondary considerations of utility are pushed forward as crucial matters of discussion. If this opinion were all there was to go on, you would scarcely know that what is being talked about is the cold and deliberate extermination of life."

46. Orlando *Sentinel*, January 28, 1973; Sass, p. 6.

47. Omaha *World-Herald*, January 28, 1973; Sass, p. 3.

48. Norfolk *Ledger-Star*, January 23, 1973; Sass, p. 4.

49. Birmingham *News*, January 28, 1973; Sass, p. 5.

50. Des Moines *Register*, January 23, 1973; Sass, p. 8.

51. Louisville *Courier-Journal*, January 24, 1973; Sass, p. 10. The editor noted that some "moral questions" still would be raised.

52. Milwaukee *Journal*, January 24, 1973; Sass, p. 12.

53. New York *Times*, January 24, 1973; Sass, p. 9. Many of these statements sound like those made by some Southern newspapers following the Dred Scott decision in 1857. Then, the Memphis *Appeal* on March 9 called the Supreme Court ruling "The most important decision, accompanied by the most learned and interesting opinion that has probably ever emanated from . . . the only tribunal which could settle the question permanently and satisfactorily to the great mass of the people." The Charleston *Daily Courier* predicted on March 10 that the decision "will exert the most powerful and salutary influence throughout the United States," and the Little Rock *True Democrat* on March 24 ran the headline, "Momentous Question Settled." Only a war truly settled the slavery question.

54. Dallas *Morning News*, January 23, 1973. The lead was, "Immediate reaction to the Supreme Court's liberalized ruling on abortion Monday seems to have people here more concerned about its mechanics than they are its morality." It was not clear which people the reporter interviewed, because the first 14 paragraphs of the story quoted speculations by unnamed doctors, and the two hospital administrators mentioned by name refused comment. The last three paragraphs of the story did quote a Catholic bishop and an anti-abortion group leader, both of whom expressed moral concerns.

55. Milwaukee *Journal*, January 23, 1973, 1C12.

56. Fort Worth *Star Telegram*, February 13, 1973, 10F13.

57. Cleveland *Press*, August 9, 1973, 64C1.

58. Oakland *Tribune*, May 4, 1973, 40A13.

59. Baltimore *Sun*, January 23, 1973; Atlanta *Constitution*, February 15; Dallas *Morning News*, February 19; Detroit *Free Press*, February 23; Des Moines *Register*, March 4, Milwaukee *Journal*, August 12. See also Dallas *Morning News*, July 2.

60. San Antonio *Light*, February 20, 1973, 11D1.

61. Atlanta *Journal*, March 18, 1973, 19G11.

62. Chicago *Sun Times*, February 28, 1973, CST files.

63. Cleveland *Press*, March 14, 1973, 19F3.

64. Detroit *Free Press*, May 7, 1973, 40B9.

65. Ibid., May 9, 1973, 40B14. The *Free Press* did better in 1974, sending female reporters undercover to 12 abortion businesses. At those businesses all of the reporters were told they were pregnant, even though they were not. The *Free Press* did not see a general problem with the nature of the abortion business, however; it praised one of the abortion businesses for being "caring, warm and sympathetic."

66. Milwaukee *Journal*, February 11, 1973, 10F4; article by Nina Bernstein.

67. Dallas *Morning News*, April 20, 1973, 31G7.

68. Houston *Post*, June 20, 1973, 48F4.

69. The Noonan and Burtchaell books examine poll data and press use of them.

70. Abortion, legal or not, was still blind surgery, generally performed by a doctor without knowledge of the patient or her medical history.

71. Los Angeles *Times*, July 5, 1976; St. Louis *Post Dispatch*, July 2; Cleveland *Press*, July 17; Chicago *Daily News*, July 2 (Sass, pp. 13–14, and Chicago *Sun-Times* files).

72. *Arizona Republic*, July 9, 1976; Sass, p. 17.

73. Providence *Journal*, July 3, 1976; Sass, p. 15. The view was "moderate" because the Court had said states could "require a woman to give her written consent before having an abortion."

74. New York *Times*, July 3, 1976; Sass, p. 16.

75. Washington *Post*, February 11, 1976.

76. Los Angeles *Times*, September 12, 1976.

77. Boston *Globe*, September 20, 1977.

78. Cincinnati *Post*, August 6, 1976.

79. New Orleans *States-Item*, February 6, 1976.

80. Milwaukee *Journal*, September 5, 1976. The *Journal* did not point out that the Supreme Court had done exactly that in 1973.

81. Rochester *Democrat Chronicle*, October 22, 1977.

82. Memphis *Commercial Appeal*, December 9, 1977.

83. Kansas City *Times*, February 4, 1978.

84. Kansas City *Star*, March 11, 1976.

85. Chicago *Sun-Times*, January 21, 1974, p. 50.

CHAPTER 13
"THAT NO FETUS WILL BE BORN ALIVE"

1. Restell advertisement in New York *Herald*, March 6, 1840, P. 1.

2. Ibid.

3. Articles and memos in files of the Pro-Life Action League.

4. Story told in Ruth Seymour, "Unwanted . . . alive," Detroit *Free Press*, January 3, 1982; Pro-Life Action League files.

5. The author was a reporter on the Boston *Globe* during the early 1970s.

6. *National Review*, March 14, 1975, pp 260–2.

7. William Nolen, *The Baby in the Bottle* (New York: Coward, McCann & Geoghegan, 1978), p. 88.

8. Ibid.

9. Ibid.

10. The best short summaries of major issues of the case may be found in Nolen, pp. 107–115 and 143–175.

11. Boston *Globe*, January 12, 1975, pp. 1, 34.

12. Ibid.

13. Ibid.

14. Ibid. Prosecution and defense also quarreled about definitions of "birth." Prosecutor Flanagan said that once the placenta was detached from the uterine wall, the child was on its own systems and therefore was born. Defense counsel Homans said a "fetus" was not a person until he or she was removed from the womb.

15. Boston *Globe*, January 16, 1985, p. 1.

16. Ibid.

17. Described by the Washington newspaper *Human Events* as "a young pro-abortionist reporter."

18. Boston *Globe*, January 17, 1975, p. 1.

19. For a similar misrepresentation see the January 18 *Globe* article (p. 1).

20. Ibid., January 21, 1975, p. 1. That report went on to say, "The prosecution contends that in an abortion by hysterotomy Edelin . . . held the fetus in the uterus for 3 minutes, thus cutting off its supply of oxygen. . . . The prosecution charges that the fetus, alleged to have been between 24 and 28 weeks in gestation, could have lived." The *Globe*, in other words, implicitly sided with the defense case by using "fetus" even when reporting the prosecution's case: "Medical examiner tells court fetus had respiratory activity. . . . Pathologist says fetus in Edelin case breathed . . . charged with the death of a fetus." (January 24, p. 1; January 29, p. 1)

21. Ibid.

22. Reporter White consistently showed such bias in word selection. For example, her January 21 story repeated misstatements: "The prosecution contends that in an abortion by hysterotomy Edelin performed on Oct. 3, 1973, he detached the placenta from the uterine wall and held the fetus in the uterus for 3 minutes, thus cutting off its supply of oxygen. . . . The prosecution charges that the fetus, alleged to have been between 24 and 28 weeks in gestation, could have lived . . . [Edelin] is charged with manslaughter in the death of the fetus during the abortion."

23. Ibid., February 14, 1975, p 1. White clearly understood the importance of terminology, as she noted that defense attorney Homans "repeatedly objected" when prosecution witnesses used the word "baby."

24. Ibid., February 6, 1975, p. 1.

25. Ibid., February 7, 1975, p. 1.

26. Ibid., February 11, p. 1.

27. Ibid., January 21, 1975, p. 1.

28. Ibid., February 13, 1975, p. 1.

29. Ibid., February 16, 1975, p. 1.

30. Ibid., February 9, 1975, p. 1.

31. Quoted in *Harper's*, March 4, 1975.

32. Nolen, p. 177.

33. Ibid, p. 179.

34. Ibid.

35. Ibid.

36. Boston *Herald*, January 6, 1975, p. 1; January 7, p. 5.; January 11, pp. 1, 22.

37. Ibid., February 8, p. 1.

38. Ibid. January 23, p. 13. See also January 28, p. 6. One variety of conservatism might have influenced *Herald* news coverage slightly: Concerned with government spending, the *Herald* showed impatience with the "snail's pace at which the trial had been moving — at an estimated cost of $3000 a day to Boston & Suffolk County" (Jan. 17, p. 8). *Herald* news stories examined the economics of abortion survival: "As wards of the state these survivors would become the total responsibility of the state. . . . If only a fraction of the million plus abortions per year now being performed in the U.S. were to involve such salvageable fetuses, the cost of

their rescue and maintenance until adulthood could entail multi-billions of dollars. Their initial care in intensive care under current hospital rates could cost upwards of $300 a day. Later, in institutions, their keep could cost according to present state rates more than $8,000 per year" (Jan. 23, p. 4).

39. Nolen, p. 217.

40. Ibid., p. 218.

41. Ibid., pp. 217–218.

42. Boston *Globe*, February 19, 1975, p. 19.

43. Ibid., February 15, 1975, p. 1.

44. Ibid. The *Pilot*, weekly newspaper of the Roman Catholic Archdiocese of Boston, attacked the *Globe* for that statement in particular, and *Globe* editor Thomas Winship apologized; Winship said, "We sent an apology to Judge McGuire and reemphasized to our staff the importance of avoiding any instance of bias against members of any religion or ethnic group."

45. Quoted in Boston *Herald American*, February 19, p. 11.

46. "Doctor, Convicted in Abortion, Charges Prejudice Barred Fair Trial in Boston," New York *Times*, February 17, 1975, p. 41.

47. Ibid.

48. Lawrence K. Altman, "Doctor Guilty in Death of a Fetus in Abortion," ibid., February 16, 1975, pp. 1, 59.

49. "Abortion Error," New York *Times*, February 19, 1975, p. 34. The *Times* did not fall for such supposed confusion—like the *Globe*, it stuck to terminology preferred by the pro-abortion defense.

50. *Harper's*, March 4, 1975.

51. Nolen, pp. 208–209.

52. "Late Abortions & the Edelin Verdict," New York *Post*, February 20, 1975, 10F11. The Atlanta *Journal* reported on February 18, 1975 (10E12) that "Edelin was convicted of manslaughter last weekend for the death of an aborted live fetus."

53. Washington *Post*, February 18, 1975; reprinted in Sass, *Abortion: Freedom of Choice & the Right to Life*, op. cit., p. 200.

54. St. Louis *Post-Dispatch*, February 25, 1975; Sass, p. 201.

55. Los Angeles *Times*, February 19, 1975; Sass, p. 202.

56. Richmond *Times-Dispatch*, February 21, 1975; Sass, p. 203.

57. *Time*, March 3, 1975, p. 55.

58. Chattanooga *Times*, February 20, 1975; Sass, p. 200.

59. Oregon *Journal*, February 20, 1975; Sass, p. 204.

60. Des Moines *Register*, February 19, 1975; Sass, p. 203.

61. Philadelphia *Inquirer*, Febraury 24, 1975, 10F14.

62. Los Angeles *Herald-Examiner*, Feb. 18, 1975, 11B9.

63. Lawrence K. Altman, "Implications of Abortion Verdict," New York *Times*, Feb. 17, 1975, p. 41.

64. Nolen, p. 207.

65. Los Angeles *Times*, February 14, 1978, part II, p. 3; Los Angeles *Herald-Examiner*, May 6, pp. 1, 5; *Time*, May 22, 1978, p. 24; material in Pro-Life Action League files.

66. Ibid.

67. Ibid.

68. Los Angeles *Times*, February 14, 1978, part II, p. 3.

69. Ibid.

70. Ibid., May 3, 1978, pp. 1, 10; May 4, pp. 1, 7; May 5, pp, 1, 7; May 6, pp. 1, 5. See also "The Ordeal of a Divided Jury," *Time*, May 22, 1978, p. 24. For a sympathetic treatment of Waddill and his life after the trial, see *Newsweek*, January 7, 1980, p. 10.

71. Ruth Seymour, "Unwanted . . . and alive," Detroit *Free Press*, January 3, 1982; Pro-Life Action League files.

72. Two examples of "dreaded complications" surviving: In Florida in 1979, a child delivered after an abortion was dumped in a bedpan without examination — but as a nurse explained, "It didn't die. It was left in the bedpan for an hour before signs of life were noticed. It weighed slightly over a pound." The child survived and was adopted. In Wilmington, Delaware, two babies were born alive, 5 weeks apart, after saline abortions. One was immediately seen to be alive and was treated; the other was discovered gasping for breath after being placed in a specimen jar. Both survived and were adopted.

73. Seymour, op. cit. The article quoted a former "abortion unit administrator" as saying, "A fetus is not a baby. This kind of report feeds the fantasies of people who imagine that abortion is baby killing. But a fetus is not a baby. . . . What is a baby? We don't know. Everybody has to determine that individually, for themselves."

74. Maria Riccardi, "Clinics are preparing for mid-pregnancy abortions," Cleveland *Plain Dealer*, June 26, 1983; clipping in Chicago *Sun-Times* library.

CHAPTER 14
IDEOLOGY VERSUS INVESTIGATION, 1978–1985

1. New York *Post*, December 16, 1976, p. 3.
2. New York *Daily News*, November 6, 1977, p. 1.
3. Ibid.
4. Chicago *Sun-Times*, November 12, 1978, p. 1.
5. Ibid.
6. Ibid.
7. Ibid.
8. Ibid.
9. Ibid.
10. Ibid.
11. Ibid., p. 5.
12. Ibid., November 13, 1978, p. 1.
13. Ibid., November 13, p. 4.
14. Ibid., November 12, 1978, Section II, p. 5; see also November 13, p. 47.
15. Ibid., November 17, p. 1.
16. Ibid., November 19, p. 1.
17. Author's interview with Scheidler, October 17, 1987.
18. Op. cit., p. 11.
19. Clipping from the Chicago *Defender* in Pro-Life Action League files.
20. Interview.

21. Chicago *Sun-Times*, November 12, p. 4; November 15, p. 4; etc.

22. Ibid., November 15, p. 71.

23. Ibid.

24. Ibid., November 20, p. 53.

25. *The Wanderer*, December 7, 1978, p. 9; letters in Pro-Life Action League files; interview with Scheidler.

26. Op. cit., November 21, p. 3.

27. Chicago *Sun-Times*, November 21, 1978, pp. 3, 12; November 22, pp. 3, 8, 56; November 23, pp. 3, 38.

28. Ibid. For additional discussion of the statistical issue and *Sun-Times* reporting, see Dexter Duggan, "Not Only Babies Die in Abortion Clinics," *The Wanderer*, December 7, 1978, p. 9.

29. Ibid., November 24, 1978, p. 5.

30. Ibid., November 26, 1978, p. 7.

31. Ibid., November 30, 1978, p. 26.

32. Cincinnati *Post*, July 2, 1986. Clipping provided by Planned Parenthood.

33. Philadelphia *Inquirer*, May 17, 1984; clipping from Planned Parenthood.

34. Cleveland *Plain Dealer*, May 9, 1985; *The Oregonian*, March 20, 1982; clippings from files of the Pro-Life Action League.

35. Hartford *Courant*, January 23, 1982: "The Hartford-Springfield area will be one of three regions where mass media campaigns to enlist volunteers to work against proposed legal limits on abortion will be launched next month . . . "

36. Noonan, p. 77.

37. The particular bill under attack by the *Times* was co-sponsored by Baptist, Mormon, Episcopalian, Methodist, Presbyterian, Jewish, Congregationalist, and agnostic legislators. Within a few years most leading publications would accept the fact that life begins at conception, but would ask questions similar to this one in *Newsweek*, January 11, 1982, p. 44: "The problem is not determining when 'actual human life' begins, but when the value of that life begins to outweigh other considerations." See also New York *Times*, July 5, 1977, p.28.

38. The National News Council, based in New York, was founded in 1974 as the result of a task force recommendation of the 20th Century Fund that an arbiter was needed to investigate complaints against the news media. The Council had no authority to regulate or impose penalties, but relied on peer review and publicity for its effectiveness. It never received much press cooperation and soon expired.

39. *Wanderer*, January 11, 1979, p. 1.

40. *The Congressional Quarterly* also received some heat when, in reporting one vote, it identified each Catholic senator and representative by an asterisk. Pat Buchanan commented in his syndicated column, "Can one imagine the fire storm if CQ placed a little yellow star of David beside the name of all Jewish members of Congress voting against F-15s for Saudi Arabia?" (*Congressional Quarterly Weekly Report*, February 4, 1978, pp. 258–267; Patrick Buchanan, "Why Catholics Get Clobbered," *Chicago Tribune*, April 18, 1979, section 3, p. 4; cited in Burtchaell, p. 113.)

41. Washington *Star* clipping in Pro-Life Action League files.

42. Sally Smith, "A child and her baby: Three seasons of strife," Detroit *Free Press*, February 21, 1982; clipping in Pro-Life Action League files.

43. Providence *Journal*, May 16, 1982. The *Journal* then presented similar snapshots of three normal cases — but instead of indicating that hard cases were 1 out of a 100, a reader was likely to think they were 4 out of 7, especially because the article continued, "There were 7,433 such cases in Rhode Island last year." The *Journal* also quoted at length and without any opposition an anonymous abortionist who charged that doctors who refuse to perform abortions "are shirking their responsibility. They are not taking care of their patients."

44. The story is told in S. Rickly Christian, *The Woodland Hills Tragedy* (Westchester, IL: Crossway, 1985).

45. Los Angeles *Times*, February 7, 1982, Section II, p. 6. See also February 6, p. II-6; Feb. 10, p. II-8; Feb. 11, p. II-4.

46. Ibid.

47. Quoted in Christian, p. 76. The law stipulated no photographs of deceased *persons*; Jeanette Dreisbach of the California Pro-Life Medical Group responded to those charging illegality by asking whether they considered the 16,500 victims "persons in the eyes of the law? If so, those abortions were murder." If officials "insist they're persons, nothing would please us more."

48. Ibid.

49. Results, which appeared initially in journal articles, are most readily available in S. Robert Lichter, Stanley Rothman, Linda S. Lichter, *The Media Elite: America's New Powerbrokers* (Bethesda, MD: Adler & Adler, 1986) p. 29.

50. Philadelphia *Inquirer*, January 27, 1985; clipping provided by Religious Coalition for Abortion Rights. The *Inquirer* story's first three paragraphs, reporting a Reagan speech about abortion, were followed by 7 paragraphs about the film, then 3 about pending legislation, then 13 paragraphs attacking the film, then 1 paragraph from Nathanson in response.

51. Ibid.

52. David Michael Ettlin and Mary Knudson, "Some doctors call film emotional and deceptive, say fetus can't feel pain," Baltimore *Sun*; clipping provided by the Religious Coalition for Abortion Rights. See also C. Fraser Smith and John W. Frece, "Legislators are shown two views of 'Silent Scream,'" Baltimore *Sun*, February 20, 1985.

53. Ibid.

54. Dale Mazzacapa, "Speaking out about their abortions," Philadelphia *Inquirer*, May 19, 1985; clipping provided by Religious Coalition for Abortion Rights.

55. Baltimore *Sun*, May 22, 1985.

56. Ibid.

57. This study, as noted, concentrates on major print media, particularly daily newspapers. Television network news during the mid-1980s may have been fairer; see Joanmarie Kalter, "Abortion Bias," *TV Guide*, November 9-15. 1985, pp. 8-27.

58. Minneapolis *Star and Tribune*, January 21, 1985; clipping provided by Religious Coalition for Abortion Rights.

59. (Portland)*Oregonian*; clipping provided by Religious Coalition for Abortion Rights.

60. Ibid.

61. Miami *Herald*, January 5, 1983; *Herald* clippings in files of Pro-Life Action League.

62. Ibid., January 7, 1973.
63. Ibid., January 24, 1983.
64. Ibid.
65. Ibid.
66. "Women tell of abuses at abortion clinic," Miami *Herald*, January 24, 1983.
67. Ibid.
68. Atlanta *Constitution*, March 11, 1975, p. 21.
69. Ibid.
70. Ibid., March 11, 1980, Classified p. 1.

CHAPTER 15
A LAP DOG FOR THE ABORTION LOBBY

1. Chicago *Sun-Times*, November 24, 1978, p. 5.
2. Ibid.
3. Ibid.
4. See Howard Moody, "Abortion: Woman's Right and Legal Problem," *Christianity and Crisis*, March 8, 1971, pp. 27–32.
5. New Haven *Register*, Jan 31, 1975, 2b2.
6. New York *Post* article in Pro-Life Action League files.
7. David Reardon, *Silent No More* (Westchester, IL: Crossway, 1987).
8. *USA Today*, July 23, 1986, p. 1D.
9. Author's survey of centers associated with the Christian Action Council.
10. Estimates by surveyed centers. Government statistics show that the number of abortions, after rising steadily for two decades, has decreased during the past 2 years. Abortion statistics are notoriously unreliable, and the decrease may be due to changes in the population cohorts, but the centers do appear to have had some impact.
11. Clippings received from survey participants.
12. Survey.
13. Ibid.
14. Ibid.
15. For a full discussion of the public relations theory and procedures involved, see my article, "Abortion Rights: Anatomy of a Negative Campaign," *Public Relations Review*, Fall, 1987, pp. 12–23.
16. Author's telephone interview with Michael Byers, February 20, 1987.
17. Byers said, "If you don't use every tool at your disposal, that mother can be left to the abortuary. 90% of the women who come here come in looking for an abortion. 80% leave deciding to continue their pregnancies. That's what the abortionists are afraid of. We estimate that 35,000 babies were saved by centers affiliated with us in 1985, at a cost of $9 million to the abortion industry."
18. Author's interviews with anti-abortion leaders and with volunteers at one "crisis pregnancy center" affiliated with the Christian Action Council. In many ways, the difference among anti-abortion groups arose out of the classic question, "Do the ends justify the means?" (Or, more precisely, "Which ends justify which means?")

19. New York *Daily News*, January 28, 1986, p. 27.

20. Telephone interviews with Sutnick, January and February, 1987, and clippings provided by Planned Parenthood.

21. Judging by the evidence of clippings from across the country, Sutnick's appraisal of her effectiveness seems accurate. She is quoted approvingly in many articles, but her fingerprints are obvious in many more. For example, she obtained a copy of the Pearson Foundation manual and distributed copies of it to reporters throughout the country; quotations from the manual figured prominently in many stories. Copies of the manual were passed around from reporter to reporter. Sutnick said she had to "keep from laughing" when a New York *Times* reporter interviewing her held out a copy of the manual and asked if Sutnick had seen it. "The copy had come from me originally," Sutnick said, "although the reporter didn't know it. I knew it was one of our copies because it had the number of our duplicating department on it."

22. RCAR is composed of members of theologically liberal groups who "have joined together to preserve the legal option of abortion." RCAR, according to a fact sheet included in its press kits, "has maintained a professional lobbying program on Capitol Hill since 1973. A national legislative alert, DISPATCH, is mailed to 25,000 key activists around the country whenever necessary."

23. Press statement provided by RCAR.

24. Telephone interview with Hodges, January 29, 1987.

25. Telephone interview with Radford, February 27, 1987.

26. Telephone interview with Perrin, February 25, 1987.

27. Sutnick interviews.

28. Perrin interview.

29. Ibid.

30. *USA Today*, July 23, 1986, pp. 1D, 4D.

31. Ibid., p. 4D.

32. Reno *Gazette-Journal*, December 5, 1985, pp. 1A, 1D; Ann Arbor *News*, December 1, 1985, p. 1A; (Portland) *Oregonian*, July 3, 1986; etc.

33. Detroit *Free Press* clipping provided by the Christian Action Council; other clippings provided by Planned Parenthood, the Religious Coalition for Abortion Rights, and the National Abortion Federation.

34. *Newsday*, December 29, 1986; article supplied by Planned Parenthood of New York City.

35. Milwaukee *Journal*, April 6, 1988, p. 1.

36. See, for example, Oakland *Press*, June 22, 1986, p. 1.

37. Chicago *Sun-Times*, May 7, 1987; article in *Sun-Times* library.

38. Ibid.

39. "Five Hundred Bodies Discovered in Michigan Avenue Dumpster," May 1, 1987, press release in Pro-Life Action League files; interview with Scheidler.

40. Iowa City *Press-Citizen*, May 7, 1987.

41. Press release, op. cit.

42. Chicago *Sun-Times*, May 7, 1987.

43. Lichter et al., loc. cit.

44. See particularly work by Herbert Gans and Stephen Hess.

45. New York *Times*, January 21, 1988, p. 11.

46. The Dred Scott decision, which led to even greater controversy, became moot within a decade.

47. Columnist Pat Buchanan reported statements that some newborn abortion victims "have been immediately iced and their body temperatures cooled to preserve the tissues. The dead (or not quite dead) baby has been hurried to the surgeon, who then removes the organs and transplants them into the adult recipients." ("Aborted infants finally wanted . . . for organs," *Conservative Chronicle*, January 14, 1988, p. 16.)

49. Ibid.

50. Noonan, p. 70.

51. Milwaukee *Journal*, May 12, 1985; clipping in Pro-Life Action League files.

52. Because much recent commentary is so loaded, young reporters wanting to research issues certainly need to go beyond their newspapers clip files of the last 25 years. As Washington *Post* columnist Colman McCarthy acknowledged concerning abortion coverage (*Notre Dame Magazine*, November, 1979), "All too often, researching an issue means walking to the morgue and 'getting out the clippings.' But what if stories of last month or last year were shallow?"

53. *Time*, October 13, 1967, p. 33.

Index

A

"Abortaria," 71
Abortifacients, nature of, 5-6
Abortion advertising, 4-9, 12, 14-18, 20-27, 31, 40-42, 45, 48-54
    attempted ban in Massachusetts, 18
    effect on news coverage, 45
Abortion and church priorities, 47
Abortion and maternal deaths, 82, 84-85, 108, 110-111
    reason for decline, 82
Abortion and political corruption, 18-19, 58, 73, 82, 84
Abortion and power, 60, 72-74, 106-107, 116-117, 180
Abortion and regular physicians, 38-39, 77, 80, 82
Abortion as oppression of women, 36, 39, 51
Abortion counseling, 41, 57, 134, 142-147
Abortion demographics, 58, 90, 98-99, 177, 179
Abortion profiteers, 134-135
Abortion public relations, 68-71, 77-80, 85-88, 103-112
    Jack Sprat strategy, 107
Abortionists, affluence of, 12-13, 26, 28, 78, 82, 84

Abortionists, effective prosecution of, 77
Abortionists, famous
    Banti, Diane, 83
    Brandenburg, Leopold, 81
    Costello, Madame Catherine, 14-16
    Duke, Louis, 72-74
    Edelin, Kenneth, 36, 124-130
    Everitt, Lancelot, 22
    Gedicke, Herman W., 35
    Hathaway, Isaac, 34-35, 39
    Howard, T.M., 119
    Mauriceau, Charles, 4, 11, 26, 27
    McGonegal, Dr., 46
    Mottard, Henry L., 62-63
    Rappaport, Nathan, 108
    Restell, Madame, 4-16, 18-19, 24, 26-27, 29, 32-33, 104, 123
    Stapler, Andre, 58-59
    Sturm, Maurice, 67-68
    Thompson, Robert, 51-54, 64-65, 166
    Waddill, William, 36, 130-131
Abortionists, "good" vs. "bad," 80-81, 84, 88-89
Abortionists, political influence of, 35, 73, 79
Abortionists, vivid descriptions of, 10-11, 19, 27, 29, 37-38, 43, 46, 52

Agenda-setting, 25–30, 75, 88–92, 94, 98–99, 109–110, 112, 150

Amen, John H., 73–77, 172

American Law Institute, 91, 109

American Medical Association, 18, 29

American Mercury, 72, 79

American Psychiatric Association, 85

Anderson, Jack, 147

Anti-abortion books, 18–19, 42–43, 47

Anti-abortion legislation, 18, 25, 30–31, 40

Anti-abortion medical leaders, 9, 18

Anti-abortion slumbering, 88

Arizona *Republic*, 121

Associated Press, 90, 95, 98, 147

Association for the Study of Abortion, 106, 113

Atlanta *Constitution*, 48, 57, 95

Austin *American-Statesman*, 148–149

B

Baltimore *Sun*, 139–140

Banti, Diane, *see* abortionists

Bedford, Gunning, 9

Bennett, James Gordon, 4, 8

Birmingham *News*, 118

Birth control and abortion, 61, 79–80, 167

Black, Algernon, 78

Blackmun, Harry, 117

Boston *Daily Times*, 153

Boston *Globe*, 121, 124–129, 187
    misreporting in Edelin case, 126

Boston *Herald*, 124, 127, 187

Bourne, Alec, 71–72

Brandenburg, Leopold, *see* abortionists

Brezhnev doctrine of abortion politics, 119

British Medical Journal, 12

Brooklyn *Eagle*, 172

Brown, Harold O. J., 153

Bruzelius, Nils, 125

Buffalo *Evening News*, 116

Burtchaell, James T., 179

Buutap, Nguyenphuc, 108

Byers, Michael, 144, 192

C

California Medicine, 117

Calvin, John, 3, 153

Catholics as "bad guys," 104, 128, 137–138, 188

Charleston *Daily Courier*, 20

Chattanooga *Times*, 129

Chicago *Daily News*, 110, 121

Chicago Medical Society, 49–50

Chicago *Sun-Times*, 110–111, 113, 120, 122, 133–137, 141–142, 147

Chicago *Times-Herald*, 48

Chicago *Tribune*, 20, 31, 42, 49–50

Christian Action Council, 144, 146

Christian Science Monitor, 118

Cincinnati *Commercial*, 17

Cincinnati *Enquirer*, 116

Cincinnati *Post*, 121, 137

Clergy Consultation Service, 105

Cleveland *Plain Dealer*, 17, 21, 113, 132, 137

Cleveland *Press*, 119, 121

Collier's, 79

Commission on Population Growth and the American Future, 117, 184

Comstock Act, 40, 50

Connecticut *Courant*, 16

Cooper, Boyd, 131

Cornelsen, Ronald, 130–131

Coronet, 88

Cosmopolitan, 144

Costello, Madame Catherine, *see* abortionists

Crisis pregnancy centers, 143–147

D

Dallas *Morning News*, 48, 115–116, 119, 185

Davis, John Jefferson, 153

De Tocqueville, Alexis, 154–155

Dellapenna, Joseph, 152, 176

Des Moines *Register*, 118, 129

Detroit *Free Press*, 113, 119, 132, 138, 144, 146, 185

"Dreaded complications," 123, 131–132, 189

Dred Scott decision, 185

Duke, Louis, *see* abortionists

E

Edelin, Kenneth, *see* abortionists

Edelin and Scopes trials, 129

Ehrlichman, John, 117

Everitt, Lancelot, *see* abortionists

F

Fetal transplants, 148, 194
Fetus and unborn child, *see* press
Finkbine, Sherri, 93–98
Flanagan, Newman, 124–125
Fletcher, Joseph, 85
Fort Smith *Herald*, 16
Fort Worth *Star-Telegram*, 119
Friedan, Betty, 107

G

Galdston, Iago, 87
Galveston *Daily News*, 42
Gedicke, Herman W., *see* abortionists
Glamour, 144
Gorov, Lynda, 147
Grant, James, alias of Robert Thompson, *see*
    abortionists
Grisez, Germain, 112, 152
Guttmacher, Alan, 78, 85–86, 91, 94

H

Hall, Robert, 106, 113
Halva-Neubauer, Jeanine, 162
Harland, Marion, 43
Hartford *Courant*, 114, 137
Hathaway, Isaac, *see* abortionists
Hellman, Louis, 117
Hilgers, Thomas W., 153, 174
Hodge, Hugh, 18
Hodges, Fredrica, 145
Holmes, Rudolph, 49–50
Homans, William, 125
Horan, Dennis, 153
Houston *Post*, 48, 83, 115, 183–184
    ideological rationale, 183–184
Howard, T.M., *see* abortionists
Howe, E. Frank, 19, 157

I

Indianapolis *Daily State Sentinel*, 17
Indianapolis *News*, 118
Indianapolis *Star*, 116

International Birth Control Conference, 69
Investigative reporting, *see* press
Iowa *Press Citizen*, 145

J

Jefferson, Mildred, 126
Jennings, Louis, 25
Jones, George, 25, 47
Journal of the American Medical Association,
    42, 62, 65

K

Kansas City *Star*, 122
Kansas City *Times*, 121
Keely, James, 49
Kellogg, J.H., 47
Kelly, J.E., 42–43
Kelsey, Frances, 93, 95
Kheel, Theodore, 107
Kinsey Institute, 90
Kleegman, Sophia, 78, 87
Kross, Anna, 78

L

Lader, Lawrence, 99, 104–105, 107–110, 115,
    137–138
Laufe, Leonard, 123
Lerner, Max, 84
Lichter-Rothman survey, 139, 147
Lidz, Theodore, 86–87
Lohman, Anna, a.k.a. Madame Restell, *see*
    abortionists
Lohman, Charles, a.k.a. Mauriceau, *see*
    abortionists
London *Times*, 72
Long Island *Press*, 114
Los Angeles *Herald-Examiner*, 129, 138–139
Los Angeles *Times*, 53, 57, 61, 68, 71, 83–84,
    89, 94–97, 121, 129, 138, 170
Louisiana *Courier*, 17
Louisville *Courier-Journal*, 118
Louisville *Daily Journal*, 21
Luker, Kristin, 167

M

Maginnis, Pat, 107
Means, Cyril, Jr., 32
Mecklenburg, Fred, 126, 127–128
Medical Jurisprudence, 9
Memphis *Commercial Appeal*, 114, 121
Mencken, H.L., 77
Miami *Herald*, 140–141
Migliorino, Monica, 147
Milwaukee *Journal*, 119, 120–121, 146, 149–151
Minneapolis *Star and Tribune*, 140
Missouri *Republican*, 21, 42
Model abortion law, 78, 91
Mohr, James, 152, 163
Moloch, 47, 62, 168
Moody, Howard, 105, 111
Mottard, Henry L., *see* abortionists
Myers, Lonny, 111

N

Nathanson, Bernard, 99, 139–140
National Abortion Federation, 145
National Abortion Rights Action League, 137, 139–140, 148
National Association for the Repeal of Abortion Laws, 105
National Committee for Maternal Health, 77–78
National News Council, 137, 190
National Organization for Women, 107, 119, 139
National Police Gazette, 10, 11, 16, 19, 23, 36–39, 44–45, 155, 164
New Haven *Register*, 142
New Orleans *Daily Crescent*, 17
New Orleans *Daily Times*, 21–22
New Orleans *Picayune*, 31, 40
New Orleans *States-Item*, 121
New York *American*, 59, 67
New York *Daily Mirror*, 73, 75–76, 89
New York *Daily News*, 64–66, 73, 80–82, 133, 144, 168, 171
New York *Herald*, 4, 8, 11–12, 40, 53
New York *Herald Tribune*, 88–89
New York *Journal*, 48, 51, 60, 62–63, 65, 68
New York *Journal-American*, 73–78, 81–82, 90, 96

New York Medical Society, 24
New York *Post*, 84, 96, 105, 133, 143
New York *Sun*, 4, 6, 8, 154, 171
New York *Times*, 12, 24–36, 38–40, 45–47, 60, 62–64, 68, 73, 77–80, 82, 89–91, 94, 96, 105, 108–110, 113, 115, 118–119, 121, 128, 137–138, 144, 148
  exposing abortion in 1871, 25–28
  pro-abortion during the 1960s, 108–110
  compared with sensational newspapers, 38–39, 63
  leaving anti-abortion battle, 46–47
New York *Tribune*, 12, 29–30
New York *World*, 67
New York *World-Telegram*, 74–75, 78–79, 82
New York *World-Telegram and Sun*, 88, 103
Newark *Evening News*, 114
Newsday, 98, 146
Newspapers, *see* press and individual titles
Nixon, Richard, 117
Noonan, John, 116, 149
Norfolk *Ledger-Star*, 118

O

O'Donnell, John, 64–65
Oakland *Tribune*, 119
Ochs, Adolph, 46
Olivarez, Grace, 184
Omaha *World-Herald*, 113, 118
Oregon *Journal*, 129
Orlando *Sentinel*, 118
Orwell, George, 96

P

Pearson Institute, 144
Penicillin and abortion, 82
"Perils of Pauline," 93–94
Perrin, Marlene, 145–146
Philadelphia *Inquirer*, 129, 137, 139–140
Pilpel, Harriet, 107
Planned Parenthood, 78–79, 90–91, 94, 106, 135–136, 137, 143–145
Polls, public opinion, 97–98, 117, 118
Population Council, 180
Portland *Oregonian*, 114, 137, 140, 144
Press advocacy of abortion, 92–150
  differential vividness, 114

significance of point of view, 97
publicity for abortion, 119–120, 137
attempts to remove abortion from agenda, 121
relaying of historical inaccuracies, 111, 184
response to power, 116–117
significance of story format, 93–94, 97
spiking of anti–abortion stories, 105, 137–139
use of ABABCCC story structure, 114
use of experts, 126, 139
use of photographs, 127
use of word "fetus," 96, 125–126, 187, 189
vocabulary, 96
Press alternatives to pro–abortionism, 95, 116, 120
Press coverage and reporters' beliefs, 147
Press overlooking of unborn child, 77, 79, 89, 114, 149
Press and agenda-setting, *see* agenda setting
Press and "neutral" abortion reporting, 77, 81
Press and solid undercover work, 25–28, 133–137
Press in the nineteenth century, 4–48
examples of hard-hitting reporting, 26–28, 39
Pro-Life Action League, 135, 147
Providence *Journal*, 121, 138

Q

"Quality of Life," 190

R

Radford, Barbara, 145
Rappaport, Nathan, *see* abortionists
Raymond, Henry, 25
Reardon, David, 143
Religious Coalition for Abortion Rights, 121, 145–146
Reporting of abortion, *see* press and individual newspaper names
Restell, Madame, *see* abortionists
Richmond *Times-Dispatch*, 129
Robinson, William, 69, 77
Rockefeller, John D., III, 107, 117
Rocky Mountain News, 48
Roe v. Wade, 32, 90–91, 121

Rosen, Harold, 85, 88, 90
Rudich, Mark, 73

S

San Antonio *Light*, 119
San Diego *Tribune*, 111
San Diego *Union*, 111, 115, 127
San Francisco *Chronicle*, 114–115
San Francisco *Examiner*, 20, 30, 41, 51–54, 57, 61, 80–81
Sanger, Margaret, 57–61, 68, 79, 104, 173
Scheidler, Joseph, 135, 147
Self, 144
"Silent No More," 140
"Silent Scream," 139–140
Springfield *Republican*, 21, 39–40, 150
St. Clair, Augustus, 25–28
St. Louis *Post-Dispatch*, 113, 118, 121
Stapler, Andre, *see* abortionists
Sturm, Maurice, *see* abortionists
Sutnick, Amy, 144–146, 193

T

Tatalovich, Raymond, 112
Taussig, Frederick J., 70, 77–78, 99
Taylor, Harold, 87–88, 99
Thalidomide, 93, 95, 97
The Abortionist, 92
The Defenders, 92
Thompson, Robert, *see* abortionists
Tietze, Christopher, 90, 99
Time, 70–71, 79, 82, 88, 98, 129
Transcendentalism, 7

U

U. S. Postmaster-General, 50
Ullman, Solomon, 73
USA Today, 144–146

V

Vogue, 144
Voyages to the moon, 84

w

Waddill, William, *see* abortionists
Wadsworth, Benjamin, 3
Warrick, Pamela, 133–137
Washington *Post*, 40, 48, 53, 89, 95–96, 107, 114, 121, 129
Washington *Star*, 138
Wattleton, Faye, 137

White, Diane, 125, 187
Wilkes, George, 10
Williams, Glanville, 85, 91, 104, 109, 175–176
"Woodland Hills Tragedy," 138–139, 191

z

Zekman, Pamela, 133–137